by John Timpson

Timpson's England
Timpson's Towns
Timpson's Travels in East Anglia
Norwich – A Fine City
Timpson's English Eccentrics
Requiem for a Red Box
Little Trains of Britain
Timpson's English Villages
Timpson's Other England
Timpson's Timepaths

Paper Trail
Sound Track

Timpson's
English Country Inns

JOHN TIMPSON

Photographs by Andrew Perkins

HEADLINE

Copyright © 1995 John Timpson (text)
Copyright © 1995 Andrew Perkins (photographs)

First published in 1995
by HEADLINE BOOK PUBLISHING

10 9 8 7 6 5 4 3 2 1

British Library Cataloguing in Publication Data
Timpson, John
   Timpson's English Country Inns
   I. Title
   647.9542

   ISBN 0–7472–0826–3

Designed by John Hawkins
Printed and bound in Portugal by
Printer Portuguesa

HEADLINE BOOK PUBLISHING
A division of Hodder Headline PLC
338 Euston Road
London NW1 3BH

Contents

Foreword

This is not intended to be another good beer guide, nor indeed another guide to good pubs, though all the inns I have selected are good ones, and they all sell good real ale. What I have primarily looked for are inns with something special about them – unusual histories, strange legends, curious characters, odd features.

Many of them date back to the days when lodging houses were built for the medieval masons working on the parish churches. They developed into alehouses, then into village inns; hence the frequent close proximity of the inn and the church. Others, out in the open country, catered mainly for the coaching trade, and a few became licensed fairly recently, after the premises had served a quite different purpose. But each of them has a distinctive tale to tell, something more than the familiar stories of secret tunnels, smugglers' hide-outs and ghostly goings-on in the cellar.

For instance, there are the unlikely items you can find in a bar. The Crown at Charlton-on-Otmoor in Oxfordshire has a seven-foot oak table once used in the church across the road for laying out corpses. The Three Horseshoes at Warham in Norfolk has on the ceiling a Norfolk twister, a kind of inverted roulette wheel. The Red Lion at Lamarsh in Essex has a bar inscribed 'To the Greater Glory of God and in Loving Memory of Alfred Bradley Rooke...' and pews, instead of benches, with a notice on one saying, 'Please leave this pew vacant during Communion.' Behind the bar of the Pack Horse at Affetside in Greater Manchester is the skull of the man who beheaded the Earl of Derby during the Civil War.

Then there are inns with strange histories, like the Pandy at Dorstone in Hereford & Worcester, built as a penance by one of the knights who killed Thomas Becket; the Leagate Inn at Coningsby in Lincolnshire, last of the 'guide houses', which still has the bracket where a torch was lit to guide travellers across the Fens; the Pack Horse at South Stoke in Avon, which has a right-of-way through a passage in the middle for coffins to be carried to the church; and the Cross Keys at Uppermill in Greater Manchester where an eighteenth-century curate went berserk and stuck a red-hot poker in the landlady's eye.

As for remarkable characters, you may have heard of Mabel Mudge of the Drewe Arms at Drewsteignton in Devon: at ninety-eight she is England's oldest licensee. But there are other magnificent ladies in the business too. Irene Jelf's family were granted the licence of the Boat Inn at Ashleworth in Gloucestershire during the reign of Charles II, and it has stayed in the family ever since, while Doris Jemison has lived at the Red Lion at Snargate in Kent all her life, preserving it just as it was when her family took it over in 1911. Among the more unconventional landlords I would pick Lacey Beckett of the Bull and Butcher at Turville in Buckinghamshire, who used to go riding dressed as Napoleon, and still sits on his favourite settle by the fire, so they say, fifty years after he killed his wife, his dog and himself in the bedroom upstairs.

There are inn names with curious origins, like the Three Chimneys at Biddenden in Kent, which has no connection with chimneys; the Chequers at Gedney Dyke in Lincolnshire, which derives its name from berries, not draughts; and the Belgian Arms at Holyport in Berkshire, which used to be the Eagle until German POWs started saluting it in the First World War.

There are unusual premises like the Crooked House at Himley in Staffordshire, which is so crooked that bottles roll upwards on the table; the Dusty Miller at Wrenbury in Cheshire, converted from a canal-side mill; and the Twenty Church-wardens at Cockley Cley in Norfolk, once the village school, the bar used for services when the church tower collapsed, now with quite a different significance to its name.

Not least, spare a thought for the Chequers at Ledsham in West Yorkshire, which only has a six-day licence because a Victorian Lady of the Manor once saw customers relieving themselves in the garden on a Sunday.

I have made sure that all these one-hundred-odd inns have a civilised, traditional atmosphere as well as a good story, and I drew the line at some which, through force of economic circumstances, have become little more than restaurants with bars. But breweries buy and sell, licensees come and go, and what may be a traditional country inn one month can become a licensed fast-food café the next, complete with piped music and electronic fruit machines.

I only hope this does not happen to any of Timpson's English Country Inns, so that you can enjoy them, and their stories, as much as I have.

John Timpson

South-Western Region

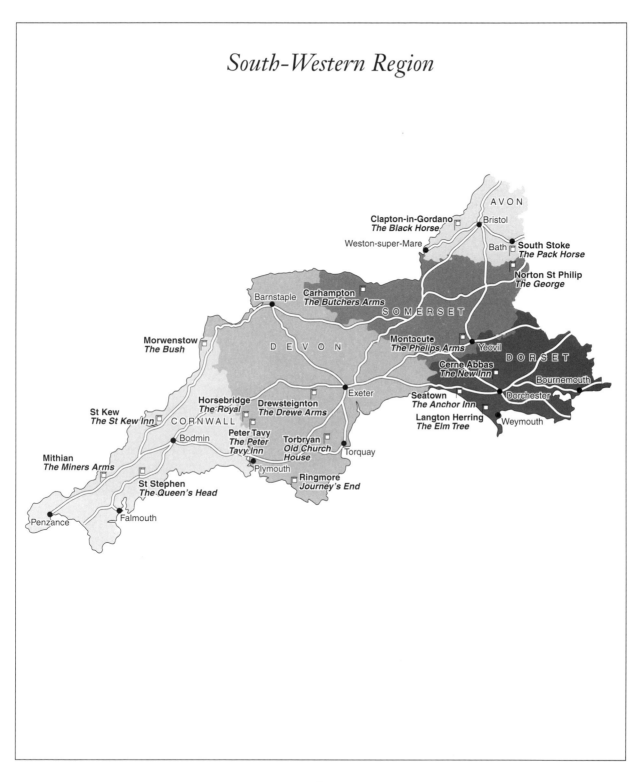

Clapton-in-Gordano
The Black Horse

Weston-super-Mare

Bristol

AVON

Bath

South Stoke
The Pack Horse

Norton St Philip
The George

Barnstaple

Carhampton
The Butchers Arms

SOMERSET

DEVON

Montacute
The Phelips Arms

Yeovil

DORSET

Morwenstow
The Bush

Cerne Abbas
The New Inn

Bournemouth

Exeter

Dorchester

Horsebridge
The Royal

Drewsteignton
The Drewe Arms

Seatown
The Anchor Inn

St Kew
The St Kew Inn

CORNWALL

Langton Herring
The Elm Tree

Weymouth

Bodmin

Peter Tavy
*The Peter
Tavy Inn*

Torbryan
*Old Church
House*

Torquay

Mithian
The Miners Arms

Plymouth

Ringmore
Journey's End

St Stephen
The Queen's Head

Penzance

Falmouth

*On the twelfth night after Christmas my true love
said to me, 'Hello wassailer!'*

The Butchers Arms
Carhampton, Somerset

Main road

Twelfth Night can be a pretty depressing occasion. The Christmas decorations have reached the ultimate in tattiness and are consigned to the loft or the dustbin, leaving the place looking naked, dusty and covered in pine needles. The festive season is officially over, and the worst of the winter lies ahead.

But it was not ever thus. The twelfth night after Christmas, the eve of the Feast of the Epiphany, used to be an opportunity for roistering, merry-making and wassailing. Originally the wassailing bit was performed on New Year's Eve, when young ladies carried the wassail bowl from door to door, drinking the health of the householders in spiced ale and getting a modest tip in return. But there was a fair amount of spiced ale around on Twelfth Night too, and wassailing was rife.

Among the apple orchards of the West Country

there was a local variation. Instead of spiced ale, the bowl contained spiced cider, and on Twelfth Night there was the ceremony of wassailing the apples, drinking a salutation to the apple trees to ensure a good crop later in the year. The Butchers Arms claims to be the only inn in Somerset which still maintains this tradition, and it does so on the original Twelfth Night, which was 17 January in the Julian Calendar before we changed to the present one. That was in 1752, so the tradition can be claimed to go back for well over two hundred years.

The Butchers Arms stands right on the main coast road through the village, so close to it in fact that the inn sign and the car park are on the opposite side of the road. This must be a problem in the summer, when the holiday traffic is continuous, but in the winter Carhampton goes into hibernation, and the locals have the inn to themselves – except, of course, on 17 January, the night of the wassail.

The decorated beam in the bar is perhaps the work of an itinerant monk. Is it ecclesiastically symbolic, or just another doodle?

It starts with mulled cider, made to a secret recipe known only to the landlord. Thus fortified, everyone adjourns to the orchard, where a bonfire is lit and songs are sung in honour of the apple trees. Shotguns are fired through the branches to drive off the bad spirits (which in apple trees take the form of grubs), and slices of toast soaked in cider are hung in the trees to attract the robins, so they will feed on any hard-of-hearing grubs that ignored the shooting. Having ensured a plentiful and grub-free harvest, the wassailers return to the bar for the rest of the mulled cider and, perhaps, a final rendition of 'Wassails in the Sunset'.

Now this is all jolly stuff, and very good for business during the slackest month of the year, but the Butchers Arms has other historical connections too, of a rather more serious nature. It was built

about 1600, first as a primitive shell with no upper storey and just a hole in the roof for a chimney. When it became an inn, probably a cider-house, in 1638 the building was 'modernised', and given an upper storey, proper fireplaces and a cobbled floor. It thus became respectable enough to be patronised by monks and other pilgrims who were heading for the ruins of Cleeve Abbey, five miles away.

Cleeve was the only Cistercian abbey in Somerset. It had a reputation for hospitality and good works, so much so that when Henry VIII ordered its dissolution with that of all the other monasteries, the local gentry appealed for it to be preserved. Henry, as was his wont, ignored them and dissolved it anyway, but much of the building remained and it continued to be a place of pilgrimage. The Butchers Arms has two reminders of those pilgrims, a decorated beam in the main bar which is thought to be the work of an itinerant monk, and a monk's prayer in one of the bedrooms, written in Old English and commending the 'pleasantness' of the inn.

The other reminder of those early days is underfoot. When the main bar was given its cobbled floor the builders incorporated the date, 1638, using what appear to be off-white cobbles. However, closer inspection will reveal that, in fact, they are bones not stones. I have seen similar floor material in the Hermitage at Bicton Gardens in South Devon, where the entire floor consists of deer knuckle-bones. These are knuckle-bones too, but they come from sheep.

Hence the name of the inn? Apparently not, according to the landlord. But it has ensured that for the past 450 years or more, every joke in the bar of the Butchers Arms has been rather near the knuckle.

Prisoners locked in the ladies' loo, Tom Jones in bed upstairs

The stone steps were built for the coaching days; now they are handy for pot plants.

The New Inn
Cerne Abbas, Dorset

14 Long Street

It would be difficult to write about Cerne Abbas without mentioning the Cerne Giant – certainly too difficult for me. So let's dispose of the nudge-nudge bit first. The giant has been described as the most uninhibited monument in Britain; certainly his virility is beyond question. The theories about him range from a mystic Stone Age fertility symbol to a Roman representation of Hercules, but I prefer the David-and-Goliath tale of the giant who came to threaten Cerne but decided to have a nap on the hillside first. A shepherd boy crept up the hill and slew him where he lay, and the villagers carved into the turf the outline of his prostrate body. Well, nearly prostrate...

It seems curious that the Benedictines should have built an abbey under the shadow of this obviously pagan image, and having done so, made no attempt to obliterate it. But the abbey has come and gone, and the Cerne Giant remains, an object of pilgrimage for young couples who believe that, if they stand on the appropriate part of his anatomy, a baby is certain to result. I suspect, though, that a few beers in one of the village inns would have much the same effect.

There are plenty in Cerne Abbas to choose from. Early in the last century, when soldiers returned home from the Peninsular War with no job and no pension, they were allowed to open beerhouses. By 1831 the twelve hundred residents had a choice of thirteen hostelries to drink in, and although the population has dwindled, the ratio remains much the same.

Some favour the Royal Oak, which was built at the time the abbey was dissolved, and acquired some of its stonework as a result. Others prefer the Red Lion, which has a Victorian façade, but actually dates from the same period. It has a sixteenth-century fireplace almost made to measure for an abbot's sitting-room. But I would plump for the New Inn, which also has stonework from the abbey and a lot more besides, including probably the oldest, and certainly the heaviest, roof in the village. It is made of Purbeck stone, and when it was dismantled a dozen years ago for the beams to be strengthened, it was found to weigh over two hundred tons. The beams must have been strengthened just in time.

It is a long while since the New Inn was new. Local legend has it that the Romans built a rest-house on the site, a Cold Harbour as it was called, where men and horses found shelter. The inn was built as a guest-house for the abbey. There is a priest's hole, now bricked up, beside one of the fireplaces, which gave the monks access to the upstairs rooms – though I am not sure why they did not just use the stairs, unless of course the guests were ladies.

It became Cerne's principal coaching inn, and reached its peak in the 1820s when the turnpike was opened. But business fell away when the railways came, and for a time the New Inn stopped being an inn and was used as the village fire station. It also acted as a court-house, with the magistrates sitting in the main bar and the prisoners kept in what is now the ladies' toilet. The first recorded case was in 1725, and it remained in use until a custom-built 'Justice

Room' was built at the police station in 1860.

In the early part of this century the New Inn had another unconvivial role. On each quarter-day the church bell was rung, and the tenants of the Pitt-Rivers Estate did not ask for whom the bell tolled, they knew it tolled for them. It summoned them to the New Inn to pay their rents to the land agent, Charles Stride. But it was not all bad news. In return for the payment, each tenant was given a threepenny beer voucher to spend at the bar. This quarterly ritual might have continued until the estate was wound up in 1919, but it was stopped at the outbreak of war under the Defence of the Realm Act. How the realm was imperilled is not very clear, but it meant

that while Mr Stride still got his rents the tenants missed out on the beer.

The New Inn, of course, has its ghosts – a figure in a monk's habit and a woman who was stabbed to death at the inn many years ago. There was also a time, some years ago, when figures in period costume were to be seen in one of the bedrooms, making energetic use of the four-poster bed, but these were no ghosts, just Albert Finney and his leading lady acting out the love scenes in the film version of *Tom Jones*. Why choose the New Inn at Cerne Abbas for such goings-on, one wonders? Could it have something to do with the Cerne Giant?

It is not only on the M5 that they go like the clappas

The Black Horse
Clapton-in-Gordano, Avon

Clevedon Lane

'Gordano' may sound excitingly continental, but to the average motorist heading for the West Country it is just another service station on the M5 motorway. If they give the name any thought while they fill their tanks and buy more crisps, they probably assume that the proprietor is Italian. Actually this Gordano, in what is officially Avon but is still regarded by the locals as north Somerset, has about as much connection with Italy as Granada service stations have with Spain.

It is, in fact, very English indeed. It goes back to Saxon times when 'gor' meant a spearhead and 'dene' was a flat plain. Gordano is a flat plain shaped like a spearhead and was originally just a saltmarsh regularly flooded by the sea. It is now a reclaimed, but still rather featureless, stretch of countryside between Portishead and the M5.

Clapton-in-Gordano is set on the hillside which overlooks this land, with origins as Saxon as those of Gordano itself. The local chief was Clappa, and this was 'Clappa's Town'. By the fourteenth century the name had been adjusted slightly; it was William de Clopton who built the parish church and the building beside it where the masons lived. Then the de Cloptons died out – they went, one might say, like the Clappas – but the church survived, and the adjoining building developed over the centuries into what is now the Black Horse.

It acquired its name in the days when Clapton was a mining village, and the mine was just at the bottom of its garden. The Black Horse probably represented a pit pony covered in coal-dust, or one of the horses which hauled the coal to the docks at Portishead. The coal would have been shipped across the Bristol Channel to Wales. One historian comments drily that it was sent to South Wales because it was too far to send coals to Newcastle. It certainly does seem strange in view of the vast coalfields in South Wales! Maybe it was its cheapness which made Clapton's coal so attractive. In the early eighteenth century the Black Horse pit was producing coal at threepence-ha'penny a bushel; in today's money that works out at 56p a ton.

It looks convivial now, but it used to be a cell – the bars on the windows are real.

The mine has long since closed, and so have all the others in Gordano, but the Black Horse remains a very tangible reminder of the rough-and-ready, and sometimes violent, lives of the miners. The lounge bar looks very snug at first sight, with its old wooden settles and the china mugs hanging from the beams, but there are still iron bars in the window from the days when it served as the village jail.

It was not unusual for inns to be used as court rooms and cells in villages which could not afford proper court-houses and lock-ups, but not many have retained the original cell bars. The Black Horse has also kept its stone-flagged floor and its traditional bar furniture, but these days there are flower baskets hanging on the front wall, and a car park where the coal-mine used to be.

Nevertheless, this is not tourist country. The tourists are all hurtling southwards on the M5, a mile or so away. Any travellers finding themselves in Clapton are either lost or looking for Cadbury Camp, another confusing name for the uninitiated. Cadbury, these days, is immediately associated with chocolate, but there are three Cadbury Camps or Castles in Somerset, all of them ancient fortifications. One is reputed to be the site of King Arthur's Camelot. The one near Clapton is reached by a footpath from near the Black Horse. It is not King Arthur's, just an anonymous earthworks with a commanding view across Gordano to the Bristol Channel. But first you have to find the Black Horse, which is tucked away down a side lane and easy to miss, as indeed I did at the first attempt, even though I knew where to look! The sign which points to it from the main street is skilfully placed so that it is virtually invisible from the Portishead direction.

However, when I was there one lunchtime there were plenty of businessmen, and other visitors, from Bristol and Portishead who had successfully found their way there. But mercifully, for those of us who like a pint in peace, all those motorists at the Gordano service station are in far too much of a hurry to look.

They all help at Auntie Mabel's;
that may be the village bobby behind the bar

The Drewe Arms
Drewsteignton, Devon

The Square

Drewsteignton has produced some notable characters during its long history, from the three young ladies who reputedly erected the massive Spinsters' Rock before breakfast (it is actually a Neolithic burial chamber) to the enthusiastic angler Major Herbert David Lewis. He died in 1982 aged ninety-three, and is described on his gravestone, rather charmingly, as the Contented Fisherman. But the most famous figures connected with the village were both there in the 1920s, and, although they came from opposite ends of the social spectrum, they did have one interest in common: the Drewe Arms.

Julius Drewe was one of the founders of the Home and Colonial Stores. Having made his fortune, he got Sir Edwin Lutyens to build him an imitation medieval castle on the site above the village where his supposed ancestor, the Norman noble Drogo, once lived. It took twenty years, and Julius died only two months after it was finished. However, while he was waiting he had the electricity cables in the village square put below ground to improve the view, and he altered the name of the Druid's Arms to his own. This was not as disrespectful as it may seem, because the village has nothing to do with the Druids. Victorian antiquarians had the misconception that the Spinsters' Rock was a Druid cromlech, or standing stone, and the inn was renamed accordingly (it was originally built to house the masons who built the church). Even a Victorian rector was taken in by this theory, and called his horse 'Druid'; it was, in fact, the only Druid that Drewsteignton has known.

About the time that Julius Drewe gave his family name to the inn, it acquired new licensees, a young man called Ernest Mudge and his wife, Mabel. Ernest died in 1951, but Mabel lives on, and on, and on... In 1994 she was ninety-eight years old, and England's oldest licensee. And so far as the locals are concerned, the Drewe Arms has changed its name again – it is known to everyone in the area as 'Auntie Mabel's'.

The legendary 'Auntie Mabel', almost certainly England's oldest licensee.

I hope that Julius and Mabel had many pleasant encounters at the Drewe Arms before he died in 1930. Although they came from such different backgrounds, they had a lot in common, and it is nice to find that both families are commemorated in the church next door – albeit at different social levels. There is a rather splendid high-backed chair for the use of the vicar, dedicated to the memory of Frances Drewe, who died in 1954; it was given by her children and grandchildren. Rather more discreetly,

in the rear pew, there is a kneeler 'in loving memory of Ernest Mudge, died March 4th, 1951, aged 69, husband of Mabel'.

The Drewe Arms, when Ernest and Mabel took over, must have looked very much as it does today. The furniture in the bar is still very simple – benches and tables, old photographs and advertisements on the walls. The beer and cider are still drawn from the wood, bar lunches are limited to sandwiches, and anyone who asks for a gin and tonic is looked at twice. But what makes the Drewe Arms special, and what has won it an award for 'the pub with the most delightful atmosphere', is not only Auntie Mabel and her redoubtable barmaid, Dorothy, it is also the friendly, but distinctly protective, attitude of its regulars. Any of them, it seems, can go through to the room behind the bar and draw a pint for themselves and their friends – and for any visitors, if they look reasonably acceptable. When I was there it was difficult to tell which side of the counter was which – there were more people sitting around the barrels than in the bar itself.

Auntie Mabel was poorly at the time, so Dorothy, who is merely in her seventies, was presiding. She simply sat in the corridor chatting with allcomers while, somehow, the inn operated itself. Yet I am sure that, at the end of the day, the till had the right amount of money, the casks were left with the right amount of beer, and nobody would have caused a vestige of trouble or offered a word of complaint – and that is not just because one of the helpers behind the bar turned out to be the village policeman.

Since then, Mrs Rudge has had to move permanently into a nursing home, but the locals have formed a 'Save the Drewe Arms' committee, hoping to ensure that, even if she is not there, it will still be 'Auntie Mabel's'.

A horsebridge without horses, and a packhorse that became royal

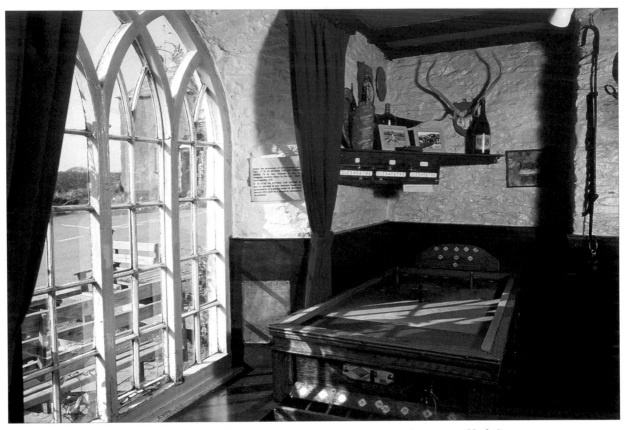

The original nuns might recognize the window, but what is that green table for?

The Royal
Horsebridge, Devon

Near the bridge

Horsebridge is in Devon, but only just. It lies on the east bank of the River Tamar, which marks the boundary with Cornwall. Centuries ago it was a major crossing point for packhorse trains and then coaches. Today most of the traffic crosses the river by the two trunk roads, at Launceston to the north and Gunnislake to the south, leaving Horsebridge comparatively undisturbed in the hinterland of little lanes that lie between. This could have been bad news for the Royal, which used to cater for the packhorse and coaching trade, but it is good news for anyone who likes unspoilt inns to remain unspoilt.

The Royal stands about fifty yards from the splendid old bridge that gives the little village its name, though, surprisingly, Horsebridge was not named in honour of horses. The original version was Haut Bridge, meaning high bridge, which it undoubtedly is. It is probably the oldest of the three medieval bridges along this stretch of the Tamar, all of them high – and narrow. They are barely twelve feet wide, which is more than enough for a packhorse and not too bad for a coach, but it does present problems for today's motor traffic.

It has meant that Newbridge at Gunnislake, on the trunk road from Tavistock to Liskeard, has had to be supplemented by a much newer one, but Greystone bridge still copes with the heavy traffic from Tavistock to Launceston. Horsebridge does not have too many problems with the local traffic from the little villages around it, but the masons who built it may have foreseen the summer rush of holiday-makers – they provided cut-waters, little alcoves along the sides of the bridge, for pedestrians to take refuge when needed.

Newbridge may have got its name because it was the newest of these three bridges, built in the early 1500s. Horsebridge and Greystone are known to have existed in the 1430s; they are mentioned during that period in the Exeter episcopal records. The See of Exeter extended across the border into Cornwall, and it was probably to enable the clergy to visit their Cornish benefices that the bridges were built. Some reference books give the precise date of Horsebridge as 1437, and about fifty years later a nunnery and rest-house were built close by it, which in due course became the Royal.

The nuns were able to enjoy the peaceful surroundings of the Tamar valley for only fifty years before Henry VIII had his disagreement with the Pope. The nunnery, like others throughout the country, was dissolved, but happily the building itself survived. After a decent interval it became an alehouse, known for obvious reasons as the Packhorse. It was in an ideal position for an inn, and the Packhorse must have prospered because, by the 1600s, it was considered sufficiently reputable to be patronised by Charles I. It is not clear why Charles was travelling around in this remote corner of his kingdom, nor is it known for certain whether he actually stayed at the inn or merely dropped in for a pub lunch, but the proprietor was so delighted to see him that he forthwith altered the name of his establishment, and it has been the Royal inn ever since. He also had the royal seal carved on the doorstep to add a little more tone.

In spite of its name, it is still easy to recognise its ecclesiastical origin. The high arched windows look more suited to a church than an inn. But once inside, the two bars follow the traditional pattern of harnesses and horse brasses on the walls, converted casks and high-backed benches to sit on, and plain old tables to sit around. One activity from its early alehouse days has also been preserved: it is one of the few village inns in the country which still brew their own beer on the premises.

I imagine the miniature aviary in the garden is entirely twentieth-century, but Fred the Jackdaw, its senior citizen, could come from any age. I think Charles I would approve.

I found just one feature of the Royal which might cause him to recoil. When the two main bars get overcrowded, there is a small third room to take the overflow. It is called – and may they be forgiven – 'The Drip Tray'.

Smugglers in the cellar, a hanging in the bar,
and a spy on the phone

A lying fisherman was lynched here and the Portland Spy plotted here; it's a lot quieter now.

The Elm Tree
Langton Herring, Dorset

—————— Chesil Bank ——————

Every old inn within sight of the sea has a smuggler's tale to tell, and the sixteenth-century Elm Tree by Chesil Bank is in there with the rest. A bricked-up hole in the cellar is said to be either an escape tunnel or a hiding-place for contraband. It has a tale of lynching too, which actually took place in the bar. The victim was a fisherman in the 1780s who lied about his catch.

So what's new, you cry! That hardly seems a lynching offence, or every riverside pub in the country would be festooned with dangling corpses. But this was more serious: it involved the cheating of his fellow fishermen. They chased him through the village, dragged him into the bar, and strung him up from a beam, which was part of a ship's mast and is still part of the ceiling.

As well as this earlier attempt at deception, there is a much more recent tale which few other inns can match – twentieth-century deception on an international scale. The Elm Tree has the dubious distinction of being the rendezvous in the sixties where the spy Harry Houghton, and his girlfriend, Ethel Gee, used to contact his KGB 'controller', Kenon Molody, better known as Gordon Lonsdale. They passed on stories which did a lot more damage than any fisherman's tale.

In centuries to come I suspect that the Portland Spy, as Houghton came to be called, will give rise to as many elaborate legends as the smugglers in the cellar and the swindler on the beam. One can get a foretaste of what is in store from an article which appeared nearly twenty years ago in the *Dorset Countryside*. It tells how Hough-ton came to the inn to receive his instructions.

'Standing at the bar and drinking heartily, he waited to receive phone calls on certain nights, and then quietly left the inn to stand on the shores of Portland or Lulworth Cove to receive dark-clad aliens who came to steal our secrets, some of them perhaps still quietly "sleeping" amongst us today...'

Gripping stuff indeed, in the same mould as the other local legend, that Napoleon once landed near here to reconnoitre a possible invasion. A farmer's wife saw a small group on the cliffs studying a map, and heard one of them, 'a short square figure, hand across breast', mutter to the others as he put away the map, 'C'est impossible'. So the invasion was cancelled, and Langton Herring had to wait another 150 years before 'dark-clad aliens' made use of its coastline again.

The earliest aliens to arrive on Chesil Bank were the Saxons. They called the beach Kiesel, meaning granite, and Chesil was derived from that. Langton Herring seems a particularly appropriate name for a fishing village, but the Herring has nothing to do with fish. Oddly enough it was previously called Langton Salmonville, but there are not too many salmon in the Chesil lagoon. Both names actually came from Norman families who settled at Langton, first the Sarmonvilles and then the Harencs. I like to think that in Roman times a centurion called Scampus lived there, and it was known as Langton Scampi.

There is no catch about the name of the Elm Tree Inn; it was not founded by a Viking called Elmut. There really was an elm tree close by, but it disappeared a long while ago. Some say it was blown up by gunpowder, but no one can suggest why. I imagine it must have gone before the lynching, or they would surely have used it in preference to the rather low beam in the bar.

Village inns and parish chur-ches often stand close together, but in Langton Herring they are closer than most. The apse of St Peter's is so close to the rear wall of the Elm Tree that, if there really was an escape tunnel between the two, it was a singu-larly short one. Some historians believe that the inn was built to house the stonemasons working on the church; they might have found it more convenient to join them up and fit a connecting door.

From outside, the Elm Tree looks a lot more recent than the church, but the older part still has a flagstoned floor and low-beamed ceiling, with the original bread oven beside the inglenook fireplace. The landlord is a former chef at the Dorchester Hotel and the food is renowned, but you can still sit on the old wooden settle by the inglenook to drink your beer, surrounded by brass and copper on the walls, and picture – if you have a macabre turn of mind – the body of the cheating fisherman dangling from the beam. And who is that furtive-looking figure on the telephone?

Should a Pole be in the penance cupboard for faking the Queen?

The Miners Arms
Mithian, Cornwall

Village centre

It is not called the Miners Arms for nothing. This is mining country, for copper and tin. It is an unglamorous occupation which left an unglamorous litter of ruined engine-houses and heaps of waste scattered across the countryside. This is not a part of Cornwall that visitors are steered into. In the guidebooks there is little mention of St Agnes, the nearest mining town, and none at all of Mithian, which makes the Miners Arms all the more of a find

in a county so largely devoted to tourism.

It is tucked away in the maze of lanes which lie between the main A30 road and the coast. There are villages around it with names like Perranzabuloe and Goonhaven, which rarely feature in the holiday brochures. The only local tourist attractions are St Agnes Head, from where you can see a thirty-mile sweep of the Cornish coastline, and St Agnes Beacon, six hundred feet high and a good lookout point for viewing the sadly despoiled countryside, including the remains of Wheal Coates, Wheal Kitty and the other local mines. The last one closed in 1917, and the miners mostly emigrated to find work elsewhere. It used to be said that wherever in the world you found a hole in the ground, inside it you would find a St Agnes miner...

Most visitors keep on heading south past the principal mining centres of Redruth and Camborne to the artistic delights and crowded streets of St Ives. Mithian is not particularly artistic, but it is certainly not crowded, and the Miners Arms has retained its village inn atmosphere, though it has been extended to include the adjoining cottage. It still has its wood-block floors, its low ceilings and its plain stone walls. It was not actually built for the miners, though generations of miners have used it. Originally it was a retreat for monks, and halfway up the stairs is a penance cupboard, which used to have a carved mahogany seat to offer a modicum of comfort for the penitent occupants, but these days it is just a cupboard.

The date 1577 is carved into one of the ceilings in the form of a rosette. It seems likely that it was added some time after the place was built, because 1577 was in Queen Elizabeth's reign, when monks were hardly being encouraged to build retreats. Quite the contrary, in fact. This was the period when England was under threat from Roman Catholic Spain, which increased the Queen's antipathy towards Catholic monks.

Mithian was about as far from the royal court as you could get, an obscure corner of a province which still considered itself independent, and the Miners

The penance cupboard on the stairs was once occupied by penitent monks; now it is just a cupboard.

Arms must have been as popular among refugee monks as among local miners. But it was still necessary to take precautions. A secret chamber was recently uncovered behind one of the fireplaces, and local legend has it that there was a tiny chapel upstairs which could instantly be converted into a bedroom. There was also a secret tunnel – isn't there always? – between the inn and the nearby manor house, where presumably the squire had Catholic sympathies. The tunnel caved in many years ago, and nobody seems to remember much about the chapel.

The feature which does still strike you, however, is the wall-painting of Queen Elizabeth, who was responsible for all the problems of the local monks. It seems a little curious that they should display a portrait of their main persecutor, unless it was a ploy to deceive visiting Protestants. But there is another explanation which I have yet to find in any of the local literature.

I had a chat with a gentleman who lives across the road from the inn; his Miners Arms T-shirt indicated that he was a regular. We talked about the chapel, the tunnel, the penance cupboard and the secret chamber, then got around to the painting. He assured me that it was not painted by one of Elizabeth's contemporaries, as most visitors assume. It was actually the work of an itinerant Polish artist who came to the village as recently as the 1950s. He had presumably seen the date on the ceiling, discovered who the monarch was in 1577, but had not appreciated which side she was on. If any of those refugee monks returned today, that painting might give them a very nasty jolt.

A folly on the hillside and Loonies in the bar

The Phelips Arms
Montacute, Somerset

Close to Montacute House

Many village inns were founded to provide lodgings for the masons building the parish church, but here is an inn, so it is believed, which was provided for masons who were merely building a house. Mind you, it was quite a house. The Phelips Arms – and it really is Phelips, not Philips – stands close by Montacute House, a magnificent Elizabethan mansion. This was built at the end of the sixteenth century by Edward Phelips, who became Speaker of the House of Commons under James I, and led the prosecution at the trial of Guy Fawkes.

It is difficult to visualise a link between the mansion and the inn, because the present Phelips Arms is built in a very different style, but it could well stand on the site of the original lodging house. Certainly it stood there in the early days of coaching, when Montacute was on the main route from London to Exeter. A number of other inns flourished in the village at that time, but by 1840 only two survived, the Phelips Arms and the King's Arms. When the railway arrived in 1853 it was the beginning of the end for the coaching trade, and the Phelips Arms was left with just the scratches by the door made by the coach wheels when the driver was in too much of a hurry to get to the stables beyond.

While Montacute still has a Phelips Arms, it no longer has a Phelips. The family was already living there when Thomas Phelips acquired the land and property of the local Cluniac monastery, after the Dissolution. It was his son Edward who built Montacute House, which remained the family home for over three hundred years, but in 1931 passed to the National Trust. The family live in Hampshire now, but they still have an interest in the estate, and I hope they sometimes drop in for a drink at the old-fashioned inn which bears their arms and their name. They can still enjoy a quiet pint without being disturbed by small children, piped music or electronic games.

The village itself takes its name from the peaked hill that rises above the inn, the *mons acutus*. This was where a Holy Cross was dug up in the eleventh century, as the result of a vision. The finder apparently believed it to be as significant a discovery as the Holy Grail, so he presented it to King Harold to ensure his victory against the invading Normans. Alas, it was not as powerful as he had thought.

Perhaps to rub it in a bit, the Norman family of Mortain, who acquired Montacute after the Conquest, built a castle on the hill where the non-Grail had been found. But history has mocked the Normans in their turn. The castle has long since disappeared, and in its place stands one of those pointless 'follies' – or 'a fancy of Georgian romanticism' as one writer more politely describes it – where the owner once managed to fly a pennon fifty-six yards long, for absolutely no reason I can think of except to win a bet or to get into the eighteenth-century version of the *Guinness Book of Records*.

The regulars at the Phelips Arms no doubt watched this performance and, perhaps, had a bet or two themselves on how long the pennon – or indeed the folly – would stay up; then they went back to their skittles. But the inn was more closely involved in another curious event in the village, which developed more dramatically.

The story goes that the village bell-ringers wanted to ring a peal on a particular saint's day, but the vicar refused permission. It may have been the same vicar who, when fives was first introduced into England, removed all the projections on the church tower so that he could use it to play against. Perhaps he felt the bells would put him off his game.

The ringers were, apparently, so incensed by his refusal that they started a riot, which became so serious that the militia had to be despatched from Taunton to quell it. The ringleaders were imprisoned in a room at the Phelips Arms, but one of them managed to get out, probably with some help from his friends. He made his way to the coast and took a ship to the colonies. I am told there is a village in Australia called Montacute which he founded – and I hope you can hear the church bells ringing there on every saint's day.

There have been no riots in Montacute lately, but the Phelips Arms still has its excitements. It does, after all, play a key role in the political life of the nation – as the local headquarters of the Monster Raving Loony Party.

Never mind the vicar's chimneys, how about the piscina in the bar!

The Bush
Morwenstow, Cornwall

Crosstown

Morwenstow still seems to live in the shadow of its eccentric Victorian vicar, Robert Stephen Hawker. Visitors to the village mainly come to see the vicarage he built, with chimneys shaped like the towers of his previous churches – except for the kitchen chimney, which is modelled on his mother's tomb. Or they climb along the cliff to visit the wooden shack where he spent much of his time, meditating and watching out for shipwrecks; it is now the smallest building owned by the National Trust.

More knowledgeable visitors may have read about his curious practice of visiting his parishioners on a mule, accompanied by his pet pig. He would wear either a yellow blanket with a hole in it for his head – a replica, he said, of the garb worn by early Cornish saints – or, on more formal occasions, a claret-coloured tailcoat over a fisherman's jersey, which had a red cross on it where the spear pierced Jesus's side.

His black socks were knitted from the wool of a favourite sheep.

He married a woman twice his age, and when she died he married again, to a girl forty years his junior. He smoked opium, studied the occult, took services wearing red gloves and, as a final gesture, became a Roman Catholic on his deathbed. Yet he was much loved by most of his flock; one of them wrote, 'Our Vicar is slightly cracked – but he's a very clever old soul.'

Against that kind of competition, other features of Morwenstow's history rather pale, but it does have another fascinating story to tell, based on its village inn, the Bush. The inn looks more like a farmhouse, and the entrance to the bar is through a courtyard where one can easily picture cattle being penned, but its history goes back much further than that. It is thought to be on the site of a small oratory established by St Morwenna in the fifth century, and the oldest part of the building dates back to about AD 950.

There is a reminder of that period at the end of the bar. Next to one of the beer-pump handles, and sometimes concealed by a flower arrangement on its cover, there is a Celtic piscina made of serpentine stone. It was used for washing Communion vessels, only a few feet from where the beer glasses are washed now.

The little chapel was occupied by Celtic hermits until the thirteenth century, then they moved out and the Cistercian monks moved in. They liked remote places and Morwenstow was about as remote as they could get, at the end of a long narrow lane which stops quite close to the cliffs. They added what is now the dining-room at the Bush, and there have been other minor additions over the centuries, when it became a cobbler's shop and then an inn. At this time it was much frequented by the local smugglers and wreckers – which meant most of the male population of the village. The atmosphere in the pub is still so placid and homely that those ancient monks and hermits would feel immediately at home. The floor is bare, the furnishings basic, the fare simple.

There are no electronic gadgets, no piped music, no children, no dogs. The landlord likes it that way, so do the locals, and so indeed do I.

The Bush, in fact, is much the same as it was in the days of Robert Hawker, who I imagine enjoyed his glass of ale as much as anyone. Inevitably the inn is said to be haunted, with strange footsteps being heard, doors being opened and the like. It would be nice to think that it was the famous vicar himself who sometimes returned to see how his parishioners were faring. Each time I visit the Bush I look hopefully at the big built-in settle by the fire, just in case I spot a figure sitting there in a claret-coloured tailcoat, a fisherman's jersey with a cross on it, and black woollen socks.

It would not be his first 'manifestation'. As a youth he startled the good folk of Bude by appearing on a rock off the coast wearing a long wig made of seaweed and an oilskin wrapped round his legs to look like a tail, and wailing plaintively to the moon. They were even more startled when the 'mermaid' finally broke into the National Anthem before disappearing into the waves for ever.

With a record like that, I would not put it past Robert Hawker to have another go. So I suggest that, if you ever pay a visit to the Bush, you keep an eye on that settle as well.

One of the little eccentricities of the Revd Robert Hawker. The chimneys on his rectory opposite the Bush are modelled on church towers

The assassin missed the Duke of Monmouth - but then came Sedgemoor

Not a lot has changed here since Samuel Pepys 'dined very well for 10s'.

The George
Norton St Philip, Somerset

The High Street

'The Duke of Monmouth was shot at here', says the caption on the picture postcards at the George. It may be a macabre claim to fame, but at least it is a welcome variation on the usual 'Queen Elizabeth slept here', 'Cromwell stabled his horses here' or – in the Lake District – 'William Wordsworth wrote a sonnet here'. A hired assassin was said to have been offered a thousand pounds to take a pot-shot at the Duke as he was shaving by his bedroom window. During recent renovations some lead shot was found in a wooden beam which may or may not confirm it. According to a local ballad the Duke was very laid-back about the whole affair. After the shot

...he gaily turned him round
And said: 'My man, you've missed your mark
And lost your thousand pound.'

28

It was only a temporary reprieve. His supporters had managed to fend off the Royalist troops in skirmishes around the village, but they failed to follow up their advantage. Instead of pursuing them they set off in the opposite direction the next day, leaving the wounded behind at the George, but they only got as far as Sedgemoor – and that was that. After their defeat the George came into use again in a different role, to house the Duke's captured followers in what is now the Dungeon Bar. In due course, along came Judge Jeffreys and the Bloody Assizes, and all of the prisoners were hanged, with the addition of an unfortunate bystander who opened the door for them and found himself joining them on the gallows.

The Pitchfork Rebellion, as it came to be known in school textbooks, was the saddest chapter in the long history of the George. It is claimed to be the oldest continually licensed inn in the country, built in the thirteenth century and with a licence dating back to 1397. Sceptics may point out that the first alehouse licence was granted by Edward VI in 1552, but the Carthusian monks who built the George were also Lords of the Manor, and quite capable of granting their own licences. Anyway, every monastery had a brew-house and supplied its guests with ale. The George was the guest-house for the monastery at Hinton, and offered hospitality to the wool merchants who did business with the monks. After the monasteries were dissolved, the George continued to function as the village inn, and the ale continued to flow, as it has done ever since.

It has to be said that few village inns look quite so grand. It has its original lower floor, with a massive Gothic doorway and a stone-built platform beside it from which waggons were loaded. The upper-storey wool hall was destroyed by fire in about 1500 and rebuilt in half-timbering. Nothing much has changed structurally since.

But in spite of its imposing exterior, the main bar is almost frugal in its simplicity. Beneath the lofty beamed ceiling and the high mullioned windows there are just long plain tables, wooden settles and a bare floor. Only the vast fireplace is a little overwhelming. The lounge is more up-market, with panelled walls and antique furniture. It all looks much the same, I imagine, as it did in June 1668 when Samuel Pepys dropped in for a meal with his wife and servants on their way from Salisbury to Bath. He seemed well pleased with the fare and with the prices – 'Dined very well for 10s' – but was rather more impressed, it seems, by the tombstone in the church down the lane to a pair of local Siamese twins 'that had two bodies upward and one stomach, and there lie buried'.

Some seventy years ago the George fell on hard times. A visitor wrote in 1926: 'The vast building is now no more than a village alehouse, and with a modern bar fitted in pitch-pine!' The exclamation mark is his; you can almost feel him shudder. 'The greater part of the interior is in a dismantled condition...and the long ranges of the upper floors are now dilapidated.'

Since then, happily, the George's fortunes have changed. It was sold in 1960, and the new owners installed a landlord who ran it admirably for thirty years. The current tenants were appointed in 1993 'with the view of renovating and revitalising this historic inn'.

The phrase 'renovating and revitalising' has an ominous ring to it. It often means pool tables, pinball machines and – shudder, shudder – even a pitch-pine bar. The most striking change, however, has been the catering. In contrast to Egon Ronay's rather dismissive comment in 1992, 'Food is secondary, but go for the daily special,' the standard menu now runs to six foolscap pages. Traditionalists may wonder whether that is good news or bad.

A letterbox with no letters, just some very odd stamps

The Peter Tavy Inn
Peter Tavy, Devon

Near the church

Peter Tavy and Mary Tavy sound a rather charming couple, but in fact they grew up as unromantic mining villages, and the hatred between them was proverbial. The story goes that a Peter Tavy man was walking beside the river which links the two villages when he saw someone in the water, shouting for help.

'Where be you from?' he enquired.

'Mary Tavy,' came the spluttered reply.

'Drown, then,' said the man from Peter Tavy, and continued his walk.

The villagers are a lot more civil to each other these days, and the villages have mellowed too. They are set right on the edge of Dartmoor, away from the main road, and they provide welcome havens for walkers on the moor. Both have village inns, but while Mary Tavy's has acquired the fanciful name of the Elephant's Nest, in honour of a past landlord of exceptional girth, in Peter Tavy nobody has devised anything more original than the Peter Tavy Inn.

It was originally a farm cottage and smithy, now much expanded with a dining-room added at the rear, but the bar itself, although recently modernised, still retains its flagstone floor and much of the old brickwork has been preserved. Even the new beams have been 'distressed' to emulate the old ones – which can be a source of distress in itself to the purists, but at least it shows willing.

The most intriguing feature of the Peter Tavy is kept behind the bar, where the beer is still tapped direct from the cask. Tucked away among the barrels are a couple of well-thumbed (and slightly beer-stained) exercise books, which are produced only if specifically asked for. The older one is inscribed on the front page, 'David, Jill and Helen – the Derriford Dreamers, August 1985'. It is full of strange, stamped inscriptions and messages, which continue into the second book. The signatures include Lady Emma and her Minder, Blind Pew, Jude the Obscure, Desperate Dan and Beryl the Peril, and, in my view, the most ingenious, 'Warren Peace' – under a picture of two friendly rabbits.

Somewhere in these pages there ought to be Alice Through the Letterbox, because these bizarre characters are all part of the Dartmoor Letterbox network, which involves many hundreds of walkers on the moor who prefer to use assumed names. It all started with a message left in a bottle on the bank of Cranmore Pool in one of the more inaccessible corners of Dartmoor. Whoever put it there gave the location to a friend, who left another message in it and set up a second 'letterbox' elsewhere. Then he told a friend, who told a friend, and the letterboxes multiplied until, today, there are over five thousand.

Most of them are concealed in trees, or down rabbit holes, or under rocks; whoever installs them is responsible for maintaining them. But about sixty are in more accessible and civilised locations, in village inns like the Peter Tavy, and indeed in the Elephant's Nest. Each inn has its own distinctive stamp, and a visiting 'postman' gets his own book stamped as well as putting his entry in the inn's.

There is an informal organisation which produces a gazetteer of letterbox locations, but it is accompanied by a stern warning not to allow it to fall into the wrong hands. Vandals could wreak havoc with the whole system if they knew where to look. These days the set-up has become so sophisticated that enthusiastic 'postmen' can acquire '100 Club' T-shirts, indicating they have visited a hundred letterboxes, and for the real elite there are T-shirts for the '5000 Club'.

This was all new to me, not being even a member of the '1 Club', but there is another story attached to

The stamp of approval – another 'posting' in the Dartmoor letterbox network.

the Peter Tavy which has a familiar ring about it; I am sure it must have been linked to other inns in other villages. But it features in the local folklore, so let the Peter Tavy have the credit for this interesting tale.

The inn is just down the lane from the church of St Peter's (hence the village's name, linked with the River Tavy). A former vicar, the Reverend McBean, would not begin morning service until he was sure there were no customers lingering in the bar. During the opening hymn, therefore, he would send his churchwarden, one Roger Mudge, to check that it was empty. But it so happened that Mr Mudge was a relative of the landlord, and as he walked slowly towards the Peter Tavy he repeated more and more loudly: 'I'm coming, Cousin Tom, I'm coming.' Not surprisingly, when he opened the door the bar was empty, and he could report in all honesty that nobody was there. As one chronicler records: 'The sermon would then commence, the Vicar at the same time congratulating himself upon his parishioners showing such a regard for the hours of divine worship.'

*A literary sheriff, a fighting parson – and a blacksmith
who hammered like the clappers*

Journey's End
Ringmore, Devon

Cul-de-sac near the church

If you are ever in the vicinity of Bigbury-on-Sea
you will feel obliged to visit the Pilchard Inn on
Burgh Island, if only to have a ride on the famous
'tractor' – the eight-foot-high platform on wheels
which can comfortably cross the hundred yards to
the island during the six or eight hours each day when
the sand is covered by the tide. The inn itself,
frequented for six hundred years by fishermen and
smugglers, is worth a visit in its own right. It is now

flanked by an art deco hotel which was a favourite
haunt of Agatha Christie, who went there to write,
and of the Duke of Windsor and Mrs Simpson, who
had other things on their mind.

However, when you have had your fill of Burgh
Island, and the swarms of sightseers queuing up for
the tractor, it is worth escaping from the tourist route
and taking the little lanes around Bigbury which lead
to a genuinely unspoilt village, a deserted cove, and

another ancient inn where another writer of the 1920s completed his most famous work.

The name of the inn is Journey's End, and indeed it would offer a felicitous end to any journey, but this was where Robert Cedric Sheriff, playwright and novelist, wrote the final scenes of *Journey's End*, his classic play about the First World War, set in the trenches in 1918. A framed programme of an early performance, signed by the cast, is in the bar.

It is difficult to imagine a greater contrast between the setting of *Journey's End* the play, and Journey's End the inn. Ringmore is one of those picture-postcard Devon villages where the black-and-white, thatched cottages really do have roses round the door, and one half expects the door to be opened by a rosy-cheeked yokel in a smock and a big floppy hat. The residents may still be rosy-cheeked, but they are a little more sophisticated these days, to such an extent that they have formed a local historical society and produced a dossier on almost every building in the village, including – conveniently – Journey's End.

It was the New Inn until Mr Sheriff passed this way, and like most New Inns it was already very old; the original building was erected in the thirteenth century. It was probably licensed as an alehouse when Queen Elizabeth set up a chain of 'New Inns' for the benefit of merchants and other travellers. Judging by the number that still claim 'Queen Elizabeth slept here', she tested most of them personally, but not even the devoted research of the historical society could uncover any evidence of her visiting Ringmore.

The inn did have an official visit, however, in 1685, when church inspectors reported that it was 'a house of good order, no cards, no dice to be used'. The rules are not quite so strict now, but the bar still preserves the traditional atmosphere that the inspectors enjoyed, back in the days of Charles II.

The bar is 'journey's end' for a programme of one of the early performances, signed by the cast.

In the eighteenth century the local elders held their meetings in what is now the restaurant and, later, part of the inn was used as a shop. Those were its official functions, but unofficially the inn must have been a popular haunt for the smugglers and wreckers who operated from Aylmer Cove, twenty minutes' walk down the valley, past a farmhouse, a cottage, and very little else.

One of the farm buildings has a cannon-ball embedded in the wall, but it is unlikely that the Customs and Excise brought in heavy artillery to mow down the smugglers. It may have been looted from a wrecked Spanish galleon, or Cromwell's men may have fired it when they landed at Aylmer Cove to capture Ringmore's fighting rector, William Lane. He had set up a battery of cannon on the main road at Aveton Gifford to halt the Roundhead advance and, when he could hold out no longer, he spiked the guns and pushed them into the river before heading back to Ringmore. The landing party burnt down his rectory, but Parson Lane hid in the church tower for three months, sustained by food from his parishioners plus, I hope, the odd pint of ale from the inn down the lane. Then he escaped to France, and eventually gained a pardon.

I am sure the inn supplied refreshment also to the enterprising blacksmith who came to the rescue when the clapper fell off one of the church bells during a wedding peal. The gallant fellow climbed into the belfry – having plugged his ears, I trust – and joined in the peal by hitting the bell with his blacksmith's hammer. Alas, during the subsequent celebrations at the inn there was a crash back at the church. His hefty blows had proved too much for the ageing bell, and having already lost its clapper it gave up the struggle completely and fell in pieces to the belfry floor.

It too had reached its Journey's End.

Why was poor Adele buried under the floor in the bar?

The St Kew Inn
St Kew, Cornwall

Churchtown

The village of St Kew is just a church, an inn, a telephone box and a tiny handful of cottages, tucked away in a fold of the hills which lie between the A39 trunk road and the north Cornish coast. To most holiday motorists the name is known only because of St Kew Highway, which is a textbook example of twentieth-century ribbon development along a main road, with a petrol station as its most exciting feature. If they are planning to turn off the road at this point, it is probably to visit the picture-postcard fishing village of Port Isaac or the sandy beaches near Polzeath. Either way, they will see nothing of St Kew itself, unless they happen to get lost in the maze of lanes which surround it, misled by signposts which seem designed primarily to confuse.

The St Kew Inn is alongside the church, which confusingly is dedicated not to St Kew but to St James the Great. It is difficult to decide which place has the more fascinating story to tell. The inn must get priority, but I will visit the church briefly later – as indeed most visitors do.

The stone walls of the St Kew Inn date back to the fifteenth century, but it was licensed only in the eighteenth. It still has a huge open kitchen range with earthenware flagons on the high mantelpiece above, and the floors are shiny Delabole slate, from the quarry ten miles away. But there is one patch of concrete in the slate, just beside the bar, a rather mundane reminder of a macabre discovery and the curious happenings which followed.

A teenage girl was buried under the floor of the bar, and occasionally her spirit returns – but at the moment nobody seems too bothered.

About sixteen years ago a new water pipe was laid in the bar and the floor was dug up. The body of a teenage girl was found beneath this spot. It had lain there, so the experts said, for the best part of a century. The landlord told me that nobody knew who she was or how she came to be there, but over the years she has become known as Adele, a curious name for a Victorian village girl.

Her body was taken away and re-buried in consecrated ground, but her spirit, it seems, remained behind. There have been various manifestations. The landlord himself has felt her pass him in the bar, and a customer who was there said she saw a girl brush past him, but could not describe her. Adele only appears, he told me, when alterations are being carried out at the inn; on that occasion a former stable was being converted into an extra bar.

Nobody seems too disturbed that the inn has a ghost. It was probably just by chance that, during the whole time I was there, even though the place was quite crowded, nobody stood on that concrete slab by the bar.

The other unusual female at the St Kew Inn is Aneka. She lives in an outhouse at the entrance to the beer garden across the lane, and monitors the comings and goings. Aneka is a Nubian goat, an unexpected animal to be frequenting a Cornish inn, and with a name almost as unlikely as Adele, but like Adele she is largely taken for granted.

The garden offers two bonuses, as well as being a useful overflow area in the peak season. It is a splendid place to sit and admire the old stone inn, with the ivy climbing up the walls and the flowertubs set out on the cobbled forecourt. Then you only have to make a quarter-turn and you can admire the Church of St James the Great, which also contains some most unusual features.

For instance: a Book of Hours dated 1623, an Elizabethan pulpit, a fifteenth-century lantern cross, a stained-glass window of the Passion dated 1469, another depicting the Tree of Jesse which is even older, around 1350 and, by far its oldest relic, the fifth-century Ogham Stone, so called because the writing on it is in Ogham, an ancient alphabet used by the earliest Celts in Britain. It is all straight lines and quite unreadable to anyone but an Ogham expert, who must be almost as rare as the language itself. One who has read the inscription, however, says it spells the name IUPTI, the Ogham version of Iuptus.

Presumably Iuptus was buried at St Kew and this was his headstone. If the same expert could come up with the Ogham equivalent of Adele, it might be appropriate to scratch it on that concrete slab in the bar of the St Kew Inn. It would provide quite a talking-point for the tourists – and for bewildered antiquarians in centuries to come.

Catching the Sunday trade with a hard sell in the churchyard

The Queen's Head
St Stephen, Cornwall

The Square

There is a St Stephens in Cornwall as well as St Stephen, which must make life difficult for postmen. It also makes it even more unlikely that you will find the Queen's Head, which is well off the tourist track anyway. If you ask a Cornishman the way to St Stephen, he will probably assume you are looking for its more picturesque near-namesake, and direct you to St Stephens, just across the river from Launceston, which was once the county capital and is still a popular tourist centre. The tourists often wander across the medieval foot-bridge to stroll around St Stephens, which is believed to have an even longer history than Launceston itself.

St Stephen without an 's' – but with the Queen's Head – is in quite different surroundings, forty miles to the south-west. It lies in that industrial area of Cornwall based on St Austell which the Cornish tourist agencies try not to think about, and tourists try to avoid. While the Midlands have their Black Country, Cornwall has its White Country, where a third of the working population are employed in the china-clay industry, and the mountains of spoil have been spreading across the countryside for nearly 250 years. It is therefore one of the few areas in Cornwall where, even at the height of the holiday season, the local inn is still used primarily by the locals – and none more so than the Queen's Head.

The village itself is not too prepossessing. You drive into it from St Austell past a moonscape of white mountains and, although there is a helpful sign

The weird 'moonscape' of china-clay workings which provide the backdrop for the Queen's Head.

on the main road saying, 'Queen's Head, first turning on the right', it is not encouraging to find the turning is marked 'No Entry'. You actually need the second turning on the right, and once you have found it the Queen's Head lies ahead of you, a sturdy square Georgian inn which was once the centre for the local coaching trade. The stables have been demolished to make a car park, and the original four small rooms on the ground floor have been knocked into one, but it is still a homely local, and there are plenty of reminders of its earlier days.

A sepia photograph shows a coach about to leave outside the inn, and there is a composite picture, dating back to the same period, of Cornish wrestlers, some of them local men with relatives still living in the village. Another photograph shows a turn-of-the-century wedding couple who look as if they have

a story to tell, but I am afraid no one knows what it is. A previous landlord bought it from a travelling dealer to fill a gap on the wall – the couple actually lived in Leeds.

St Stephen has had a quiet existence and rarely hits the headlines, but there was one occasion when the Queen's Head achieved a modicum of fame, even notoriety. A report appeared in the *Royal Cornwall Gazette* in 1832 about an incident at the parish church, which stands just up the road from the inn.

'The congregation was astounded on Sunday last, on their leaving the church, by the crier announcing the following intelligence in the churchyard: "Good beer is now selling at the Queen's Head at four pence per quart".' And the *Gazette* adds disapprovingly: 'This is civilisation with a vengeance!'

I cannot help admiring the landlord, though, for displaying such enterprise. I imagine he had to compete with the King's Arms, which is just around the corner and has the advantage of standing on a busier road with more passing trade. Four pence a quart may have been an early version of an introductory special offer, and full marks for publicising it so effectively – even if the *Cornish Gazette* (and probably the vicar) took a poor view of it.

The pleasant young couple who now hold the licence have not resorted to commercials in the churchyard yet, but they do make full use of one of the natural advantages of the Queen's Head. The garden has been made accessible to customers, and it has a most striking view across the valley. In the foreground are lush green meadows, typical of the scenery found in Cornwall's more touristy areas, but in the background there is that startling mountain range of white china-clay spoil, much more attractive when seen at a distance, and the kind of extraterrestrial vista which few Cornish inns can match.

Sitting in the garden, the only 'foreigners' at the Queen's Head even at the height of the summer season, it seemed a different world from the traditional attractions of the other St Stephens – and it appealed to me just as much. I reckon this is a classic case of 'Even Stephens'.

The locals got the treasure ship's treasure –
and the Anchor got the anchor

The Anchor Inn
Seatown, Dorset

Next to the beach

On the night of 16 January 1748, while returning from Curaçao to Amsterdam, the Dutch ship *Hope* ran aground on Chesil Beach in huge seas. The foremast snapped and providentially fell towards the beach, so the entire crew was able to scramble along it to safety. They left behind a shattered hulk which was partly washed out to sea and partly buried under the pebbles – together with gold, silver and other valuables worth £50,000. By the following morning two hundred locals were plundering the wrecks; within the week, ten thousand people were taking part in West Dorset's biggest-ever treasure-hunt.

It was more than two hundred years later, however, that the *Hope* gave up its last relic. In 1985 a fisherman was trawling off the beach when his net picked up an unexpected catch, a hefty anchor which was identified as belonging to the Dutch treasure-ship. It was not gold or silver, alas, but it was of sufficient historical interest to be acquired by David Miles, the landlord of the fortuitously named Anchor Inn, which was actually built at about the time of the wreck. The anchor stands outside the inn today, a reminder of more rumbustious times when Seatown was tech-nically a fishing village, but fishing was just the day job...

The cove on which it stands was ideal for smugglers. It lies below Golden Cap, the highest cliff on this part of the Dorset coast and ideal for a smugglers' lookout point. One of the local gangs was led by a man known only as the Colonel, who was strongly suspected to be the local squire – which is perhaps why he was never apprehended. Smuggling was so rife that in 1750 Seatown qualified for its own resident exciseman, who lived in a guardhouse in the village. It must have been one of the most uncomfortable postings in the excise service, and indeed one of the unfortunate officers who landed the job is said to have been murdered at the top of the stairs in the Anchor Inn, perhaps while eavesdropping on the conversation in the bar. He is said to haunt it still.

Later four coastguard cottages were built to strengthen the arm of the law in Seatown, and there is a reminder in the Anchor Inn of one of their successes. Among the many old photographs which practically cover the walls in the bar is one of the village wheelwright and undertaker in the 1930s, a Mr Hussey, whose grandfather was not as lucky as the mysterious Colonel. He was apprehended with

The last relic to be recovered from the eighteenth-century treasure ship Hope. *A fisherman trawled it up two hundred years later, and it was acquired by the fortuitously named Anchor Inn.*

contraband in his possession, and sentenced to six months in Dorchester prison, where he died before completing his sentence.

Seatown is, of course, very close to the sea, but in no sense is it a town. With a resident population of twenty-five it is hardly even a village. The lane which runs into it from Chideock, half a mile away on the main road, passes only a handful of houses before it ends at the Anchor Inn, virtually on the beach. But during the summer months the population is multiplied a hundredfold, thanks to the vast caravan site which lies just up the lane from the inn.

Regular visitors look back nostalgically to the days when there were just a few holiday chalets along the beach, thirty-odd years ago. At that time the Anchor Inn had a memorable landlady called Veron-ica, much admired by the male holiday-makers. Her evening barb-ecues on the beach are recalled with particular relish. These days, I am afraid, there is more sophisticated entertainment. A fruit machine is brought out during the summer months to help amuse what one writer calls 'the cheery crush of caravanners and scantily clad beach people', so if you prefer an inn which lacks all these features, then the time to visit the Anchor Inn is out of season, when the fruit machine is put away, there is space to play cribbage and dominoes, and the landlord has time for a chat.

He may well tell you about the lady who lived many years ago in the Anchor Cottage, next to the inn, who was famous for her 'furmity', a special kind of porridge, sweetened and spiced. She sold the standard product at a halfpenny a portion; the de luxe version, which included a tot of rum, was sold for a penny.

Nobody ever asked where she got the rum.

Funeral processions passed through the inn - and had a beer with the bier

Not just the entrance to the inn, it was the route to the churchyard for funeral processions.

The Pack Horse
South Stoke, Avon

Near the church

There are steep roads to negotiate in South Stoke in order to reach the church, but even so, in years gone by, there must have been keen competition to act as pallbearers when anyone died in the village. The route of the funeral processions lay right through the centre of the Pack Horse inn, past a convenient serving hatch where the deceased had usually left provision for a round of drinks.

The passageway and the serving hatch are still there, but these days there are doors at each end, and funeral processions are not encouraged. The back door is the original one erected in 1647, and it still opens on to a path which leads through the beer garden to a side gate of the churchyard, but the path has been diverted round a modern building, and the side gate is kept locked. It is easy to visualise, however, how convenient it must have been for funeral cortèges coming up the hill or emerging from the Packhorse Cottages across the road – and the prospect of a free beer *en route* was a bonus.

It is not unique, incidentally, for a right-of-way to pass through an inn. The Fox at Bucks Green in West Sussex, for instance, was built across an old bridle-way, and every Christmas Day a horseman rides through the bar to maintain the ancient right of free passage. But the Pack Horse probably has the only one which combined biers with beer.

The present Pack Horse dates back to 1489, when an earlier guest-house, erected by the monks of South Stoke Priory, was rebuilt 'with two fair chambers upon the ground floor and the same upon the first' – and, of course, the passageway in between. Some of the timber work dates back to that period, and most of it is at least three hundred years old.

An early licensee, Nicholas Scudamore, joined Oliver Cromwell's army just before the battle of Naseby and volunteered to carry the regimental colours. Nobody had bothered to tell the new recruit, I suspect, that standard-bearers made easy targets, and the poor chap was shot dead in his first battle. It is not recorded whether he made his final journey through the Pack Horse passageway.

There is some doubt, in fact, whether in his day the Pack Horse occupied its present premises, or whether it was situated in what is now Pack Horse Farm. The title may have been transferred in 1825, when the original packhorse trail, which wound up the hill from the farm, was replaced by a straighter and steeper road, which now climbs through the centre of the village and passes the front door of the inn. But whichever premises were occupied by the ill-fated Mr Scudamore, there is no doubt that the Pack Horse was on its present site when the Rose family took over the licence in 1888 and held it for the next hundred-odd years.

Their activities are well documented, starting with the first Mr Rose who was the earliest resident of South Stoke to install gas – but he was so horrified when he got the first bill that he stopped using it. His son left a more lasting legacy, the heavy wooden shutters which are still fitted to the windows. He installed them during the First World War to protect his customers from the Zeppelins – though why the Germans should have wanted to bomb the Pack Horse is not too clear.

The Roses are reported to have grown rhubarb in the chimney, and there is also a cupboard in the fireplace where they were said to deposit drunks until they had sobered up. Under the hearth there is reputed to be the usual tunnel linking the inn with the church, but funeral processions much preferred the passageway, and there is no trace of it now. These days the fireplace is used only for fires, and very splendid log fires at that, fitting in with the black-beamed ceilings and the old oak settles on the quarry-tiled floor. The modern outskirts of Bath are only a mile or so away from the Pack Horse, but happily they remain centuries apart.

Monks brewed, masons built, but who played
skittles on the ceiling?

The panelled wall in the bar – from the old church across the road, or a sea-captain's cabin?

Old Church House
Torbryan, Devon

Opposite the church

There were a great many Church Houses in Britain in medieval times, built to house the masons working on the local church, but it seems to be only in South Devon that the inns they developed into are still called by that name. There is a little cluster of them around Totnes, each one with a similar background but different features.

Church House at Holberton is probably the most elaborate, since it also served as a monks' chantry house, complete with chapel. The great hall where they ate and slept, and probably taught the local children, is now divided up, and the monks, of course, have long since left, but the inn remained linked to the church until it became a free house less than fifty years ago.

Church House at Rattery is probably the oldest, dating back to the eleventh century. Its spiral stone staircase is said to date from 1030. This is a little confusing since, according to some reference books, it was built to house the craftsmen working on the

Norman church, but the Normans did not arrive in Rattery for another forty-odd years. Perhaps this is an exceptional example of forward planning. It also took a little time to find an incumbent, since the first vicar is not recorded until 1199. But it was plain sailing after that, and a complete list of incumbents from that date is hanging in the bar.

My favourite in this group, though, is Old Church House at Torbryan, a remote little village hidden in a fold of the South Devon hills. There is just the church and the inn and a score of cottages, but at one time, astonishingly, it was on the main stage route to Plymouth, and was one of the largest and most important parishes in Devon. Up to the turn of this century there was horseracing at Torbryan, and sheep-shearing feasts attended by thousands of people.

It is difficult to associate today's sleepy little village with such goings-on. Even the church has succumbed to the change in population and is now in the hands of the Redundant Churches Trust. Happily, it is being extensively restored, and the original occupants of Old Church House would view this with approval, since they were engaged on the same exercise five or six hundred years ago.

It is believed the building was also occupied by monks, who ate and slept upstairs and brewed ale below – which must have been very handy for the masons. Sir John Betjeman passed this way, and confirmed that what looks like an upstairs window was originally a door to the upper storey, approached by outside steps which have long since disappeared. The steps behind the bar which lead up to the modernised bedrooms are probably original, and are still too narrow for two monks to pass.

Old Church House has been having its renovations as well as the church across the way. When the present landlord arrived, about ten years ago, the rear of the inn was roofed with corrugated iron. He has replaced this with slates; although the adjoining cottage is thatched, the inn always seems to have been different.

He has also done a little detective work on the

impressive oak panelling which covers one wall of the bar. One reference book suggests that it was a screen salvaged from the original church when it was burnt down in the fifteenth century – which was the reason the masons were called in and Old Church House built. One might think that in a fire disastrous

enough to destroy a church, a wooden screen would not stand much chance of surviving, and it is interesting to find, on closer inspection, that there is a curved mark underneath a hook in the panelling, remarkably like the mark which a ship's lantern would make as it swung against it with the movement of the ship.

There is scarcely an inn anywhere near the coast which does not claim to contain ship's timbers, but a ship's panelled screen, perhaps from the captain's cabin, is something of a novelty, particularly as Torbryan is a dozen miles inland and has no particular connections with the sea. The debate continues.

There is no doubt, however, about the identity of the curious wooden objects hanging from the ceiling of the bar. They look like overgrown doorstops, large and round and dumpy, but they are actually old-fashioned skittles, perhaps three or four hundred years old. They must have needed a particularly powerful blow to knock them over. There is no sign of a skittle alley at the inn, and one wonders where they were used, and by whom. But at least there is no suggestion they came from a ship.

Southern Region

Swindon

Chippenham

Lacock
The
George
Inn

Heddington
The Ivy

WILTSHIRE

BERKSHIRE

Holyport
The Belgian Arms

Frilsham
The Pot Kiln
Reading

Windsor

Beckhampton
The Waggon and Horses

Binfield
The Stag and Hounds

Guildford

HAMPSHIRE

Winchester

Salisbury

Southampton

Shere
The White Horse

SURREY

Chiddingfold
The Crown

WEST SUSSEX

Withyham
The Dorset Arms

Pluckley
The Dering Arms

Maidstone

KENT

Canterbury

Margate

Royal Tunbridge
Wells

Biddenden
The Three Chimneys

EAST
SUSSEX

Folkestone

Dover

Aldington
The Walnut Tree

Stopham Bridge
The White Hart

Langstone
The Royal Oak

Portsmouth

Chichester

Worthing

Dragons Green
The George and Dragon

Brighton

Hastings

Eastbourne

Snargate
The Red Lion

Smugglers in the attic and a skull in the cellar –
it's just the Aldington Blues

The 'secret' room above the fireplace, accessible only by ladder, was originally a
children's bedroom, but the smugglers found it useful too.

The Walnut Tree
Aldington, Kent

Roman Road, opposite village hall

Aldington might seem an unlikely place for smugglers. It is six miles from the sea, and these days it has a detention centre on its doorstep and the M20 motorway only just out of earshot. But it stands on high ground, looking out across the flat expanse of Romney Marsh, and a light set in the attic window of the Walnut Tree could be seen as far away as the Channel coast, to provide a warning or an all-clear. This was, in fact, the headquarters of the Aldington Blues, the most notorious gang of smugglers in Kent, and during the early years of the last century they operated along a stretch of the coastline from Camber to Sandgate, and sometimes as far as Dover and Deal.

Aldington consists largely of modern houses these days, but the Walnut Tree still looks the part, its small leaded windows and sturdy doors a match for any exciseman. Inside it is full of nooks and crannies and confusing passages. Above the bar there is a secret room which can be reached only by ladder, and a convenient tunnel in the cellar is supposed to have led to the church, more than a mile away. The oldest part of the building is said to date from the days of Richard I, and the upper storey was added in the fifteenth century – including the secret room, which was not intended to be particularly secret, just a bedroom for the children.

By the end of the seventeenth century a brew-house had been added, and it was licensed for the sale of ale and cider in 1704. Even at that stage there was a walnut tree in the garden, and the inn was registered as the Walnut Tree in 1749. Then came the nineteenth century, the Napoleonic Wars – and the Aldington Blues, later to become the Ransley Gang.

Romney Marsh still has reminders of Napoleon – the Martello towers at Dymchurch built to repel an invasion, the Royal Military Canal from Appledore to Hythe, dug to cut off the marsh if a landing was successful. But reminders of the old smuggling days are less obvious. Dymchurch does have a festival in memory of their notorious parson Dr Syn, but he was just a fictional smuggler, created by the local author Russell Thorndike. The Aldington Blues were very real, but the Walnut Tree is their only memorial.

Their first leader was Cephas Quested, but in 1821 he was spotted with contraband at Camber by the preventive officers known as the Coast Blockade. They pursued him across Walland Marsh and captured him at Brookland, along with Richard Wraight, brother of the landlord of the Walnut Tree. Another member of the gang was wounded but reached the inn and hid there successfully. Wraight was acquitted but Quested was hanged, and the smugglers were left without a leader. Another Aldington man, George Ransley, took over, and for

the next five years the Ransley Gang ruled the marshes, bringing ashore virtually whatever contraband they fancied. If there were any brandy-loving parsons in that part of Kent, they were probably sure of an unlimited supply.

But in 1826 the Ransley Gang went too far – as far as Dover beach, in fact, where they killed a quartermaster of the Coast Blockade within sight of his barracks. They are said to have used long duck-guns, which must have been tricky to manoeuvre but very unpleasant to be shot by. A £500 reward was offered, a quite astonishing sum in those days, and it proved too much for one member of the gang to resist. He turned informer, and in the early hours of an October morning there was a full-scale raid on Aldington and the Walnut Tree by Bow Street Runners and members of the Blockade.

The whole gang was captured, including Ransley himself, but curiously none of them ended up on the gallows. Perhaps all those brandy-loving parsons had friends where it counted. At the trial nine men were found guilty of smuggling, but the death sentence was reduced to transportation for life, and Ransley was sent to Tasmania. His wife and children followed, and in 1838 he was given a full pardon on condition he never returned to England. By then he was not too bothered; he was doing very nicely in Tasmania, became a prosperous farmer, and lived well into his eighties.

All exciting stuff, and you still get a flavour of it in the period atmosphere of the Walnut Tree. But there is a much more macabre tale attached to the inn as a bonus. About fifty years ago a skull was dug up in the cellar, possibly that of a member of the gang who was buried there secretly, but it was never identified. The story developed that whoever it was could not bear to leave the cellar, and it was left undisturbed. Thirty years later, however, a tidy-minded landlord put the skull in a rubbish skip. All manner of unpleasant things happened, to such a degree that the landlord had to move out and live in a hotel. The inn was exorcised, and the skull was retrieved and given a Christian burial. There have been no problems since.

A ghostly waggon, a grey lady, and Charles Dickens's 'human' chair

The Waggon and Horses
Beckhampton, Wiltshire

On the corner of the A4 and A361

The Waggon and Horses is often regarded as a coaching inn, which is borne out by its key situation at the junction of the old Bath Road and the one linking Salisbury with the Midlands – both much quieter now better routes are available. But as its name suggests, it was originally more of a waggoning inn, a stopping place for the massive waggons which were the sixteenth-century equivalent of a heavy goods vehicle. The waggons were big and heavy enough to need eight-foot wheels to support them and a team of cart-horses to haul them, with quite often a couple more horses at the back to act as brakes on the hills. The inn had a smithy where the horses could be reshod, and over the road there were stables, with hay lofts which served as overnight accommodation for the carters while the horses slept below.

Inevitably, there is a ghostly coach story, but in this case it is a ghostly waggon, which is driven past the inn on each anniversary of an accident in which it overturned, coming too fast down a hill. The horses fore and aft, the driver and a couple of passengers all died. The version I heard was that it crashed into a roundabout, which sounds slightly suspicious – there were not too many road roundabouts in the sixteenth century. But perhaps it happened where the roundabout now is, a few yards up the road from the inn.

If you are still suspicious of the ghostly waggon, then how about the ghostly nun? She committed suicide in the tack room at the Waggon and Horses, and there have been various sightings of the 'Grey Lady' since. A woman customer who was told this story by the landlord some months ago promptly contradicted him. 'It's not a Grey Lady,' she said, 'it's a man – over there by the fireplace.' And she described in great detail the clothes and general appearance of a person the landlord was totally unable to see. This is the sort of problem you get when you start telling ghost stories.

Charles Dickens might have sat in this settle composing the Pickwick Papers ; *the inn certainly tallies with the Bagman's Tale.*

But it was a different kind of ghost story which Charles Dickens told, or rather the Bagman did, in *Pickwick Papers*, and which is also associated with the Waggon and Horses. It is thought to be the original of the inn in 'The Bagman's Tale', where a commercial traveller called Tom Smart took shelter after driving his gig one wild night across the Marlborough Downs. 'It was a strange old place, built of a kind of shingle, inlaid as it were with cross-beams, with gable-topped windows projecting completely over the pathway, and a low door with a dark porch, and a couple of steep steps leading down into the house...'

During a bibulous evening he became very envious of another customer who was chatting up the landlady – 'a buxom widow of somewhere about eight-and-forty or thereabouts, with a face as comfortable as the bar' – and he was still pondering ways of chatting her up himself as he went to bed. In his room he noticed 'a strange, grim-looking high-backed chair, carved in the most fantastic manner, with a flowered damask cushion, and the round knobs at the bottom of the legs tied up in red cloth, as if it had got the gout in its toes'.

During the night he woke up to see the chair turning into a gnarled old man, who revealed he was the landlady's guardian and wanted to save her from the customer in the bar. He told Tom the man was married and had left in a wardrobe a letter from his wife, begging him to return home. In the morning the chair had turned back into a chair again, but Tom found the letter in the wardrobe and showed it to the landlady. She duly spurned his rival and, in due course, they were married – and on the day of the wedding Tom noticed that the chair was creaking very noisily, 'but he couldn't say for certain whether it was with pleasure or bodily infirmity...'

Alas, I found no creaking chair at the Waggon and Horses as evidence, and indeed according to the story Tom and the widow went to France and the old house was pulled down. But as well as looking like the inn in the story – the 'kind of shingle' walls are actually broken-up stones from the nearby Avebury Circle – there would appear to be another similarity. It is said that in Dickens's day the inn had a very attractive landlady and, for reasons that can only be guessed at, she always gave him the best room in the house.

It is not difficult to visualise Charles Dickens, or even Tom Smart, in the bar of the Waggon and Horses. He could be sitting on the high-backed curved settle, surrounded by the stuffed squirrels in glass cases, the Victorian pictures, and the 1876 newspaper cutting on the wall reporting a penny-farthing ride from London to Bath. The only items out of period are the fruit machine and the piped music, but when I was there the music was by the Carpenters, and the romantic Tom Smart might have quite fancied that.

Don't bother to count the chimneys, just remember the French for 'road'

The Three Chimneys
Biddenden, Kent

On the A262 towards Sissinghurst

This corner of Kent is picture-postcard country, and Biddenden is almost too good to be true. If the houses are not half-timbered they are clad with mellow red tiles, and in the case of the Cloth Hall you get both – one side of the Hall is black-and-white timber and plaster, the other is red tiles with gables and oriel windows. The whole village looks straight out of a film set.

By comparison, Sissinghurst looks a little more lived-in. The houses are mostly white weatherboard, and the church, instead of dating back to the fourteenth century like Biddenden's, is a Victorian building which one expert has described as 'a poor thing with a lean west tower and a stunted chancel'.

On the other hand, the only famous figures connected with Biddenden, and depicted on the village sign, are the unfortunate Biddenden Maids, Siamese twin sisters who were joined at shoulder and hip. Sissinghurst, however, had Sir Harold Nicolson and his wife Vita Sackville-West, who created the renowned garden at Sissinghurst Castle and brought the village international fame.

Set between these two contrasting villages, and enjoying the best of both worlds, is the Three Chimneys, a successful combination of down-market 'local' and up-market inn for the tourists. Like the rest of Biddenden, which it officially belongs to, it looks good enough for a picture postcard, whitewashed and half-timbered. Inside there is a network of little rooms with beams and oak panels and flagstoned floors. The public bar remains basic, and geared to drinking, not eating, but the Garden Room, separate from all the others, has menus which the guidebooks drool over. However, it also serves a

down-to-earth ploughman's lunch for which you can see and select your own cheeses and watch them being cut – and the home-made pickle is excellent. So, somehow, the Three Chimneys manages to satisfy both ends of the market, and it has a tale to tell which is good enough to satisfy me too.

It is, of course, the story behind its name. Although it is called the Three Chimneys, it has always had only two. The inn sign does not feature any chimneys at all. Instead, it shows a signpost where the three lanes meet outside the inn, and beneath it, looking rather wistful, is a uniformed figure, a French prisoner-of-war. For him the signpost marked the *trois chemins*, the crossroads, the furthest point he is allowed to wander from his quarters at Sissinghurst Castle. It was the mispronunciation of *chemins* by the non-French-speaking locals which gave the inn its name.

The story dates back to the Seven Years War, in the middle of the eighteenth century. The castle already had two hundred years of history behind it; Queen Elizabeth really did sleep here, as a guest of the man who built it, Sir Robert Baker. It was not

actually a castle, just a fortified manor house, but judging by what remains of it, the fortifications were formidable.

The brick gatehouse is the most prominent part that survives, a splendid twin-turreted tower four substantial storeys high, and there are two other sections, the Priest's House where the local writer Richard Church lived, and South House, where Harold Nicolson wrote his biography of George V. It was all derelict when the Nicolsons bought it in 1930, and its decline probably began when it was used to house French prisoners. One reference book notes that they did 'much damage'.

The same book states that the castle housed three thousand prisoners, which is a very large number of prisoners even for a very large castle. There could hardly have been a rapid turnover, since I assume the only ways prisoners left were by escaping, which was rare, or feet first. It would require quite a dramatic death rate to account for so many prisoners; after all, the Seven Years War only lasted seven years.

Reports of life as a Sissinghurst captive vary. According to one, there was extensive ill-treatment by the guards which, in one instance, drove a prisoner to deposit a bucket of water on one of them from the top of the gatehouse tower. He did not just pour the water, he dropped the bucket as well. But if the guards were so tough and the prisoners so rebellious, how were they allowed to stroll down to the Three Chimneys? I suppose the answer is that this privilege was accorded only to the officers, who were treated very differently from the men. I doubt it was an officer who dropped that bucket.

If all were told, I am sure the story of the prisoners of Sissinghurst Castle would be as gripping as that of another castle-cum-prison in a much later war. But I doubt there is a *bierhaus* near Colditz called the Three Roads.

Let's tie another story round the old elm tree

The Stag and Hounds
Binfield, Berkshire

Forest Road

The Stag and Hounds looks more like two inns than one, built in different periods and different styles. The older half, said to be partly fourteenth century, is all oak beams, low ceilings and snug little rooms. The second half was added a few centuries later, with high ceilings, tall windows and well-proportioned rooms. They form the king-size equivalents, I suppose, of the public 'snug' and the lounge bar of an orthodox village inn – and king-size is appropriate, because the inn was once a royal hunting lodge, used by Henry VIII and, inevitably, slept in by Elizabeth.

The gnarled old hollow tree-trunk opposite is supposed to mark the centre – and if the tree is anything to go by, the dead centre – of Windsor Great Forest. The poor thing is so twisted and deformed it is hardly recognisable as a tree. When the current landlord took over a few months ago he thought it was an oak, but all the records identify it as an elm – the Centre Elm, in fact – and its decrepit appearance is hardly surprising. It has been ring-dated as more than eight hundred years old, which means it could have been planted by Richard the Lionheart, or more probably by his successor King

John, since Richard spent most of his time hunting Saracens, while John preferred killing things that couldn't hit back.

The inn is not quite so old as the elm, which must have already been there for a couple of hundred years when it was built, possibly as an operational headquarters for the royal verderers and warreners – the medieval version of gamekeepers – before it was used as a hunting lodge. They meted out summary justice, holding their own courts and carrying out their own sentences. Anyone who killed the King's deer was hanged – which is where the elm might have come in handy. Merely being found in possession of a weapon or a trap meant losing a hand.

As the elm grew older it is thought that fugitive poachers might have hidden inside its hollow trunk though, in view of its proximity to the verderers' base, it seems a rather foolhardy choice. It is also said to have hidden some of Cromwell's men, an interesting reversal of the Charles II-in-the-Boscobel-Oak story. Perhaps they were not fugitives, just using it as an observation post for a commando raid on the royal lodge.

In more recent times the hollow elm tree is supposed to have been a popular tryst for courting couples, though they must have looked a little conspicuous from the windows of the Stag and Hounds as they clambered in and out. The only certainty is that, given a hollow tree, somebody is going to hide in it – you can take your pick who they might have been.

The history of the Stag and Hounds is a little more precise. The records say it became an inn in 1727, when the coaching trade was building up. The Regency extension was built during the boom years, and William Cobbett may have enjoyed its comforts when he turned up on one of his rural rides in 1822. 'Set out for Reading and stayed at the Stag and Hounds at Binfield – a very nice country inn.' He was not so civil about nearby Bracknell: 'I have never set eyes on so bleak and desolate a heath.' If only he could see it now...

Much of the Great Forest has disappeared, but the Stag and Hounds still officially stands on Forest Road. Binfield has managed to preserve its village atmosphere, and the village green still sees the occasional Morris Man, but it lies inside the angle formed by the M4 and the motorway arm linking it with Bracknell, and the New Town is only two miles away. Not many stags are now seen at the Stag and Hounds, and even the hounds rarely visit, now that the local hunt has stopped meeting there.

It has seen better days but it is still a piece of English history. The Centre Elm was planted eight hundred years ago to mark the centre of Windsor Great Forest.

But successive landlords have tried to preserve the hunting connection. Some old wallpaper depicting a hunting scene was uncovered during redecoration, and a section remains on view behind protective glass. Hunting horns and horses' leathers have come and gone in the bars. And in the 1960s a landlord had the bright idea of producing Stag and Hounds ties, featuring a golden stag's head and the heads of two hounds on a maroon background, and selling at fifteen shillings.

The inn has one feature unconnected with hunting which no one seems able to explain. A portion of a stained-glass window, said to have come from Westminster Chapel after it was bombed, is set into the oak panelling, but without any indication of why. My own theory is that it was a thank-offering. After the bombing it was taken by a souvenir-hunter who was spotted, pursued all the way to Binfield, and escaped only by hiding – of course – in the old elm tree.

It failed to feed the four thousand, but it did know how to spell Jhon

The Crown
Chiddingfold, Surrey

By the village green

It is difficult to believe the Crown was once a mere alehouse, but that was its description in 1383, when it was granted a licence – the earliest in the county, and one of the earliest in England. Even to call it an inn seems over-modest. It looks more like a medieval manor house of the grander kind, 'rightly revered', as one guide puts it, 'as one of the finest examples of medieval timber-framing in the country'. Inside are massive oak timbers up to two feet thick, all manner of panelling, some elegant stained glass, and a massive stone fireplace dated 1584 and inscribed with the name JHON KNIGHT. That was not necessarily a mistake by the

stonemason; I gather the name was often spelt that way in the sixteenth century, and when you think about it, Jhon is just as logical from a pronunciation point of view as John – and neither of them makes as much sense as Jon.

The Crown started life about 1285, not as a manor house, but as a guest-house for pilgrims heading for Winchester or Canterbury. They must have been rather superior pilgrims – I doubt that Chaucer's jolly band would have qualified. It was also used by Cistercian monks on their days off. Then it went somewhat down-market with the granting of an alehouse licence to a Richard Godfayre, whose name preserved the ecclesiastical connection. Mr Godfayre, though, was not the entirely upright and God-fearing landlord his name implies – he was prosecuted four times for offences ranging from overcharging to giving short measure.

History finds little to record about this establishment for the next century or so. Perhaps Mr Godfayre's successors shared his propensity for short measures and tall charges, and preferred to avoid publicity. It is not until 1548 that the Crown is first mentioned by that name, when the building was remodelled to its present appearance, with an eye, perhaps, to attracting a better class of customer – and landlord. In which case it certainly succeeded, because in 1552 it entertained its most illustrious guest, Edward VI.

The King was only fourteen at the time, and was hardly likely to have selected it himself from the *Good Royal Inn Guide*. Indeed, at that age he would probably have preferred somewhere with the Tudor equivalent of a juke-box and a pool table. But whoever did choose it rather over-estimated its bedroom accommodation, because Edward brought with him a retinue of four thousand, headed by the Lord Treasurer, the Lord Privy Seal, and even the Lord High Admiral, whose presence seems a little superfluous with the nearest coastline thirty miles away.

This Gilbert and Sullivan extravaganza descended upon Chiddingfold literally like an invading army. Most of them had to camp out on the village green; even the Lord High Admiral may have finished up in a tent beside the duck pond. Local food supplies were soon exhausted, except for the lucky ones with the King at the Crown, and drastic decisions had to be made. Instead of waiting for natural wastage – through starvation – a system of compulsory redundancy was introduced, and the retinue was reduced overnight from 4,000 to 140. I trust the Lord High Admiral was one of the first to go.

Chiddingfold was a lot more important then, or the King would not have bothered to stay there on his Royal Progress through the southern counties. It was a centre for the iron and glass industries, and a lot less picturesque than it is today. The most vivid impression King Edward must have had when he arrived was the smell and smoke from the iron-smelting furnaces; the glass works were probably almost as bad.

The first mobile phone? An eighteenth-century yuppie would be gratified to know that his sedan chair is now fitted with a telephone.

There is some impressive stained glass at the Crown, but not from the local works. Not much of that has survived, and the only local example of any note is a window in the church, made up of four hundred pieces recovered from the old refuse pits around the village. Much of the surrounding forest was used up as fuel but, happily, there has been an extensive replanting programme in recent years, not of the ubiquitous conifer but of oak and ash. The ash is in honour of the local walking-stick-makers – I bought my first stick close by Chiddingfold, a marvellous knobbly affair like an overgrown shillelagh, and it impresses my rural neighbours still.

I had another 'first' at Chiddingfold, my first taste of roast pheasant, enjoyed with my wife during our earliest 'bargain break'. Hence my rather rosy memories of the Crown, which manifestly is not your average alehouse, but does ensure that the eating does not encroach on the drinking. You can still enjoy a quiet glass of beer at your leisure without being overawed by the surroundings. And, oddly enough, my most abiding memory of the Crown is not the splendid beams and panels and stained glass – or even the roast pheasant – it is the eighteenth-century sedan chair just outside the bar, still with its immaculate brocade upholstery but converted, with the utmost discretion, into a telephone kiosk.

If you seek a memorial to poor Walter Budd, look beside you

*The memorial in the beer garden is a sad reminder of clerical prejudice,
parental devotion, and a bizarre manoeuvre to flout the vicar.*

The George and Dragon
Dragons Green, West Sussex

Near Shipley, on the green

Dragons Green is little more than a cluster of cottages around a tiny green, with the George and Dragon as the focal point, but a few hundred years ago its population would regularly increase several hundredfold – if you include sheep. This was the assembly point at one end of the drove road which ran southwards through nearby Shipley to Ashington, and on through the gap in the South Downs at Findon to the coastal plain around Worthing. It was used to bring up the sheep to the rich pasture land in the Weald and, indeed, Shipley gets its name from 'sheep clearing'.

Dragons Green, one assumes, got its name from the George and Dragon, and there may have been an inn there since the earliest days of droving, but the present building was probably erected in either 1577 or 1677, depending on how you interpret the date on one of the massive beams in the bar. The figures have been worn down over the years, probably by constant contact with the heads of tall customers. The ceilings and doorways do take a bit of negotiating for anyone over six foot, as I know to my cost, but it is worth the effort. There is a pleasant period atmosphere to the place, and if you find yourself too close to the fruit machine you can always escape into the extensive gardens.

If you choose the front garden, you may well find yourself sitting next to an unlikely garden ornament, a substantial memorial cross which would look much more at home in a churchyard than a beer garden. That, indeed, is where it came from. A notice reads: 'This cross was erected on the grave [of Walter Budd] in Shipley churchyard and removed by order of H. Gorham, vicar. Two globe wreaths were placed on the grave by friends, and after being there for two years, were removed by E. Arkle, following vicar.'

One can sense the depth of bitterness that lies behind a notice like that, and the story of Walter Budd and his banished memorial must have been one of the major ecclesiastical talking-points of the 1890s. It involves prejudice and persecution, clerical bigotry and insensitivity, parental devotion, and a final bizarre manoeuvre which is still evidenced a century later by that incongruous cross at the George and Dragon.

The principal inscription on it reads: 'In loving memory of Walter, the albino son of Alfred and Charlotte Budd, born February 13 1867, died February 18 1893.' Walter's white hair and pink eyes made him something of a freak in this tiny village, back in Victorian days, and his occasional epileptic fits made matters worse. When he was suspected, quite unjustly, of a petty theft, the taunts and mockery turned into accusations, and it all became too much for him. He killed himself by drowning.

His parents erected the marble cross over his grave in the churchyard. On it, under the details of his birth and death, they added the inscription: 'God forgive those who forget their duty to Him who was just as afflicted.'

Enter H. Gorham, vicar. Not only was the wording offensive, he said, but he had also decided – rather belatedly, one might think – that a marble cross, a symbol of sacrifice, was inappropriate for someone who had taken his own life. It is true, of course, that suicides in those days were usually buried in unconsecrated ground, often by a public crossroads, but having permitted his burial, his carping over the cross might seem a little insensitive.

Certainly, Mr and Mrs Budd thought so. They were duly compelled to remove the cross – but they removed it only as far as their own front garden, which happened to be the garden at the George and Dragon. They were not just the licensees, but the owners of the inn, and nobody could stop them re-erecting the memorial there, complete with its explanatory notice. When H. Gorham, vicar, was succeeded by E. Arkle, following vicar, the new incumbent decided to show solidarity with his predecessor and ordered the removal of wreaths which had been placed on Walter's grave in the churchyard, thus qualifying himself for inclusion in the notice.

Shipley church has had a happier history since this unfortunate affair. The village is mainly associated with Hilaire Belloc, who owned the splendid smock mill which was restored in his memory. The inscription over the door expresses more tranquil sentiments than poor Walter's: 'Let this be a memorial to Hilaire Belloc, who garnered a harvest of wisdom and sympathy for young and old.'

The churchyard where Walter lies, in a now unmarked grave, was much loved by the composer John Ireland, who lived some miles away but expressly asked to be buried there – and there were no arguments over that.

Meanwhile, out at Dragons Green, the sad saga of the suicide's memorial has not been entirely bad news. The newspaper reports at the time attracted much extra custom for the George and Dragon, and the marble cross in the beer garden has continued to attract the curious ever since.

The brickworks and pottery have long since gone: now just enjoy the view

The Pot Kiln
Frilsham, Berkshire

On the Yattendon-to-Bucklebury road

It is the inn with the finest view in Berkshire, claims one enthusiast, and I would not argue. This part of the country is attractive anyway, but sitting in the front garden of the Pot Kiln, looking across the valley at strategically placed cows in the opposite pasture, with the woods surrounding it and no other building in sight, is like facing a film set for Merrie England. Any minute a procession of fresh-faced wenches and straw-hatted yokels could dance hand-in-hand across the sward. Even the cows look poised to copy the formation dancing in that butter advertisement. It is an idyllically peaceful corner of rural England – with the M4 motorway less than a mile away.

Not many strangers to the area find the Pot Kiln unless they are actually looking for it. They are likely to get no further than the Royal Oak in Yattendon, on the far side of the motorway, noted for being the inn where Cromwell is supposed to have planned the battle of Naseby. For a Puritan, he seemed to spend an awful lot of time in bars. These days the Royal Oak 'straddles the frontiers between pub and restaurant', as one guide delicately puts it, but its centre of gravity is well on the restaurant side. There is a choice of thirty starters and ten puddings with the bar meals, and you probably have to book a table to select them.

The Pot Kiln, on the other hand, makes no attempt to straddle any frontiers. It has remained basically unchanged for more than half a century, and its workaday origins are not disguised by floral arrangements or cosy cushions. It was built in the sixteenth or seventeenth century in front of the old brick kilns, and its distinctive chequer-board façade of red and black bricks dates from the century after that. It was in the hands of the Scottish Barr family for nearly two centuries, until Charlie Barr retired about a dozen years ago. They owned the inn, the brickworks and the surrounding land, and one can trace how the family businesses grew and prospered over the years from old copies of *Kelly's Directory*.

In 1895 they had obviously made little impact on the village – their name is not even mentioned. But in 1899 Thomas Barr is recorded as 'brick maker', on a par with William Austin, head gardener to Sir William Cameron Gull MP, of Frilsham House. Four years later Sir William has lost his Parliamentary seat and is merely a JP, but Tom Alfred Barr is expanding his business rapidly; he now has a brick, tile and pottery works, and he has gone into the timber trade too.

These various interests continue to flourish until the First World War, when Tom Barr cuts back on the timber business and concentrates on his bricks, but the postwar years see another expansion, with Mrs Eliza Barr being listed for the first time alongside Tom as 'beer retailer, Frilsham pottery'. Presumably, this was when the Barrs obtained their first licence, and Mrs Barr sold ale as well as pottery in the house, while Tom kept the brickworks going at the back. Incidentally, Austin Williams is still head gardener at Frilsham House, having outlived Sir William and reached the shortlist for the title of Frilsham's oldest inhabitant.

Alas, he succumbs in the next few years, but the Barrs are still going strong throughout the 1930s, Tom with his brickworks and Eliza with her beer and pottery. In 1939 Mrs Barr's establishment is listed under a new heading, as the Pot Kilns public house. Since then, it seems, the only change at the Pot Kiln has been the loss of the 's'. The old settles and benches in the two front rooms, the narrow passageway in between with the serving hatch at the end, must be much the same.

The brickworks closed down after the last war, and there is little evidence now of the kilns where Tom Barr baked his bricks and tiles and pots for more than forty years. And while the Pot Kiln is still essentially geared to the locals, the present licensees, Philip and Linda Gent, do offer an efficient, if uneffusive, welcome to visitors. You will not find thirty starters and ten puddings on the bar menu, but I did find a ploughman's lunch with the pickle and fresh butter served on separate dishes, thus avoiding the common hazard of the chutney merging into the coleslaw and the nasty little foil-wrapped butter-pats disappearing among the lettuce leaves. Mrs Gent's maiden name was Hoppenbrouemans; maybe Continental ploughmen are more discerning than ours. But they can't beat that quite delightful, utterly English, view.

Did the Royalists have time for a quick one at the Hedera helix conglomerata?

The Ivy
Heddington, Wiltshire

Stockley Road

The Ivy got its name from the creeper that used to cover it. It got its sign from the chairman of Wadworth's Brewery, John Bartholomew, who happily prefers to have pictures on his inn signs, rather than just a name – and he likes to design them himself. It is a rather erudite sign in this case, featuring three different varieties of ivy, with the names helpfully provided underneath. Ivy buffs may like to know they are *Hedera helix conglomerata*, *Hedera colchica variegata* and *Hedera helix sagittaefolia*.

To me they just look like ivy, and I was enormously impressed by the chairman's botanical expertise – until he explained that he had just copied them from a book on plants.

He does, however, take a personal interest in the Ivy, as one of his favourite inns, and I can understand why. The exterior is the quintessential, archetypal, English village pub; black timbers and white plaster, thatched roof and porch, tiny upper windows and a chimney at each end. In place of the original ivy, a passion fruit tree now climbs up the wall and over the thatch. (Should the inn be renamed the *Passiflora quadrangularis*, I immediately wondered – these plant books are gripping stuff.)

Inside the front door the bar has been opened up to make it larger and lighter than earlier drinkers used to know, but the beer is still served straight from the cask, there is no background music, and the bar snacks are genuinely just snacks – the most elaborate offering when I ate there was a corned beef and tomato roll.

This is a remote little inn in a remote little village, well away from the recognised tourist routes and with only one brief mention in the only guide I could find: 'Surprisingly we don't get more reports on it,' says the entry, but this is an undiscovered little corner, and although Devizes is only a few miles away, there is no direct route linking the two.

It was not always as quiet as this, and at one period in its history Devizes was rather too close for comfort. The earliest conflict in that area was when the Iron Age Celts arrived and a couple of hill-forts were built at nearby Oldbury and on the southern boundary of Heddington, on a hill known as Oliver's Camp. It was a later Oliver, however, who put Heddington on the map – in the form of crossed swords, the recognised symbol for a battlefield. The date underneath them is 1643.

In the summer of that year a Parliamentary force under Sir William Waller was laying siege to Royalist-held Devizes, when news arrived that a relief force of 2,500 cavalry was on its way from the King's headquarters at Oxford. Waller moved his forces on to the Downs, and the two armies met on the hillside above Heddington. The Royalists gained the upper hand, and with the Devizes garrison coming up to give them additional support, Waller could see himself being trapped between them by the steep slopes of Oliver's Camp, which strategically

became Charles's Camp instead. Oliver's commander decided to save the cavalry at the expense of his infantry, and ordered a withdrawal towards Bath, leaving the foot-soldiers to their fate.

This may well have been the occasion when a new set of initials came into Army parlance, the PBI; any ex-soldier will know what they mean. The PBI held their ground gamely while the cavalry disappeared from the scene, but the victorious Royalists turned their own cannon on them, the Devizes garrison arrived from the other direction, and they laid down their arms.

Remarkably, casualties were very low on both sides, perhaps fewer than fifty. Only twelve skeletons have been found which can be linked with the battle. And although the Royalists did go on to capture Bristol, Sir William Waller was soon back again with his cavalry and a fresh supply of infantry. He recaptured all the ground he had lost and finally took Devizes. So, in historical terms, the Battle of Heddington was not enormously significant, but it has not been forgotten in the village – and nor has Oliver Cromwell.

When the roof of the Ivy was being rethatched and the ivy was removed, a curious relic was uncovered. It was a heavy pottery head, slightly smaller than life-size, hollow, with the top of the scalp removed, and holes in the large protruding ears. No one at the inn was sure what it represented, but I was reminded of the carved head of Cromwell over the door of the Guildhall in Worcester, between the statues of Charles I and Charles II. The ears on the head are large and protruding – and they are nailed to the wall. Worcester was a Royalist city, and that is what they thought of Oliver Cromwell; could the Ivy have had Royalist sympathies too?

On the other hand, you may say, it could just be a hanging pot for plants. But I know which theory I prefer.

This story is true: the name has been changed to avoid embarrassment

The village pond at the end of the garden was useful for filling the fire brigade's hand pump when they were based at the inn.

The Belgian Arms
Holyport, Berkshire

On the green

The story of how the Belgian Arms got its name is so engaging that it has to be true. When William Brakspear bought it in the 1860s for £390 it was called the Eagle, and a Prussian eagle glared down from the inn sign at passers-by. Then came the First World War, and the passers-by included German prisoners-of-war from a nearby camp, who were allowed out for exercise runs. Their route took

61

them past the Eagle, and one of them spotted their national symbol overhead. He halted beneath it, stood to attention, and saluted.

The idea soon caught on, and each party of prisoners followed suit, perhaps as a joke, perhaps in all sincerity, but more likely just to annoy – and they were entirely successful. The landlord was embarrassed, the locals were furious. Brakspear's Brewery agreed to take down the eagle and re-christen the inn the Belgian Arms, in honour of the area where the fiercest fighting was taking place. So the prisoners-of-war stopped saluting, and no doubt devised some new way of irritating their captors, while the Belgian Arms has retained that name ever since.

It has also kept its homely character, though Holyport is now less than a mile from the nearest junction on the M4 motorway, and this is very much commuter country. I originally visited it on a Friday evening, when it becomes a sanctuary for weary City workers. They had swopped their suits for sweaters and slacks and were exchanging the week's stories –

very loudly – at the bar. But during the day the Belgian Arms is rather more peaceful. It stands on the village green, tucked round a corner to make it invisible from the main road so that passing traffic is more likely to patronise the larger, and more obvious, George Hotel.

In honour of its First World War transformation,

the bar of the Belgian Arms is decorated with postcards and paintings of Belgian soldiers from various eras, but its history goes back a couple of centuries earlier. It started life as a hatmaker's, and somewhere underneath the hundred-year-old wisteria on the front wall it is said that the words 'Registered Hatmaker' are burnt into one of the beams, but even the landlord wasn't sure where.

The theory is that coaches used to be driven into the village pond at the bottom of the garden to make the wooden wheels swell, and during their wait the passengers patronised the hatmaker's, either buying a new hat or having their own brushed and cleaned. Eventually, it dawned on the hatter – who was anything but mad – that these travellers might be thirsty too, so he laid in a barrel or two of ale to refresh them. Thus, the inn was born. The tale seems rather less plausible than the saluting prisoners-of-war, but a notice in the bar takes it seriously.

Certainly the proximity of the pond provided another function for the inn. For many years it was the village fire station, and the horse-drawn hand pump was housed behind the bar. The water for the pump was drawn from the pond.

It may also have been useful for baptisms by total immersion, if the story is true that one of the upstairs rooms at the Belgian Arms was once used as a Nonconformist chapel. Holyport certainly had a Wesleyan chapel by 1928, according to *Kelly's Directory*, but it does not suggest it was sited at the inn – and the current landlord has no inkling of it.

The pond's only use these days is to provide a pleasant view for the patrons in the beer garden, enjoying their 'salmon shanties' – the Belgian Arms's upmarket equivalent of fish and chips. On the Friday evening I was there it took four or five people behind the bar to keep up with the demand, and I imagine weekends are fairly hectic too, but during the week its traditional old-fashioned bar, snug and stockbroker-free, with its garden set beside the peaceful pond and green, provides something of a rural oasis in what is now a motorway-marred urban belt.

So I salute it.

It looks a show village, but it could be a dog's life in the kitchen

The spit in the fireplace was operated by a dog running around inside the wheel for hours at a time. No wonder they called it a dog's life.

The George Inn
Lacock, Wiltshire

4 West Street

Lacock unashamedly lives on tourism, which might be considered a good reason for avoiding it. The whole village, including two of its three inns and the magnificent Lacock Abbey, is owned by the National Trust, and its stone-built, stone-roofed houses are preserved in show-piece condition. It does not merely look like a film set, it frequently is. On my last visit the streets had again been covered with sand and earth for another period drama – or so I was told. The place was so packed with spectators I could not get close enough to make sure.

No, Lacock in the tourist season, and particularly Lacock in the filming season, is not for me. But I cannot ignore it altogether, because when there is space and time to enjoy them it has three very pleasant old inns, and one contains a curiosity which may be unique in such a setting.

The George Inn is probably the oldest, as well as the most interesting, of the three. It dates back to 1361, and it has had a continuous licence since Cromwell's time, when it was known simply as the Inn – which suggests there were no competitors worth worrying about. It has kept its period flavour, with its old benches and tables, and the centre-piece is a vast open fireplace with a roasting spit – and a dog wheel.

I had not come across dog wheels before. They were the canine equivalent of a treadmill, but in many ways far more unpleasant. The principle was

very simple; as long as the dog kept walking, the wheel kept turning, and so did the spit connected to it. But this was not like a gentle stroll in the park. It took three hours or more for a good-sized joint to roast, and if the dog stopped for a breather, one side of the meat was charred. The cook therefore had a whip handy to keep it on the move, and a more callous method was to put a hot coal in the wheel with the dog, so it rolled against its feet if the wheel stopped turning.

The standard dog wheel was about thirty inches across and the gap inside was less than nine inches, so the dog had to be not only extremely fit but extremely small. A special breed was developed which became known as a turnspit. They were described as 'long-bodied, crooked-legged and ugly dogs, with a suspicious, unhappy look about them' – which was quite understandable, considering what they had to put up with. A drawing of the dog wheel at the George Inn shows a jolly little puppy prancing about in it with what looks like a broad grin on its face, but the grin would not have lasted for long.

Nobody can be sure who first devised this gruelling use of dog power – probably an enterprising kitchen boy who got fed up with turning

the spit himself. Certainly it existed in Tudor times; a sixteenth-century writer gave the earliest description of how dogs helped to cook the dinner. 'When any meat is to be roasted, they go into a wheel where they, turning about with the weight of their bodies, so diligently look to their business that not drudge or scullion can do the feat more cunningly.'

The turnspits were still diligently looking to their business in the 1700s, when John Gay wrote 'The Turnspit Taught', a blow-by-blow account – literally – of how they were trained to turn the wheel. Fists and cudgels and even broomstick handles were involved. A few lines of his poem might be termed the Turnspit's Lament:

Was ever cur so cursed (he cried)!
What star did at my birth preside!
Am I for life by compact bound
To tread the wheel's eternal round?

I am afraid he was. It took a century or more for the lament to be heard. Dog-lovers began to take a poor view of the dog wheel, and the turnspit found champions like the Revd Henry Crowe, who wrote in 1822: 'Enclosed in a wheel from which they cannot escape (indeed the lash prevents any) and oppressed by the heat of the stove, their fate is well nigh that of Ixion, except that he was not doomed to toil by a fireside in hot weather.'

Many people shared this view, even if they had never heard of Ixion – who was tied to a perpetually revolving wheel by Zeus for making passes at his wife. However, it was not public sympathy, but the arrival of the mechanical roasting-jack, which finally released the little dogs from their wheels. Three of them finished up as pets of Queen Victoria at Windsor Castle; another achieved a sort of immortality by being stuffed and put in a museum at Abergavenny.

As for the dog wheels, only a handful survive – which is why, even at the height of the tourist season, it is worth struggling through the crowds to see the fireplace at the George – and be reminded of what 'a dog's life' was really like.

Well placed for smugglers and barge-spotters, not so handy for cars

The Royal Oak
Langstone, Hampshire
End of High Street

'Parking at all close may be very difficult,' warns one guide. For 'very difficult' I would substitute 'frequently impossible'. The Royal Oak has to be reached on foot along the narrow flag-stoned sea wall, and the little High Street nearby is generally full of parked cars anyway. But I am not complaining. It is an enormous relief to leave the busy main road which is the only access to Hayling Island and find a haven which cars cannot reach.

There was a time when customers parked on the foreshore at low tide, but it was a chancy business which could end, at best, with a wetting and, at worst, with a submerged car. There is now a barrier across the end of the High Street to limit its use to residents who live beyond the Royal Oak, whose access to their garages depends entirely on the state of the tide.

In a setting like this, it is not surprising that the Royal Oak was popular with smugglers. It was frequented by the notorious Langstone Gang, who towed their contraband into Langstone Harbour on submerged rafts so it could not be spotted from the shore. Other smugglers adopted more direct methods to achieve the same end. In 1792 a Revenue man called Thomas Gloge was offered £50 to stay at home on a particular night, while contraband was landed. The offer was made by the bos'n of a convict ship lying in the harbour who, in his turn, had been paid by one James Hunt, of Southsea Castle. Mr Gloge, however, politely declined: 'It is against my conscience to suffer any such thing.' Instead, he tipped off his colleagues, who raided the castle and in the cellars found cavities containing nearly a thousand casks of spirits.

No smugglers were ever arrested at the Royal Oak, perhaps because there is a priest's hole, which could equally have been made a smuggler's hole, in what is now a bathroom, and there were three staircases from the days when it was three cottages, which could have provided useful escape routes. The biggest haul in the vicinity was recovered when the smack *Rambler* was seized in the harbour in 1834, with over a hundred casks hidden in the bilges. There is a sporting chance that some of them were destined for the Royal Oak's cellar.

The inn's position on the quayside was handy not only for smugglers, but for Hayling Island customers who were caught on the mainland by the tide, before the bridge was built in 1824. For nearly a century before that the Royal Oak held a 'tidal licence', which meant customers could drink there until the tide was low enough for them to use the causeway, known as the Wade Way, which linked the mainland with the island.

About the time that the bridge was built, the causeway was breached and a channel dredged to allow barges to be towed between Chichester Harbour and Portsea Island. It was part of an inland waterway route between London and Portsmouth, using the now defunct canals between the Wey and Arun rivers, and from the Arun to Chichester. The idea was to avoid the attention of Napoleon's ships in the Channel, though by the time it was completed the war was over. Some of the barges regularly carried bullion, guarded by four armed redcoats on each barge. It must have been a mouth-watering sight for the smugglers as they sipped their ale outside the Royal Oak, but they presumably drew the line at piracy because the bullion always got through.

Incidentally, a few years ago a writer mused on the loss of the causeway and commented that 'if the tidal licence was still in force today, the landlord would indeed have to keep long hours'. He could not have foreseen the introduction of the all-day licence, which the landlord now holds.

It is not known when the Royal Oak got its name, though Langstone does have a tenuous link with the tree-climbing King Charles II. While he was in hiding after the Battle of Worcester, two of his friends, Lord Wilmot and Colonel Gounter, came to the harbour hoping to book him a passage to the Continent. They failed, but they sought solace in a dish of oysters in the village 'and much enjoyed their frugal fare'. There is no evidence they ate at the Royal Oak, but it was once a bakery as well as an inn, and could well have had an oyster bar too.

The inn has had its ghostly manifestations, from chairs being scraped on the stone floor of an empty bar to footsteps in an empty corridor. A previous landlady's dog used to sleep in the bar until one night it fled upstairs in a frenzy of fear and never entered it again. On a more mundane note, buttons were mysteriously detached from a cardigan and re-appeared in another room.

Things have been pretty quiet lately on the supernatural front, but no matter. Any inn can have a ghost – and most of them do. The Royal Oak has its smugglers' tales, its unspoilt homely bar, its splendid position on the quayside – and no cars.

Even the inns got memorial windows – but the church got bogus brasses

A Dering window at the Dering Arms, where they look their best with leaded lights and a stone surround.

The Dering Arms
Pluckley, Kent

Near the station

To be honest, I actually went to Pluckley to visit the Black Horse, which stands in the centre of the village and looks as though it ought to be a typical, traditional village inn. The producer of *The Darling Buds of May* must have thought so too, because its exterior was used in the television series, disguised as the Stag and Hounds, and it is full of photographs of Ma and Pa and their unbelievably idyllic family.

But I doubt the cameras ventured too far inside, because the Black Horse has succumbed completely, alas, to the eaters rather than the drinkers. It not only announces 'Food All Day' – words that always chill me – but serves the food all through the open-plan bars. I felt distinctly out of place with my glass of beer and no steaming plate to go with it. So I left the Black Horse to the lunchers and headed, none too hopefully, for the Dering Arms, which stands beside the railway station about a mile outside the village.

Anything less like the average station hotel is difficult to imagine. It is a lofty, rather gaunt building which was once a hunting lodge dating back to the seventeenth century, and it still looks rather aristocratic and exclusive. But here again, appearances deceived, and this time the surprise inside was a pleasant one. The bars are traditional and homely, with unfussy chairs and tables on stone floors. It can be up-market when it wants to be – I gather it has regular black-tie dinners with seven gourmet courses – and the bar menu has some elegant touches too, but there are sandwiches and ploughman's lunches, and, best news of all, the food does not interfere with the drink. While I was in the little public bar, not a plate was in sight.

Happily, the Dering Arms has the same unusual feature that attracted me to the Black Horse, the distinctive Dering 'thanksgiving' windows, tall and narrow and round-arched. It was through such a window that a Dering made his escape from the Parliamentary forces during the Civil War, and to celebrate his good fortune all the cottages on the estate, including the one that became the Black Horse, were given windows of the same design. The family hunting lodge got the same treatment, and the Dering windows provide a welcome touch of individuality in the plain walls of the Dering Arms.

The actual window through which the fugitive leapt was presumably in the family mansion, which was largely destroyed by fire in 1952 after being occupied by the Derings since the days before the Tudors. The line could have ended abruptly when the head of the family, described as 'the greatest learned man in England' at the time, told Queen Elizabeth to her face that she was wrong to encourage 'the whoredoms of hawkers and hunters, dicers and carders, and morrow-mass priests!' Obviously powerful stuff, even if these days it is not too clear what he was on about, but astonishingly the Queen did not order his immediate execution, and he survived. Maybe she was baffled too, and assumed it was some sort of learned joke.

The church is full of Dering memorials and brasses – but seven of the eight brasses are ingenious forgeries. They were put there by Sir Edward Dering, 'whose passionate love of family overcame the scruples of truth', as one critic put it. Like Queen Elizabeth I am inclined to take a more generous view; it might be some sort of learned joke.

The Derings have left Pluckley after thirty generations, but they may not have gone entirely, because the village has another claim to fame as well as its fancy fenestration; it is said to be the most haunted village in England. It has at least a dozen spectral inhabitants, including some of the Derings. The burnt-out mansion is said to be haunted by the White Lady Dering, while the Red Lady Dering roams the churchyard looking for her unbaptised child. Also around the church is the 'smiling monk', who was executed at Tyburn but doesn't seem to care, and the lanes are haunted by a high-wayman who never reached Tyburn but was pinned to a tree by the sword of an intended victim who declined to stand and deliver.

Then there is a gipsy woman who fell asleep smoking her pipe and burnt herself to death, and at the disused brickworks is the 'screaming man' who fell into a mixing trough filled with knives and never emerged in one piece. A phantom coach makes regular appearances, and the Black Horse has a girl who was killed by a ball in a skittle alley. That was in premises previously occupied by the inn, but when it moved during the last century to its present site, she came with it.

The Dering Arms looks as if it should be haunted too, but I found no mention of smiling monks, screaming brickworkers, impaled highwaymen or incinerated gipsies. Not even the Derings are represented – but when I see those distinctive windows I can visualise a ghostly figure leaping through them, and that laugh in the next bar may be the Elizabethan Dering, still chuckling at how he ticked off the Queen and got away with it.

Never mind all the food, the inn itself is still a shere delight

The White Horse
Shere, Surrey

—— Middle Street ——

Once upon a time, in the days before the M25 motorway, the best way of skirting London to the south was to use its more modest 'numbersake', the A25, which passed through the middle of Shere. The traffic, inevitably, was quite intolerable and, happily, the village was bypassed before they built the motorway; if the M25 had come first, they might not have bothered with the bypass. Shere regained a modicum of peace, and during the week, particularly in the winter, it can seem almost as remote as the Shere of the eighteenth century, described by Sir Max Pemberton as 'one of the wildest parts of Surrey'.

It still has plenty of half-timbered houses, a seventeenth-century Old Prison House, a church that dates back to the Crusades, and, of course, the White Horse, built around 1475. The more recent buildings blend in quite reasonably – one convincing half-timbered shop was actually built by Sir Edwin Lutyens in 1892. Shere is, in fact, a pretty little village which survives in an area now mostly devoted to commuter homes, and so pays the inevitable penalty of an influx of visitors during summer weekends.

This is, of course, good news for the White Horse, where most of the visitors gravitate, and this has not escaped the notice of Mr Chef and Mr Brewer, who concentrate on the lunch and dinner trade. In other circumstances this would have frightened me off, but the original structure and appearance of the old place have mercifully remained unchanged, it still manifestly takes a pride in its history, and it is quite an achievement to survive at all in this developer-prone corner of Surrey.

I was there before official opening time, and that is probably the best time to see it. I was allowed to wander through the heavily timbered bars with their stone floors and oak settles, and admire in comfort the wattle-and-daub wall which has been left exposed over one of the massive fireplaces. Another one has a mantel which turns out to be Elizabethan carved chalk-stone, and there are old parchment documents on display dating from 1650, though it is not too clear what they say.

One of the splendid fireplaces which have survived the hazards of time and changing owners. Some of the original wattle-and-daub walls have survived too.

When the documents were found during renovations they also discovered a pair of Elizabethan shoes, not abandoned by some absent-minded guest but placed in a cavity behind the wall to bring good luck – a rather more civilised symbol than the live cat which was sometimes walled into new buildings for the same reason.

The shoes must have been put there when the building was first modernised, not when it was originally built, a century before the Elizabethans were disposing of their footwear on building sites. It was first a farmhouse, with a ground floor open to the roof. For a structure like that, little more than a shell, they did not bother with elaborate foundations, but apparently drove ship's timbers into the ground, to wedge it into place. It was an interesting variation on their normal use, to prop up ceilings, but, judging by the number of 'ship's timbers' in our old country inns, the supply in those days was inexhaustible.

The farmer, it is said, grew a few hops to make his own supply of beer. He must have hit on a winner, because he turned all his farm over to hops and made his home into an alehouse. Interestingly, the White Horse still sells ale from the Mortlake Brewery, which was founded about the time that the farmer went into the business; perhaps they exchanged a few tips.

The alehouse prospered and became an inn, with an upper floor added to accommodate guests. Access was by a barn ladder through a hole in the bar ceiling, so for once there is no suggestion that Queen Elizabeth slept here – she would not have fancied the ladder in those skirts. Nor, indeed, did anyone else of any note until Samuel Pepys passed that way in the seventeenth century, by which time I trust there was a staircase.

The weight of the extra storey must have put quite a strain on the submerged ship's timbers, and a young Australian lady at the White Horse assured me quite seriously that they were slipping gradually down the hill into the river, but it still looks remarkably stable.

In the eighteenth century the clientele was largely poachers, sheep-stealers and smugglers, and when the cellar was repaired in 1955 a second cellar, containing casks of smuggled brandy, was uncovered. These days you are more likely to find sausage and Stilton pies or a beef casserole at the White Horse, but if the sight and smell of food is too much for you, there are always the benches and tables in the cobbled courtyard outside, with a good view of the trippers trying to find a parking space. You can also keep an eye on the White Horse itself, to see if the young Australian lady really was joking.

The goal-runners have long since gone, but one left his drawers behind

The Red Lion
Snargate, Kent

On the B2080 by Romney Marsh

The Red Lion is not just unspoilt, it has remained virtually unaltered for over a century, and that is because, for nearly all that time, it has been in the hands of one family. Doris Jemison is the current representative, and apart from opening up a private room to provide a little more space, she has not changed anything of any consequence since her family took over in 1911. Stepping into this simple village inn is like stepping back into the days before the First World War, when bars were marble-topped, pub games like toad-in-the-hole were as common as darts, and running drawers were long enough to cover the knees.

The Red Lion still has examples of all three. The marble bar has been given some handsome hand pumps, but they could have been put there only as a gesture – the beer and cider are still drawn from the cask. Toad-in-the-hole is a local version of penny-tossing, but more tricky. Four brass counters have to be tossed into a hole in a bench, but they must not rebound into it off the lead backing, and the hole itself is only fractionally larger than the counters, so great accuracy is required. There must be few sounds more gratifying to a player than the bell underneath the hole going 'ping!' when a successful counter drops on to it.

There are other old bar games too: nine men's morris, bat-and-trap, miniature bar skittles with pins only an inch or so high. But the most unusual form of recreation at the Red Lion has now, alas, died out. Doris Jemison's father was a member of the Snargate Goal-Runners Club – which brings us to the calf-length running drawers. She has one of his pairs on show, alongside the flag of the SGRC.

Goal-running, as she explained it to me, sounds like a lethal combination of maypole dancing, musical chairs and Rugby football. There are two teams of about twenty players – the number, it seems, is not important – and they run round and round their own flag, until one player makes a dash for the opponents' flag. I am not too clear how the opponents are permitted to stop him, but it sounds rather like scoring a try with the odds stacked overwhelmingly against you. The wear and tear on the players must have been considerable; perhaps the game died out just because they ran out of volunteers.

Snargate is the sort of village where one can visualise these home-grown contests taking place. It is right on the edge of Romney Marsh, and it must have been a remote little corner, left largely to its own devices. It came into existence because a sluicegate was needed in the thirteenth century to maintain a waterway between Appledore and Romney; it lies about halfway between. The sluicegate, or snaregate, was built in 1254, and the waterway was still in use 150 years later, when a new gate was installed. A little community grew up beside it, with a church dedicated to a local hero, St Dunstan, an early Archbishop of Canterbury. The name of the village was originally spelt Snergate, but the first syllable rhymed with Hertford or Derby, so in due course the spelling was helpfully adjusted to make life easier for BBC announcers.

The Red Lion is said to be 450 years old, which means that early sluicegate operators went thirsty, but it was certainly around when smuggling was rife along the Channel coast, and the marsh was a popular hiding-place for smugglers and their contraband. There is little doubt they came to Snargate. Apart from its isolated position, there is the painting of a ship which was discovered under a layer of whitewash in the parish church. It is a four-masted vessel of about eight hundred tons, and experts say that it has a forecastle, upper, half and quarter decks, and is of a design used between 1480 and 1520, but the significant feature about it is its position. It is on the north wall opposite the church door, and there was a tradition on the marshes that this meant the church was a safe place to hide smuggled goods. The Red Lion is only a few hundred yards up the lane, and it seems very likely that the smugglers called there too.

But it is the more recent history of the inn which makes it so special. Kent is a populous county these days, and too many historic old inns have been gutted and refurbished to supply burgers rather than beer. They are described elegantly as 'dining pubs', but 'licensed restaurant' or 'restaurant with a very small bar' might be nearer the mark.

The Red Lion is definitely not a dining pub, and if Doris Jemison has her way it never will be. If ever a banner was erected over the doorway saying MEALS ALL DAY, I have a feeling that her father's running drawers would grab the flag of the Snargate Goal-Runners Club and disappear with it for ever into the depths of Romney Marsh.

Doris Jemison has changed nothing of any consequence at the Red Lion since her family took it over in 1911. It still has its marble bar.

A bridge too small - twice: and for thirsty militiamen, a wait too long

The White Hart
Stopham Bridge, West Sussex

Just off the A283 between Petworth and Pulborough

In 1977 a travel writer observed of Stopham Bridge: 'Although narrow, the bridge manages to cope adequately enough with today's traffic, and it is to be hoped that it will never be thought necessary to build a second bridge beside it, for that would quite spoil the setting.'

How opinions, traffic and scenery can change in less than two decades. There is now a modern concrete bridge alongside the medieval one. It is hardly as picturesque, but it does provide a safe and speedy passage for the increasing traffic on the A283 road between Petworth and Pulborough, plus peace and quiet for the White Hart in what is now a secluded cul-de-sac. Before it was built, crossing the road from the inn to its pleasant riverside garden must have been hazardous in the extreme; now the traffic is confined to customers' cars, and only walkers continue past the inn to admire the old bridge.

It is not the first major change that the inn and the bridge have seen. The White Hart is in Domesday Book, though not under that name, and the bridge's history goes back even further. Its foundations were laid in Roman times, and the medieval bridge is a fourteenth-century replacement for a wooden one built by the Saxons. It was restored a century later, and there was probably a house of refreshment beside it by then, but no great excitements seem to have occurred until 1807, when a large party of militiamen arrived at the White Hart, decided the service was too slow, and started a riot which ended in a pitched battle with the locals, involving several serious injuries and, in some reports, two deaths.

There is a painting of this unfortunate incident in the bar, and an account of how it happened. During the Napoleonic Wars volunteer militiamen were offered a bounty of £7 10s to transfer to the regular regiments of the line. Five hundred of these volunteers had marched from Lancashire to Sussex to sign on at Chichester barracks. At the end of their lengthy trek the army told them they had to go another forty-odd miles to Horsham to collect their money. More than a little miffed, they set off again on their march, and about halfway to Horsham a large party of them stopped at the White Hart for a drink.

'We're going to Stop'em!' A constable's posse from Pulborough arrives to deal with rioting customers.

The landlord, not surprisingly, was a little overwhelmed by this sudden influx of thirsty, bad-tempered soldiers, and the delay proved too much for them. They started to wreck the place, and the landlord sent an SOS to the constable at Pulborough, a mile or two away. This stalwart fellow rounded up a posse of locals, perhaps with the rallying cry 'We're going to Stop'em', and armed with pitchforks and staves they hastened to the relief of the White Hart. It was a violent encounter, which rendered several militiamen exempt from any further military service. It is not recorded whether the others continued to Horsham to sign up, but after all this hassle I would probably have gone back to Lancashire and left the southerners to fight Napoleon on their own.

The wars brought other activity to the White Hart as well as a riot. Because of the French threat to British coastal vessels in the Channel – and also in hopes of a handsome profit – a scheme was devised to link the River Arun with the River Wey by canal, thus creating a safe new route by water between London and the south coast. Barges could then sail up the Thames from the Port of London to the Wey, join the canal to the Arun, then sail down to Arundel, where another canal was dug to Chichester Harbour, and the Portsea Canal provided the final link across Portsea Island to Portsmouth.

Unfortunately, by the time all these canals were completed the wars had ended, and merchants found it a lot more convenient to send their goods round the coast than pay the tolls on the new canals and negotiate all the locks. The coming of the railways was the final blow, and the Wey and Arun Canal closed in 1871, ending the through traffic to London.

For the fifty-odd years that it was open, however, it brought a boom in trade for the White Hart, where a wharf provided a regular stopping place for the barges. It also brought a drastic change to Stopham Bridge, which had to have its central arch heightened in 1822 to take the larger long-distance barges, at a cost of £286. The next time the bridge proved too small for road-users, the remedy cost a little more.

When there was only horse-drawn traffic the long, low building alongside the White Hart was a forge. Now it is a restaurant, but it remains separate from the three little bars, and they have lost none of their character. Even the forge conversion has been complimented as 'modern but relaxingly cottagey'. It is a popular resort for artists and fishermen, and it can get very busy in the summer, but the landlord and his staff try to make sure the service is brisk; there is always the memory of those militiamen to keep them on their toes.

First came William the Conqueror's butler,
now here comes Fuggle the Frog

The Dorset Arms
Withyham, East Sussex

On the B2110

It is confusing at first to find so many inns in this corner of Sussex called the Dorset Arms. You will look in vain for an Earl of Dorset in *Who's Who*, but it was one of the titles acquired over the centuries by the Sackvilles, who have been associated with Withyham since Sir Jordain de Sackville married a female descendant of William the Conqueror's chief butler, eight hundred years ago. In those days a royal butler did rather more than open doors and pour the port, and this one owned most of Withyham. In 1604 Thomas Sackville became Earl of Dorset, but when the fifth Earl died in the nineteenth century he was succeeded by his sister, Countess De La Warr, and the De La Warr side of the family have lived there ever since, at Buckhurst Park; the entrance is close by the Dorset Arms.

Baron Buckhurst is another family title, so presumably the inn might have been the Buckhurst Arms, the De La Warr Arms, or even, to borrow another family title, the Cantelupe Arms, though that might be mistaken for a melon. But Dorset was the popular choice, and the Dorset Arms in Lewes, for instance, was built on land leased from the family. There was another Dorset Arms at Hartfield, just up the road from Withyham, but two inns with the same name so close together must have been confusing, and the Hartfield one is now the Anchor. I checked to see if there was a Viscount Anchor in the family, but that is one title they missed.

Apart from its genealogical interest, the Dorset

Arms has quite a history of its own. It was built around 1556 as Somers Farmhouse, and it did not become an inn until the eighteenth century, when it was called, simply, the Ale House. It was about that time that it must have acquired its present Georgian

Most of the memorials bearing the Sackville name are in the nearby church, but the Dorset Arms has a couple of reminders too.

façade. Trade could not have been too brisk in the early days, because in 1810 an official survey described the road which passes it as 'bad for carriages and in winter impassable'. But, as the alehouse was owned by the family at the Big House, along with the rest of the village, profits were probably not too important, so long as refreshment was available for the Earl's visitors. There were cattle fairs at Withyham too, which must have helped.

Since then the road has improved, to provide a scenic alternative route between East Grinstead and Tunbridge Wells along the edge of Ashdown Forest, and quite recently the Dorset Arms was acquired by the Lewes brewery of Harveys, which incorporated it in the curious ritual known as the Harvey Hop. It was launched by a band of energetic Morris Men in 1990 to mark the brewery's bicentenary year. In a one-day marathon they danced at more than thirty inns from Midhurst to Maidstone, covering nearly 250 miles between 10 o'clock in the morning and 10.30 at night, finishing under floodlights in the brewery yard, and collecting a thousand pounds for charity *en route*.

The idea caught on – not the dancing but the visiting – and other people started making the circuit,

albeit in twelve weeks or months rather than hours. Two years later the Hoppers' Club was formed, a Sussex version of the Dartmoor Letterbox network, although that takes in 'letterboxes' on the moor itself too. Participants have their books stamped at each inn they visit, until they have collected the complete set – then they start all over again. In Devon it is done mainly for fun, though they can acquire the odd T-shirt after a while, but in Sussex and Kent the brewery awards a range of trophies, from polo shirts and tankards to cricket jumpers and golf umbrellas, all emblazoned with the Hoppers' Club emblem, Fuggle the Frog.

This is not entirely altruistic on the part of the brewery. To get their books stamped, members have to buy a pint or the non-alcoholic equivalent. But a lively social club has grown out of what started as a publicity stunt, and they hold regular barn dances, pub games nights, and even a Hoppers' Ball – a cut above your average 'hop'.

Withyham is something of a Mecca for admirers of one of the most famous Sackvilles, the poet Victoria Sackville-West. Her ashes were buried at the church which stands on the hill near the Dorset Arms, and her memorial is alongside the imposing Sackville monument which was erected as part of the restoration work after the church was struck by lightning in 1663. This is also Pooh country; A.A. Milne wrote many of the Pooh stories at his home in nearby Hartfield. Turner visited Withyham, but he was only eighteen at the time and omitted to paint it, so he is rather less of a draw. But it is a popular area, and the Dorset Arms has adapted accordingly.

It has acquired a restaurant to cope with the extra trade, but mercifully the bar remains unspoilt, with its original wide wooden floor-boards of unvarnished local oak, its low-beamed ceiling and its splendid Tudor stone fireplace. The oak beams on the walls were once hidden by matchboard partitions covered with wallpaper and plaster, but they have long since been uncovered. The last Earl of Dorset, if he ever dropped in, would feel very much at home – except for the occasional appearance of Fuggle the Frog.

South Midland Region

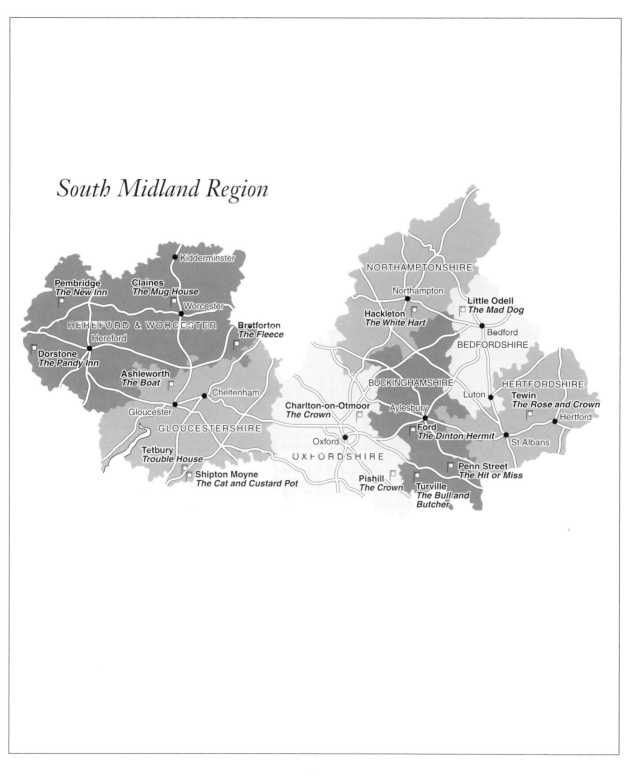

Kidderminster

Pembridge
The New Inn

Claines
The Mug House

Worcester

HEREFORD & WORCESTER

Brotforton
The Fleece

Hereford

Dorstone
The Pandy Inn

Ashleworth
The Boat

Cheltenham

Gloucester

GLOUCESTERSHIRE

Tetbury
Trouble House

Shipton Moyne
The Cat and Custard Pot

NORTHAMPTONSHIRE

Northampton

Hackleton
The White Hart

Little Odell
The Mad Dog

Bedford

BEDFORDSHIRE

BUCKINGHAMSHIRE

Aylesbury

Luton

HERTFORDSHIRE

Tewin
The Rose and Crown

Hertford

Charlton-on-Otmoor
The Crown

Ford
The Dinton Hermit

St Albans

Oxford

OXFORDSHIRE

Pishill
The Crown

Penn Street
The Hit or Miss

Turville
The Bull and Butcher

One family for over three hundred years - all in the same boat

The Boat
Ashleworth, Gloucestershire

The Quay

Amile outside the main part of Ashleworth village there is a little group of venerable and very handsome buildings. The church still has its fourteenth-century buttressed tower, Ashleworth Court dates from about 1460 and looks as grand as ever, and the massive stone tithe barn, built about fifty years after Ashleworth Court by the monks of Bristol Abbey, retains its original walls and its splendid timbered roof, thanks to the National Trust.

They make an imposing trio, and many a pilgrimage is made to see them. But just around the corner, down a little lane that ends at the River Severn, there is another venerable building which is humble rather than handsome, but attracts its own special kind of pilgrim, those who relish a genuine old English inn with an unusual story to tell.

The Boat was just a cottage when Ashleworth Court and the tithe barn were built, so the masons were too early for a drink, but it was granted a licence under Charles II and, astonishingly, it has been held by the same family ever since. Even in the case of a great house like Ashleworth Court it is unusual for the same family to be in occupation for over three centuries; in a modest alehouse it may well be unique. And the line shows no sign of dying out. When Mrs Irene Jelf retires, her niece and joint licensee, Jacquie Nicholls, will take over.

The rights to the ferry across the Severn were granted to the family at the same time as the licence, and for many generations they supplied transport across the river as well as refreshment at the inn, but I imagine the Boat was more profitable than the boat. This is a sparsely populated area on both sides of the river. Ashleworth is only a small village, well off the main road, and Ashleworth Quay, as the ferry slipway is rather grandly call- ed, is tucked away very discreetly down its narrow winding lane. On the far bank there is nothing much to be seen except fields. The nearest village on that side is Sandhurst, which looks no larger than Ashleworth, and hardly attracts the same volume of traffic as its famous military namesake. If someone on the Ashleworth side wants to visit Gloucester, the bridge on the main road into the city is only three miles downstream.

The ferry's main customers, I suppose, would have been the farm workers on the opposite bank who wanted a drink at the Boat, but as they had to pay for the ferry as well as the beer it would have been cheaper to drink elsewhere. Not surprisingly, the ferry has long since ceased to function. But this is great walking and bird-watching country; there are public footpaths along the river bank, and there is a wildfowl reserve not far away. Mrs Jelf thinks it is just possible that the ferry will come into its own again – and she still holds the rights if it does.

Meanwhile, the twenty-five steps leading down to the river from the high embankment which protects the Boat are very useful for customers coming along the river by boat, and for the fishermen who gather there each spring to catch the migrating elver. Some of the catch is exported to the Continent, to grow up into European eels.

A pub lunch in the Boat is like eating in Mrs Jelf's private living-room. It has been in her family for three hundred years.

The Boat itself still looks more like a cottage than an inn, except for the picnic tables with their coloured umbrellas which are put out during the summer. Even the old brew house in the front garden looks like just another outhouse, handy for storing a cart or next winter's logs.

Inside the front door it is like stepping into Mrs Jelf's front parlour – which indeed it is. There is a modest bar counter, but the beer is served from the cask and there are no elaborate bar menus, just filled bread rolls and the sort of ploughman's lunch which a real ploughman would appreciate – especially the home-made chutney. The open range still has its bread oven, and there are well-worn armchairs to relax in, and well-worn magazines to read. Rush mats cover the flagstone floor, and a high-backed settle looks as if it was installed when the cottage was built.

The back parlour is much the same, except that the floor is tiled instead of stone, but there is also a splendid grandfather clock. It is a reminder that, in spite of appearances, time has not stood completely still at the Boat.

Her rocking-chair may still rock, but Lola doesn't live here any more

The Fleece
Bretforton, Hereford & Worcester

The Cross

The licensed trade has thrown up some memorable characters over the years, but few can match the late Lola Taplin, for thirty years licensee of the Fleece, until she died in 1977 at the age of eighty-three. Her final act was perhaps her most remarkable; she left the inn, complete with its contents and garden, to the National Trust, on condition that it continued to be run as an unspoilt country inn.

Miss Taplin's family had lived there for more than five hundred years, but it was only in 1848 that her great-grandfather, Henry Byrd, sold the land they owned and turned the farmhouse into an inn. He made no structural alterations, and the family furniture remained in use in the bars. It is hardly surprising that when Lola Taplin eventually took over the Fleece she still regarded it as the family's private home. Customers were carefully vetted, and had to obey the strict rules of the house.

The present licensee, Mr Griffiths, remembers her well. 'She either liked you or she didn't; she lost as many customers as she had. If you moved a piece of furniture or anything like that, then she told you to leave.'

Some of the villagers, probably those she had turfed out, muttered darkly that she was a white witch, and indeed there are witch-marks in two of the bars – circles which used to be chalked on the hearth to keep evil spirits from coming down the chimney. However, the depth and age of the marks show they were there long before Lola, and probably the most bewitching thing about her was her exotic Christian name.

They do say, though, that strange things have happened since her death. One girl who worked at the Fleece found the old lady's rocking-chair rocking in an empty room; she was so frightened she never returned to the inn. An alarm near the chair used to go off three or four times a week, so each night when he closes up, Mr Griffiths moves the chair out of its range; it hasn't gone off since. There are also two clocks which sometimes stop simultaneously at three in the morning, which is just about the time Lola Taplin died.

The pewter collection is said to have been left by Oliver Cromwell in exchange for the family silver. It is not a complete set, but they were probably glad to get anything.

As she had no children to succeed her, distant relatives may have cherished some expectations about the Fleece. Younger folk in the village may have hoped that their local would be equipped with electronic games and piped music. They were all disappointed. The National Trust has followed her wishes, and although Mr Griffiths is not quite as tough with his customers as she was, the rules are still quite strict, and understandably so.

There is some magnificent antique furniture in the Fleece, and the decorations are not exactly standard pub issue. The pewter collection, for instance, is said to have been left by Oliver Cromwell in exchange for the family silver which he appropriated to pay his army. The pewter is not a complete set – some of it was made in Worcester, a few pieces in London, and most of it at Bewdley near Kidderminster – but I doubt anyone liked to ask him where he got it. The family probably thought themselves lucky that he gave them anything.

The collection is in what used to be the farm kitchen, and the fireplace still has its roasting spits and the large pan which caught the fat as it dripped from the meat. Alas, the roasting equipment is no longer complete; the clock-work jacks which turned the spits were stolen at the time of Miss Taplin's death, along with the original set of brass candlesticks on the mantel-piece.

In the room which was formerly the brew-house, and before that the farm dairy, there are antique Victorian liquor measures in brass and copper, and in the 'Dug-out', once the pantry, there is a coffin-like table with a hinged lid in which dough was kept before being baked. That is just a small selection of the Fleece's furnishings.

Small wonder, therefore, that the National Trust calls it a 'living museum', although it does make it sound pretty depressing. It is actually a very cheerful, lively pub, and in the summer when the trippers overflow into the orchard garden there is all manner of entertainments, from Morris dancing to sheep-shearing. In the winter the Fleece reverts to its traditional role, described by the landlord as 'an old farmer boys' drinking hole'. It has achieved, in fact, a happy balance between a noted tourist attraction and a village local. That rocking-chair hasn't moved for some time now, so I think Lola Taplin approves.

The locals laid out on the bar table were not dead drunk, just dead

The seventeenth-century oak table in the bar was originally used in the church across the road for laying out corpses.

The Crown
Charlton-on-Otmoor, Oxfordshire

Opposite the church

Otmoor is not quite on the same scale as Exmoor or Dartmoor. It is only about five miles long and three miles wide, and the villages which border it are almost within sight of each other across it. But this strange little area of marsh and fen and tiny streams is quite as desolate as its big brothers in the West Country, and its situation is far more unusual. It lies only a few miles outside the Oxford ring road, and there could hardly be a greater contrast than Oxford's dreaming, but traffic-surrounded, spires and 'sleeping Otmoor cast under a spell of ancient magic'.

The few people outside the area who have heard of the moor will probably know it because of the eighteenth-century Boarstall duck decoy, still in working order, and the much older Boarstall Tower, once the gatehouse to a long-forgotten manor house and now preserved by the National Trust. They may also know the picturesque Nut Tree at Murcott, a thatched inn which was frequented by Cromwell's soldiers as they prepared to besiege Oxford. They are not so likely to know the less-fashionable Crown at Charlton-on-Otmoor.

The Nut Tree does have an unusual feature, the weird gargoyles which dangle from the walnut tree in the garden, said to portray some of the regular customers of yesteryear. But as one guidebook puts it, 'the whole mood of the place is sort of smartly idyllic', and that meant that when I arrived in mid-morning all the tables in the bar were being laid with cutlery and glasses and serviettes, and nobody seemed very interested in the gargoyles. When I mentioned that the inn used to be known as the Nut Hatch, they seemed rather shocked. I am sure the Nut Tree is a great place for salmon in a prawn, lobster and brandy bisque, one of their regular bar lunches, but it does not have quite the atmosphere that Cromwell's soldiers knew.

So I continued round the edge of Otmoor to Charlton, where the church weather-vane bears a webbed foot to symbolise the kinship between the villagers and the boggy moor, and where the Crown, an unpretentious building, backs on to the moor itself.

This really is an unspoilt village local, set immediately opposite the church as so many village locals are. It lacks the traditional secret tunnel between the two, but it does have a link with the church which is a lot more valuable, and must surely be unique. In the bar there is a splendid seventeenth-century oak table, seven feet long and far too heavy for one person to move. These days it is handy for beer mugs and ashtrays and the odd game of cards, but originally it was in the church of St Mary's, and it was used for laying out corpses.

Nobody knows why the table crossed the road. It is about the same period as the church pulpit, which is dated 1616, and it could well have been installed at the same time. But while the only alteration to the pulpit has been the removal of its overhead sounding-board in the last century, by a rector who, presumably, reckoned he had a loud enough voice without it, the table must have been considered redundant, or got in the way when the pews were moved. Perhaps a churchwarden who enjoyed his pint suggested that it went to the Crown.

One landlord attempted to sell it, but there was a mighty outcry from the locals, and it stayed where it was. Its ownership is still unclear, but there is a gentlemen's agreement that it is included in the valuation when a new landlord takes over, and it will not be removed from the inn. The current landlord spent £900 on restoring it, and it has been valued at £6,000, which is a lot of money for a bar table. It has become such a familiar object among the regulars who sup their beer around it that I doubt they ever visualise it in its original role, bearing a shrouded corpse.

At the time of the highly unpopular Enclosure Acts the Crown was the headquarters for the Otmoor resistance movement; there the ringleaders planned their night-time forays on to the moor to prevent it being enclosed and drained by the gentry. On moonlit nights they would blacken their faces and sally forth with axes and spades to smash down fences and block up ditches. Sometimes they were spotted, and bloody fighting ensued, but their efforts were not in vain. Otmoor is still an open moor.

The Crown, having led the battle against the gentry, continues to hold out against gentrification. That splendid oak table has yet to experience a plate of salmon in a prawn, lobster and brandy bisque.

Secret assignations on consecrated ground - did Queen Elizabeth join in?

Not everyone agrees that the Mug House stands on consecrated ground, but the church is only just outside the window.

The Mug House
Claines, Hereford & Worcester

The churchyard

Road maps can be deceptive. They generally show Claines on the edge of the black blob which is the city of Worcester, marooned inside a triangle of busy main roads, and not the sort of place to harbour a quiet country inn. The village, it is true, is sufficiently built-up to be described as 'highly favoured suburban Worcester', but the parish church lies down a quiet little lane away from the busy roads, and the Mug House is further on beyond it, along a

drive which leads round the churchyard.

It is a lovely old brick-and-timber-fronted building, with a section of the original wattle-and-daub preserved in one of the bars. It manages to cater for the nearby camping site without losing its traditional rural flavour, and there are no juke-boxes or electronic games. If you do hear any music it is probably accompanying the Morris dancers.

It has a ghost, of course, which throws glasses off

shelves, switches off beer pumps and tramps about in the upstairs rooms. Its most unusual feature, however, may make it unique. Many a village inn was built close to the site of the church, to provide shelter and refreshment for the masons who were working on it, but the Mug House claims to be the only one which actually stands on consecrated ground.

I have to record that not every expert seems to agree. One reference book describes it as 'almost in the churchyard', which casts a certain doubt on the holiness of its position. But I am happy to accept the landlord's claim, and also his explanation of why it was built there, which does provide an intriguing alternative to the usual lodgings-for-masons story.

Claines church dates back to the twelfth century, a couple of hundred years ahead of the Mug House, and the next major influx of stone-masons did not occur until 1886, led by Sir Aston Webb, a distinguished local architect who built the north aisle and north porch. No doubt his men refreshed themselves at the Mug House in accordance with tradition, but the inn was actually built for a much more up-market clientele. It provided a convenient meeting-place for any local aristocracy who had to travel some distance to attend church. That is the official version.

But Claines is so close to Worcester that one wonders why the aristocracy did not go there instead, where there were plenty of places of refreshment available. The answer, so it is hinted, was that Claines provided more discreet surroundings for assignations in which church-going was only secondary. A room at the 'Mug' was reserved for this purpose and, according to a local historian, 'that room could tell a few tales of love, scandal, and perhaps even challenges to mortal combat'. Which sounds rather imaginative for an historian, but why not? The thought that these goings-on were taking place on supposedly consecrated ground must have added extra spice to the encounters.

It is a fact that Claines has a well-documented connection with the highest echelons of English nobility. The first Queen Elizabeth visited the village in 1575 on her way from Hartlebury to Worcester, and spent the night there – not at the local inn, for once, but at the timbered mansion called Ports Mill. Her visit was a mixed blessing for the parishioners, because they had to provide twenty-four fowl to feed the royal entourage, and she was presented with a £40 gold cup and another £20 in cash. In return they got the chalice which is still in use in the church; I hope they felt it was worth it.

Again, with Worcester so close, one wonders why the Queen did not complete her journey and sleep in the city. Is it possible that she too had a secret assignation at the Mug House, having heard of its reputation from her courtiers? It may even be that a silver coin dated 1562, which was found many years later when that special room was restored, was the tip she left behind for the landlord, which he kept as a souvenir. It would be difficult to prove the theory wrong – and I bet that imaginative historian wished he had thought of it first!

For a penitent knight, the pandy came in handy

The Pandy Inn
Dorstone, Hereford & Worcester

The village green

It was that famous cry by Henry II which started it all.

'Will no one rid me of this turbulent priest?' he demanded, exasperated by the activities of his former friend, the Archbishop of Canterbury.

The question, it seems, was meant to be rhetorical, but four of his knights took him at his word, and we all know what happened after that. They found Thomas Becket in the cathedral, tried to drag him outside and, when he refused to budge, killed him with their swords on the altar steps.

It is not recorded what Henry said next, but it could well have been 'Whoops!' Filled with remorse, he walked barefoot to the crypt of Canterbury Cathedral to be soundly thumped by every monk and bishop who could find something hard to hit him with. That apparently made everything all right again, and he ruled England for another twenty-odd years. But what about the four knights?

They were sent off to the Crusades, where no

86

doubt it was hoped they would meet their just desserts. But one of them at least survived, Richard de Brico, and perhaps in thankfulness, perhaps in further penance, he built the parish church at Dorstone in 1185, fifteen years after the murder. He also built accommodation for the workers, and that was the origin of the Pandy Inn, which claims to be not only the oldest inn in the country, but also the earliest licensed alehouse in Britain.

That sort of claim is always hazardous, but certainly the Pandy was up and running in time for both Cromwell and Charles I to visit it – fortunately at different times. It has another, more macabre, link with the Civil War. The village green by the inn was once covered by the gravestones of those who were killed in the local fighting. When the stones were removed they were used as shelves in the larder-dairy at the inn, where the womenfolk of the village learned their dairy skills earlier this century.

The name of the inn comes from a much earlier era. In the fourteenth century the building was used by local weavers to thicken the weave of their cloth into flannel. The stream which ran by it, now diverted, drove a water-wheel and operated trip-hammers which pounded the treated cloth. Such mills were known as pandys, from the Latin *pannus*, meaning cloth.

When the mill at Dorstone was licensed it was still known to the locals as the pandy, and it has kept that name ever since. It has also kept its traditional atmosphere in the main bar, with its flagstoned floor, heavy beams and open log fire. The noisier activities, including an ageing juke-box, are hived off

Drinkers have been enjoying a glass of ale round the fireplace at the Pandy since it was licensed in 1603.

into a separate games area.

Dorstone lies in the Golden Valley on the River Dore, and there is a theory that all three names are connected with the Norman 'd'Or', meaning golden. However, dor is also the Welsh word for water, which seems a more likely explanation, if less romantic. But there is no lack of historical romance in the Golden Valley. It has the ruins of two castles, one of them close to the Pandy, and on the hill above the village is Arthur's Stone, a Neolithic tomb of about 3000 BC – which is a lot earlier than King Arthur, but that is what historical romance is all about. You will also find an Iron Age hill-fort, mystical ley lines, and stories about Queen Elizabeth and the Earl of Leicester, to whom she gave one of the castles. In fact, the Golden Valley is a Golden Treasury of tales and legends.

And of course, ghosts. The Pandy has had its quota of mysterious presences and drinks leaping off tables, which occurred during the early days of the current licensees, Chris and Margaret Burtonwood. 'These strange happenings carried on until we opened up a room at the rear of the pub which had been closed off for years. Everything seemed to go wrong while this was taking place, until one night we sat down and talked to the room for a couple of hours, saying how much more comfortable it would be when it was finished.

'After that night, nothing else happened at the Pandy. In fact we quite missed the activities, because we never felt threatened; it was obviously friendly.'

I wondered if the ghost at the Pandy was called Andy – but one doesn't joke about such things.

The judge's clerk who took early retirement (into a cave) and fell for leather

The Dinton Hermit
Ford, Buckinghamshire

Just off the main street

If you ask a local the way to the Dinton Hermit, you will be directed not to Dinton but to Ford, a village over a mile away, where a rather elegant hermit looks down at you from the sign at the village inn. But three hundred years ago you would have been directed to a cave in the grounds of Dinton Hall, where the hermit spent the last thirty-odd years of his life – and the figure you would have found there bore little resemblance to that sophisticated character on the sign, with his velvet breeches, long cape and jaunty wide-brimmed hat.

In fact, the connection between the Dinton Hermit and the inn named after him is so obscure that not even the landlady could tell me what it was. The building itself dates back to the fifteenth or sixteenth century, judging by the age of its stone walls, so it was certainly there in his day. He may well have passed it on his summer strolls up into the Chilterns. But even if it was already an alehouse, it is unlikely he would have patronised it, because he always carried his own supplies in three leather bottles hanging from his belt. Two contained strong beer and weak beer, so he could enjoy a mild-and-bitter, and the third contained milk – for milk stout?

It would not have been out of character to mix his drinks like that, because the Dinton Hermit had some rather odd tastes – particularly in his dress. His clothes consisted almost entirely of little leather patches, layer upon layer, from his strange hooded cloak down to his remarkable shoes, which had patches up to ten layers thick, held together with nails. One of his shoes, now in the Ashmolean Museum, Oxford, is thirteen inches long and six inches across; even in its dried state after three hundred years it weighs over four pounds. Just standing up must have been quite a feat; actually walking in such shoes, let alone climbing up the Chilterns, must merit some kind of Olympic medal.

But the Dinton Hermit was not ever thus. His name was John Bigg, born at Dinton in 1629, well educated, and clerk to the squire at Dinton Hall. It so happened the squire was Simon Mayne, strong supporter of Cromwell, MP for Aylesbury, and one of the judges who signed the death warrant of Charles I. John Bigg may have handed him the pen.

Local legend has it that he did rather more than that. John Bigg, they say, was actually the masked executioner who beheaded the king. But this seems wildly improbable. Why should a twenty-year-old clerk from an obscure Buckinghamshire village be drafted in to chop off the king's head? It was, after all, no job for an amateur. Maybe he just boasted that the pen he handed to his master to sign the death sentence was mightier than the axe that carried it out, and the story developed from there.

When the monarchy was restored, Simon Mayne is said to have hidden in a secret chamber at Dinton Hall, reached by a tunnel under the staircase, but eventually he gave himself up, was found guilty of regicide, and committed to the Tower. He died there of ill health a year later, and his widow was allowed to bury him at Dinton church, 'without ostentation'.

John Bigg escaped any retribution for the modest part he played; the Royalists obviously did not believe the masked executioner story. However, he sank into a deep melancholy, and retired into a cave in the grounds of the Hall. He lived there for the rest of his life, adding more patches to his clothing, taking occasional nips from his three leather bottles, and providing the locals with a little gentle amusement. He died in 1696 and was buried in the churchyard near his master.

As John Bigg was born and bred in Dinton, and lived there all his life – albeit in a cave for much of that life – it might have been more logical to name the pub in the village after him, rather than one which is over a mile away. Dinton certainly had an inn in his day, the Seven Stars, which was established in 1640, during the reign of Charles I. Perhaps its landlord was a Royalist, who disapproved of Bigg's involvement in the king's trial, obscure though it was.

Whatever the reason, the Seven Stars has retained its original name, along with its nice old snuggery, a nice old fireplace and some nice old varnished settles – but without the nice old Dinton Hermit.

Don't pass the cheese, throw it! But mind the well under the bar

The White Hart
Hackleton, Northamptonshire

80 Main Road

Hackleton is just too far out of Northampton to make it a convenient lunch venue for city workers, which is a cause for regret to the landlord, who would naturally welcome the trade, but a cause for relief to those like myself who want to enjoy their pub lunches in peace. But be warned: the White Hart is a member of the Northamptonshire Skittles League, and if you think ordinary skittles can be noisy, try sharing a bar with a Northamptonshire skittles match. This does not affect the peaceful pub lunches, but on a match evening I imagine you need to be a skittles enthusiast if you are in the public bar.

Happily for the White Hart, there are a great many such enthusiasts around, and I now count myself among their number. The game involves not balls but wooden 'cheeses', and you do not bowl them, you hurl them at the pins from a distance of some seven feet. The pins stand on a table, with a miniature soccer goal behind them to prevent too much damage to the furniture and fittings, and the hurler stands at the oche, a mark on the floor like the one used by darts players.

The technique, as I understand it, is to skim the cheese towards the pins like skimming a stone on water, to get the maximum destructive effect. I have tried it both forehand and backhand, with equal lack of success. There are three cheeses and nine pins, so the maximum score is twenty-seven; my best effort was four. However, it is always exhilarating to throw things at other things, and to the thrower, if not to the casual passer-by, the noise it all makes is enormously satisfying.

It was not only the skittles which took me to the White Hart; they can be found in many other Northamptonshire inns. There were also the mementoes in the bar of the landlord's father, Frank Eli French, a versatile blacksmith, who not only made his own tools but also served as a mechanic in the Royal Flying Corps during the First World War. I am not sure how the pilots reacted when they discovered their planes were being tuned up by a village blacksmith, but there is no doubt about the opinion of Mr French's fellow villagers at Little Houghton, not far from Hackleton. After his death a few years ago, his son unearthed a certificate which they had presented to him, and which now has a place of honour in the bar, alongside his handmade tools.

'They desire to record their admiration for the worthy part he played in the struggle for liberty and justice, and to express their sincere wishes for a future of happiness and prosperity,' it reads. Their wish was fulfilled, and he lived into his ninetieth year.

His son Richard is the latest landlord of the White Hart, in a line which dates back to 1739, when Robert Holt was the first recorded licensee. According to the local records, 'Hackleton supported several outlets for spirituous liquors, but the White Hart was almost certainly the oldest.' The landlords and their families must have liked the place; in the century-and-a-half between Robert Holt becoming the licensee and 1888, there were only four different families running the inn.

They were also long-lived. William Elliott, who took over in 1907, held the licence for forty-four years. Richard French has been there only since 1986, but in view of his father's longevity, he may hold it even longer.

The bars of the White Hart have been modernised and extended over the years, but the inn has preserved a reminder of its earlier days, in an unusual location. As you lean on the bar you can look down into a well nearly forty feet deep, conveniently illuminated and with the water at the bottom clearly visible. It was still in use in the days of the last landlord, supplying the pump which stands outside on the patio.

The well could provide quite a hazard for unwary drinkers, if the glass cover were removed, and an absent-minded barman might well try to use it for dirty glasses. The cover also prevents any joker trying to combine Northamptonshire skittles with pitch-penny to create a new pub game. But if Cheeses Down the Well ever becomes popular, the White Hart will be first in the field.

Northamptonshire skittles require a miniature goalpost, a good throwing arm – and earplugs.

A dog with two tales – it should be pleased, not mad

The Mad Dog
Little Odell, Bedfordshire

West end of village

The Mad Dog is not the most inviting name for a traditional village inn, and the dog on the inn sign looks as mad as they come. Perhaps to offset it, a children's fairground roundabout occupies a prominent place in the front garden. This may prove counter-productive for die-hard drinkers who will probably prefer the company of mad dogs to small children but, inside the inn, Englishmen can drink in peace – it is the children who go out in the midday sun.

There is a convincing story behind the name. In 1724 a distinguished physician and poisons expert, Dr Richard Mead, took as his second wife the daughter of Sir Rowland Alston of Odell Castle. They made their home at Harrold Hall – also owned by Sir Rowland. About halfway between the two residences was the thatched alehouse now known as the Mad Dog. Dr Mead enjoyed the odd glass, and on one occasion found himself without the ready cash to pay for it. Instead he gave the landlord his recipe for curing the bite of a mad dog, a gruesome concoction involving ground liverwort and black pepper. The inn has been called the Mad Dog ever since.

Yes, a convincing story, and I ought to leave it at that, but there are some odd little inconsistencies. There is no record, for instance, of what the Mad Dog was called before this transaction took place. In fact, it seems to be its original name. When the first application for a licence was made by Thomas Wells, whose family continued to hold it for the next two hundred years, the chairman of the Bench – Sir Rowland Alston, of course – asked him what he would call the alehouse. Thomas, it seems, had no idea. 'Why not call it after your mad dog recipe?' suggested Sir Rowland, and he did. But if this was the first licence, how could Dr Richard Mead have had a drink there already?

Why, in fact, did he hand over the recipe at all? Surely he could have put the drink on the slate – the landlord could hardly refuse credit to Sir Rowland's son-in-law. And was the recipe worth the price of a drink anyway? It did not do much good for a villager called Thomas Bailey who, some years later, features in the parish register – 'died mad, occasioned by the bite of a mad dog'.

But this did not discourage the Wells family. Until recently a board over the inn door proclaimed: 'George Wells of the Mad Dog has a recipe for the bite of a mad dog WHICH HAS NEVER FAILED.' Maybe Mr Bailey patronised a different inn.

Apart from the curious aspects of the hydrophobia cure there were other strange goings-on at the Mad Dog. Gas cylinders turned themselves off, the framed price-list by the bar leapt from the wall, the locals saw 'a loosely caped shape' near the inglenook fireplace, and the landlord's children felt someone brushing past them in the upstairs passageway.

Then, in 1986, the bar ceiling was taken down during structural alterations, and behind it was found a leather-framed sepia photograph of a youngish woman. It was taken by a photographer with a Colchester address, and an expert dated it in the 1870s.

There are two theories about it. The more mundane one involves a landlord's daughter who dallied with a roadman, became pregnant and was sent away to Colchester to have the baby. It was brought back and looked after by the landlord, but the daughter remained in Colchester. The photograph might have been a reminder of her – but people have said the woman in the photograph is not the daughter, which rather spoils the story.

I prefer the second version, that a stranger came to the Mad Dog after the bar had been altered, saw the photograph on the wall, and identified the woman as Margaret Bowden, a notorious Victorian virago who visited pubs, observed the customers to select a likely victim, and then waited outside and killed him for his money. She was eventually caught and hanged.

So was Margaret Bowden the cause of all those curious occurrences? Was the photograph an early form of 'Wanted' notice, or did the landlord have a soft spot for her, and kept her picture hidden after she was hanged, thus imprisoning her spirit until the ceiling was taken down a century later?

I rather fancy the idea of an inn being haunted by a female footpad, and if a future landlord finds the present name of the inn off-putting, he could always change it to the Margaret Bowden, and use the photograph as the basis of the inn sign. Meanwhile it continues to be the only Mad Dog in England, so the landlord believes, and he is very pleased to keep it that way. The Mad Dog should be pleased, too; it is after all a Dog with two tales.

Shall we one day hear the patter of tiny ghostly feet?

The New Inn
Pembridge, Hereford & Worcester

Market Square

Pembridge is one of those picture-postcard villages where every building seems to be timber-framed. The bad news is that it lies astride the A44, the route which the mail coaches took from London to Aberystwyth, and which is still the main trunk road into mid-Wales. The good news is that the New Inn lies off this road, in a little cluster of old buildings around the open-sided market hall, where the pillars still bear the notches for the stalls of the medieval wool traders.

Except for the church, the inn is the oldest building in the group. Like most 'New Inns' it is very old indeed, built in 1311 as a farmhouse, later a coaching inn and court-house – the cellar used to be the dungeon. One gazetteer dates it as early 1600s, but that was probably when it was restored to look as it does today, timber-framed like its neighbours with a projecting upper storey. It is straight out of an illustration for the *Pickwick Papers*, although Pembridge was rather beyond the range of the Pickwick Club.

It was well within range, however, of the fighting which broke out fairly regularly along that particular stretch of the Welsh border. Offa's Dyke is only four miles to the west, so it was mostly the Welsh fighting the English, but the Wars of the Roses got this far too. One of the battles was fought only three miles away at Mortimer's Cross. The Yorkists won, and legend has it that a treaty between the two sides was signed in the court room at the New Inn. Alas, it did not have much effect. A fortnight later there was another battle at St Alban's in Hertfordshire, which the Lancastrians won, and the fighting dragged on for another twenty-odd years.

Things quietened down in Pembridge for a century or two, until Cromwell appeared on the scene, and the New Inn was close to the front line once again. The west door of the church is still scarred by Roundhead bullets, and the pagoda-like bell tower in the churchyard, with its massive timbers inside and the convenient slits in the thick stone walls, proved to be ideal as a lookout point and mini-fortress.

Happily, the New Inn survived the Civil War unscathed, and parts of it have changed very little since. The main bar still has its original flagstones and oak doors with peg latches, and the splendid curved-back settle by the fireplace looks as though it has been there just as long, though some believe it started life as a section of a circular cockpit.

For a change there is no suggestion that either Cromwell or Charles I slept here, nor any of the other principal participants in earlier battles, but the New Inn does have its own wartime legacies. Every reference book seems to agree that there are two ghosts in residence at the inn. One is a young red-coated soldier who paces the corridor, sometimes carrying a sword, but more often beating a drum. The other is a young lady who waits patiently for her man to come home from the war. Opinions differ as to whether he has been killed or merely lost interest.

There have been the usual strange happenings at the inn, though it is difficult to know whether to attribute them to the deceased drummer or the languishing lady. Lights are turned on, and beer pumps are turned off. The landlord has never seen anything, but an overnight guest with an interest in the psychic said she felt a very unhappy presence in her room.

The two ghosts are apparently unconnected, and may even originate from different wars. To add to the confusion, the girl manifests herself only to other women, so it is quite likely the spectral soldier does not even know she is there. It is sad to picture these two lonely souls sharing the same premises unaware of each other's presence. When I first heard about them, some years ago, I hoped that somehow the barriers of time and invisibility would come down, the soldier and the girl would make each other's acquaintance at last and, in due course, the New Inn would hear the patter of tiny ghostly feet.

I am still waiting.

In cricketing country, should an artful bodger make deckchairs?

The Hit or Miss
Penn Street, Buckinghamshire

In main street opposite cricket ground

Village inns and village cricket are so closely associated in English rural life that it is not surprising they sometimes become an integral part of one another. There are any number of village inns called The Cricketers, with variations like The Three Willows at Birchanger in Essex where, instead of the usual sign, there are three lifelike batsmen representing different eras in cricketing history,

perched on top of a post.

The Hit or Miss goes a stage further. It not only has a cricketer on its sign – a Victorian gentleman wielding a curved bat in front of two stumps – but also a collection of cricketing memorabilia in the bar, its own cricket team, and a cricket ground just across the road for them to play on, the gate emblazoned with the initials of the Hit or Miss C.C. The ground is actually owned by Earl Howe, whose family have been squires in these parts for many generations, but the club members help to preserve it. A certificate in the bar records that they raised £1,050 to help the proprietor of the Hit or Miss to repair the pavilion roof.

This part of the Chilterns is very cricket-orientated. Only a few miles away at Holmer Green there is another inn called the Bat and Ball, and village cricket teams abound. Penn Street does not like to be confused with Penn, the larger village on the main road two miles away, and if their teams meet, I imagine there is keen competition to establish which Penn is mightier on the sward.

Nobody is quite sure how far back the cricketing history of the Hit or Miss extends. According to a potted history in the bar, the inn was still two cottages in the 1730s, and it was first leased as a cottage tenement or public house called the Hit or Miss in 1798. That would make it one of the most senior cricketing inns in the country; even the famous Bat and Ball at Hambledon, headquarters of the original Hambledon Cricket Club, can only claim a history going back to the 1760s.

Unfortunately, the notes in the bar go on to say that 'Hit or Miss' is first mentioned in 1840, which I found rather confusing. The present landlord was unable to help me. He had bought the inn about twelve months before, but it had stood empty for some time, leaving much to be done, and he had not got around to any historical research. 'That was very low on my priorities,' he told me rather crisply.

The cricketing activities at the Hit or Miss have survived the interregnum, and so have its cricketing trophies. There are three well-worn bats by the bar, two of them so well-worn that any signatures they once bore are now illegible. The third has the signatures of the England and Pakistan teams in the 1987 Test series; the connection with the Hit or Miss is not explained. The rest of the wall is occupied by *Punch* cricket cartoons and a notice-board displaying the team list for the next match. Owners and landlords may come and go, but cricket is immortal.

However, if you find the game immensely boring – and I am told that some folk actually do – then the inn can offer mementoes from another traditional activity which was even more widespread at one time in this part of Buckinghamshire. Since the eighteenth century the locality has been famous for its chairs – not deckchairs, which would go so appropriately with cricket, but wooden household chairs made from the beech trees which once covered thousands of acres in Buckinghamshire and still surround Penn Street.

The chairs were made by 'bodgers', who turned the legs and struts and rails on their lathes so accurately that each fitted perfectly into the other. They were highly skilled craftsmen who might not appreciate being commemorated in an inn called the Hit or Miss, but it was owned at one time by a nearby chair factory, and the bar contains more implements for making chairs than for making runs. The tools of the trade are displayed over the fireplace, alongside a set of metal printers' blocks illustrating the different chair styles.

Maybe one day cricket will fall completely out of favour in Penn Street, the chair-making connection will surreptitiously take over, and the Hit or Miss will be re-christened the Artful Bodger. But I rather think the Victorian gentleman on the inn sign will be defending his wicket successfully for a good many years to come.

Priests came here to hide, from only a Stonor's throw away

The Crown
Pishill, Oxfordshire

B480 - main road through village

Let's get the name straight first. Locally they pronounce it Pizz'l, and they don't approve of visiting jokers who split the syllables into separate words. But, in fact, the jokers may be right. There is a theory that when horses and waggons climbed the hill past the Crown, they stopped at the top for the horses to relieve themselves, and that is how the village got its name. It seems as good an explanation as any, but if you are visiting the Crown I would recommend sticking to Pizz'l.

Not that there are many locals left these days to take offence. There is little more to Pishill than a church, a pillar-box and the Crown, set on a hillside in idyllic rural surroundings, with a splendid view across the valley from the front porch. But eight or nine centuries ago there was a thriving monastic community here, and ale has been available on the site of the Crown since the twelfth century. The present building dates back to the 1400s, and now incorporates a farmhouse, cottages and a large thatched barn, used for functions and dinners. The foundations of more cottages were found recently when the garden was landscaped, another indication of how the village population has decreased.

But, while Pishill shrank, the neighbouring Stonor estate expanded. Stonor Park is a mile or so down the road from the Crown and their histories have become entwined over the centuries. The first house was built there by a Stonor eight hundred years ago and the family has lived there without interruption ever since, acquiring more and more land, and building a bigger and bigger house. But one feature of the original building remains, the little flint and stone chapel with its brick tower.

It is a reminder of the Catholic origins of the Stonors, who remained faithful to their religion throughout the period of persecution which began under Henry VIII. They refused to take the Protestant oath and for years had to pay substantial fines and other penalties to survive, sometimes as much as £50,000 a year in terms of modern currency.

The ghost of a monk who hanged himself at the inn is said to haunt the bar on each anniversary – but no one seems quite sure when that is.

But they continued to conduct their services in the chapel and they gave shelter to other Catholics, among them the Elizabethan Jesuit Edmund Campion, preacher and pamphleteer, who produced his religious tracts in an upper room at Stonor Park until he was eventually captured and martyred.

There came a time, however, when even Stonor Park was too dangerous a refuge, and many a Catholic priest was smuggled up the hill and hidden in a priest's hole in the attic of the Crown. The attic survives, but the priest's hole does not – and nor did at least one of its occupants. His name was Father Dominique, and there are two versions of how and why he died – neither, incidentally, having anything to do with religious persecution.

The less generous one is that he permitted himself to be seduced – or vice versa – by a serving girl and, filled with remorse, he hanged himself. The other, which I much prefer, is that he tried to protect the girl from molestation by a drunken customer, and was murdered by her assailant. Either way, his ghost is said to haunt the Crown on the anniversary of his death – but nobody seems quite sure when that is.

As for the Stonors, prosperity and honours returned, a barony was inherited, and the present occupant of Stonor Park is the seventh baron, Lord Camoys. The Crown also prospers, thanks to the period atmosphere of its oak timbers, its panelled walls, and its three imposing fireplaces, capable of consuming a ton of coal a week, so it is said, when the weather turns particularly cold.

There are also, needless to say, all mod. cons. – so forget about those horses up the hill.

The Romans would have enjoyed the ale - but did their cats like custard?

The Cat and Custard Pot
Shipton Moyne, Gloucestershire

The main street

When the Emperor Claudius built the Fosse Way to mark the boundary between occupied Britain and the land to the west he had yet to conquer, he only narrowly missed Shipton Moyne. The Fosse still runs past the village as a green lane, straight as a die to Cirencester, and it still forms a boundary, a more peaceful one these days, between Gloucestershire and Wiltshire. If the Roman legions

re-materialised and retraced their steps along the Way, they would do well to ask for a breather where it crosses the lane from Shipton Moyne to Malmesbury, and take a glass of ale at the Cat and Custard Pot.

The name, I suspect, would baffle them, as it has baffled many visitors since. Actually, it has been the Cat and Custard Pot only since 1928. Until then it was an off-licence simply called the Alehouse. The bottles had wax seals to prevent them being opened on the premises, but the customers did not take them very far. The present landlord, fifth generation of the family which has held the licence for 130 years, remembers being told how the regulars went no further than the hedge across the road to sit and drink their cider.

The brewery that bought the Alehouse turned it into a village inn, and a new name had to be devised. It might have been appropriate to call it the Roman Legionary or the Centurion. Or, even more whimsically – and to confuse American tourists – Caesar's Palace. But the chairman of the brewery had been reading a novel called *Handley Cross*, by the Victorian author R. S. Surtees, which he rather fancied. The name of the book is hardly remembered today, but its main character was a cockney grocer called John Jorrocks, who

made enough money to become a country squire and joined the local hunt. His bizarre exploits in the hunting field were in the P. G. Wodehouse mould.

The chairman took the Cat and Custard Pot from one of his exploits. Jorrocks sacked his huntsman for being drunk, went hunting without him on Cat and Custard Pot Day, and managed to catch the fox without help. On one side of the inn sign he is shown twirling his cap in triumph, on the other is a cat with its head in a custard pot.

On the face of it, a logical and rather mundane explanation. There is even a tenuous link between the Jorrocks story and Shipton Moyne, since the village is in the heart of hunting country – though Surtees lived in Yorkshire and the story is set in Surrey. There is one reference in the story, however, which continues to baffle me. What the dickens is Cat and Custard Pot Day?

Are cats really so fanatical about custard that on certain days of the year they are liable to get their heads stuck in custard pots, like monkeys who put their hands in jars to get sweetmeats, then cannot get them out? Or is there some strange link with the Romans, who used to have cats, and certainly knew about custard. The first-century cook Apicius has left behind a recipe for it, which contains not only milk, eggs and sugar but wine, honey and stock – a potent concoction geared more to casseroles than cooked fruit. Was it also geared to cats?

The inn itself stands in the main (and virtually only) street in Shipton Moyne, which has won an award as the county's best-kept village, but is not too ostentatious about it. In its off-licence days the front of the alehouse was covered with creeper, and there is a photograph in the bar to prove it. Today it has the modern equivalent, hanging baskets of flowers. Inside there is an open fireplace between the bar and the eating area, and if you call around opening time on a winter Saturday evening you will probably find the local football team recovering from its exertions on the field – it is sponsored by the inn.

On the evening I was there they were uncommonly quiet for a football team; perhaps the game had gone against them. But whatever the fortunes of the team, the Cat and Custard Pot seems to be thriving under its fifth-generation licensee, and judging by the very civil farewell I was given by the young lad who was playing in the front garden – 'Good evening, sir' – it should thrive under the sixth generation too.

If you are looking for trouble, the inn sign says it all

Trouble House
near Tetbury, Gloucestershire

On the A433 towards Cirencester

The sign has a body hanging from a noose, a hand waving despairingly as it disappears under the water, a waggon in flames with farm workers and soldiers battling beside it, and a nonchalant Cavalier and a solemn Roundhead eyeing one another from each side of the general mayhem. Yes, if you are looking for trouble – in the historical sense – you need look no further than Trouble House.

The sign is comparatively new. Major John Bartholomew, head of the family brewery which owns the inn, has replaced several of the plain name-boards on the company's houses with more imaginative pictorial signs, and Trouble House acquired its dangling corpse and the other macabre decorations only in 1954. But its troubles go back much further than that. Its history is not so much a chapter of accidents as a chapter of disasters.

It has been an inn for over three hundred years, and for much of that time it was called the Waggon and Horses. It was a very logical, if rather mundane, name for an inn which stands on the main road from Tetbury to Cirencester, and has always seen plenty of passing traffic. There came a time, however, when the waggoners stopped patronising it, though nobody quite knows why. The house fell into disrepair, and its troubles began.

A new owner endeavoured to restore the building, and borrowed far more than he could afford. It all became too much for him, and he hanged himself from a beam. His successor fared no better; he too got into debt, gave up the struggle, and drowned himself in a nearby pond. By this time nobody called it the Waggon and Horses any more. This was Trouble House, haunted by two suicides, and renowned throughout the licensed trade, I would think, as the most disastrous investment in the business.

There are various versions of what happened next, but they all involve the introduction of mechanical haymaking and threshing machines in the last century, which replaced the farm workers just as tractors and combines replaced a later generation. It seems that a waggon passed through Tetbury, ostensibly carrying hay, but someone spotted that the hay was concealing a haymaking machine, and raised the alarm. An angry mob surrounded the waggon on the Cirencester road, set fire to it and beat up the driver. Then they rampaged round the farms in the area, wrecking any machinery they found, until troops were summoned to put a stop to it all.

This is where the details vary. The most dramatic version is that the waggon was attacked just outside Trouble House, and the flames spread from the waggon to the thatched roof. It was subsequently restored with tiles instead of thatch, just in case another waggon caught fire beside it – that sort of thing seemed likely to happen at Trouble House. Alternatively, the troops clashed with the farm workers near the inn, and since everyone knew that

Trouble House meant trouble, it was the inn that got the blame for all the subsequent arrests and harsh sentences.

As for the Roundhead and Cavalier on the sign, there were plenty of skirmishes in the vicinity during the Civil War, and if the inn was actually functioning as an inn at the time, no doubt it sold the odd tankard of ale to one side or the other. If both sides turned up at once, then there would have been more trouble at Trouble House.

With a record like that behind it, it seems astonishing that anyone would be game enough to

take on the licence. I am glad to record that the present licensee has been at Trouble House for thirty years, he has seen no ghosts nor experienced any ghostly happenings, and he has experienced no more trouble than any of his colleagues in what is currently a troublous trade. He is also amazingly cheerful, and so are his customers. If it were not for the sign outside and the name over the door, trouble would not spring to mind.

They still climb the outside stairs to play skittles in the alley above the bar four times a week, and the bar itself is very snug and convivial. But I have to confess that I did duck more carefully than usual to avoid the low beams – and I suspect the local constabulary has no problems with late-night drink-drivers. Who on earth would look for trouble after an evening at Trouble House?

The poachers' cupboard survives, but no more drinks on the slate

The Rose and Crown
Tewin, Hertfordshire

The green

It is not easy for a village to remain a village when a 'garden city' is built a couple of miles away, and the nearby coaching road has been transformed into the A1(M) semi-motorway, bringing it within easy commuter reach of central London. Given such circumstances, many Hertfordshire villages have become little more than dormitory suburbs, but Tewin is still unmistakably a village, and the Rose and Crown on the green still struggles to be a village inn, even though the tower blocks of Welwyn Garden City are visible over the treetops.

Inevitably, it has to cater for the occupants of those tower blocks, who need only drive for five minutes along a winding country lane off the main Hertford road to find themselves in rural surroundings for a convivial pub lunch. Indeed, when I was there, an office party was celebrating somebody's birthday, or promotion or – given the present climate –

involuntary redundancy. But they were enjoying themselves without disturbing the locals who were supping their quiet pints at the other end of the bar. In spite of the city suits, and in some cases the dashing braces, it was not too difficult to visualise the days when the saloon bar was the taproom, with high-backed wooden settles by the hearth, and when poached game was hidden in the discreet little cupboard by the fireplace.

The Poachers' Cupboard, as it is still called by the locals, is a reminder that before 1919, when the town-planning ideas of Ebenezer Howard caught on and the garden city was created, Tewin was in the heart of open country, set on a hill above the mellifluously named River Minram. A village fair was held on the green outside the Rose and Crown, skittles were played in what is now a store-room round the back and, when a gamekeeper hove in sight, the empty cupboard was suddenly full.

The cupboard by the fireplace was used by poachers to hide their stolen game; now it is just used by the cleaner.

Gamekeepers are not entirely daft, and I cannot help thinking they knew about the Poachers' Cupboard as well as the poachers, but perhaps the inn was regarded as a kind of sanctuary, and so long as the game was kept out of sight, it was also kept out of mind. In any case, a gamekeeper who tried to extract a poacher from among his friends in the village inn must have been asking for trouble.

The history of the Rose and Crown goes back at least to the early eighteenth century. A change of ownership was recorded in 1738, when it was used for sessions of the manorial courts. It became the meeting-place of one of Hertfordshire's first Friendly Societies, and one of its landlords was John Carrington, whose father was a noted Hertfordshire diarist. It was, in fact, a place of considerable importance, much more than just a village inn, but in 1820 John Carrington went bankrupt, and since then the Rose and Crown has been owned by brewers, which has not proved entirely beneficial.

During the course of extensions in recent years the inn lost an historic link with the past; not the cupboard, of course, which could hardly be removed without demolishing the entire fireplace, but the original 'slate', the traditional method of granting customers credit and recording their debts.

It was a very civilised system, devised to preserve the confidentiality of the debt until it became overdue for payment. The slate was not just a blackboard, it was hinged like a door. The debts were chalked on the inside, and it was kept discreetly closed until each Friday, when the customers received their pay. If they did not clear their debts that evening, then the hinged slate was opened, for all to see.

Alas, six or seven years ago the brewers extended and refurbished the bar, removed the slate, and filled the empty space with fuse-boxes – very practical, but singularly unromantic. I have enquired what happened to it, but the brewers do not seem to know. The only people who could possibly have been glad to see it go were the customers whose debts were recorded on it at the time.

The locals still remember the slate, and they remember the great oak door which was also a casualty of the refurbishment. Happily, the rest of the frontage is unaltered, with its red-and-blue chequered brickwork, and the village green still survives, though modern 'desirable residences' have sprung up around it. It would be nice to think that, next time I visit the Rose and Crown, I may even find a brace of pheasants hidden in the Poachers' Cupboard.

Chitty-chitty has gone back to the city, but Lacey is still around

The Bull and Butcher
Turville, Buckinghamshire

Valley Road

Until the mid-1960s, Turville slumbered peacefully in its deep green valley in the Chilterns, and the regulars at the Bull and Butcher rarely saw a stranger in the bar. Then along came an outsize sports car with retractable wings – not just mudguards, real flying-type wings – accompanied by a vast film crew and a phantasmagorical cast, and the place became known in every guidebook and gazetteer as 'the village where they filmed Chitty-Chitty Bang-Bang'.

The black-and-white, heavily timbered Bull and Butcher, every American film producer's dream of a traditional English inn, became almost as familiar to fans of Julie Andrews and Dick Van Dyke as the windmill high on the opposite hill, which also featured in the film, and they came in their droves along Buckinghamshire's narrow lanes to see the originals.

It was Chitty-Chitty boom time at the Bull and Butcher though, to some villagers who preferred their peace and quiet, Chitty-Chitty was rather a pity. But the famous car and its occupants did not return from the big city, and, although other film crews have been there since, Turville has done its best to resume its slumbers as its fame has gradually faded. These days the inn relies for its regular trade on the villagers, the riding stables next door, and the walkers who tramp to Turville over the hills, as evidenced by the 'Please Remove Muddy Boots' sign on the door. Lacey Beckett, eccentric landlord of the Bull and Butcher for over forty years, may well find time to occupy his favourite high-backed settle by the fire.

Mr Beckett, I should explain, has been dead for over half a century. During the war, when the inn was also the village shop, rationing and coupons proved too much for him, so it was said, and in 1942 he shot himself after killing his wife and dog. It later transpired that the head pains he complained of while trying to sort out his books for the government inspectors were actually caused by a brain tumour, which may account for his violent suicide, but his other exploits can hardly be blamed on that.

Lacey Beckett's favourite fireside settle – until he killed his wife, his dog and himself in the room upstairs. The locals say he still sits there, and strangely, the photographer's exposure meter refused to function for this shot. And what is that arc of light from the settle to the room above?

He was, to say the least, a little odd, and it seems his oddness is still in evidence. He is inclined to move objects around in the bar, and even upstairs; the present landlord's father is positive he saw some nail-clippers move across the dressing-table of their own volition. On one occasion a very thorough barman tidied the bar and left it immaculate, then returned to find the towels crooked on the pumps and white powder in the newly cleaned ashtrays. Lacey Beckett explained to the locals from his seat by the fire – where he holds forth regularly to those who can see and hear him – that his wife had been a very tidy person, and he could not bear to be reminded of her. His audience, I gather, found that quite a logical explanation.

There was probably a logical explanation too for his choice of riding garb. A 1930s photograph in one of the bars shows Lacey Beckett astride an embarrassed-looking pony outside the Bull and Butcher, dressed as Napoleon and carrying a home-made whip. Next to the photograph is a more macabre reminder of him, the newspaper cutting which describes how P. C. Goldsmith was called to the inn, where the doors were barred and the black-out drawn. He climbed a ladder and entered the front bedroom window. Inside were the bodies of the landlord and his wife and dog, with a letter saying he hoped God would forgive him.

The bar containing his favourite settle, where he is still reputed to sit, was originally his private lounge. The shop adjoined it on one side, the public bar was on the other, and he had a system of bells so that he could sit by the fire in comfort until the bells told him which room needed his attention. It was a useful labour-saving device; Mr Beckett may have been eccentric, but he wasn't daft.

The inn has managed to preserve its period atmosphere, dating back to 1617, when masons restoring the church demanded refreshment, and downed tools till they got it. The owner of a cottage at the end of the village saw an opportunity of serving God and Mammon, and undertook to supply them – plus the rest of the village. Thus, the Bull and Butcher was born. In 1781 it was bought for £70 by an up-and-coming Henley brewer who married into the Brakspear family; it has been a Brakspear house ever since.

It is still a peaceful haven when the film crews are not about – but before you sit on that settle by the fire, make sure that it is empty.

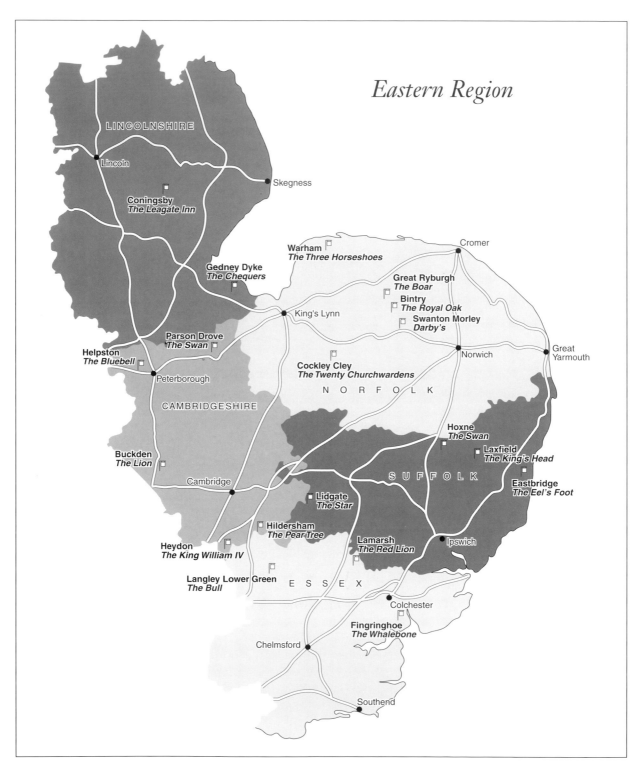

Eastern Region

LINCOLNSHIRE

Lincoln

Skegness

Coningsby
The Leagate Inn

Warham
The Three Horseshoes

Cromer

Gedney Dyke
The Chequers

Great Ryburgh
The Boar

Bintry
The Royal Oak

Swanton Morley
Darby's

King's Lynn

Parson Drove
The Swan

Norwich

Great
Yarmouth

Helpston
The Bluebell

Peterborough

Cockley Cley
The Twenty Churchwardens

N O R F O L K

CAMBRIDGESHIRE

Hoxne
The Swan

Laxfield
The King's Head

Buckden
The Lion

S U F F O L K

Eastbridge
The Eel's Foot

Cambridge

Lidgate
The Star

Hildersham
The Pear Tree

Lamarsh
The Red Lion

Ipswich

Heydon
The King William IV

Langley Lower Green
The Bull

E S S E X

Colchester

Fingringhoe
The Whalebone

Chelmsford

Southend

It may look unremarkable - but what about the feller in the cellar?

Lizzie the Great Dane is one of the unusual characters at the inn;
Roger the Roundhead declined to make an appearance.

The Royal Oak
Bintry, Norfolk

The main street

The nice thing about Bintry and the Royal Oak is that both the village and its inn are unpretentious, unspoilt and relatively unknown. They lie just within what I think of as Norfolk's 'magical triangle', the un-touristy area midway between Norwich and King's Lynn, bounded by Fakenham to the north and Swaffham and Dereham to the south. It is an area which Noël Coward – 'Very flat, Norfolk!' – could never have discovered, a rolling landscape of woods and parkland as well as beet and barley, of winding lanes and hidden streams, of villages like Bintry and village inns like the Royal Oak.

The only feature which attracts the casual visitor is Bintry Mill, on the River Wensum. You often find little groups of painters scattered along the river bank, and even the occasional film crew, but the village itself is two miles from the mill, and few of them stray that far. Nor does anyone else, and nothing much has happened in Bintry since a former vicar, the Revd R. W. Enraught, was imprisoned under the Public Worship Regulation Act 1880, for reasons which have faded into obscurity. In recent years the only controversy has been over the spelling of its name. The Diocese of Norwich and other official bodies seem to like Bintree, but the locals say it has always been Bintry, and that is good enough for me.

The Royal Oak looks as unremarkable as the rest of the village, a typical little Norfolk pub with no frills. It stands in the main street, which used to be the Norwich–Fakenham road. It has been bypassed now and Bintry has resumed its pre-motor age slumbers. The inn's two bars have been merged into one, but the central serving counter still separates the pool players from the pub luncheons, and there are enough nooks and crannies to make it cosy, as well as a vast open fire.

The locals are very familiar with the two unusual characters that live at the Royal Oak, Lizzie and Roger. One of them you cannot miss – Lizzie the Great Dane is almost the size of a Shetland pony, and on her hind legs she is taller than the landlord. But she is a sociable soul, and even when customers trip over her as she sprawls in front of the fire she will only mutter to herself quietly.

Roger is rather more elusive. He lives mostly in the cellar, and only one customer, a student of the psychic, has actually seen him. The customer was asked if he could find out why gas taps were being turned off, and why the landlord's wife and daughter had such a strong feeling that their presence was resented when they went into the cellar that they no longer went down there.

He saw a figure in long thigh-boots like a Roundhead trooper's, who told him his name was Roger (would a Roundhead have heard of Roger the Lodger, I wonder?) and he was there to 'support' the inn – though his pranks with the gas taps seemed an odd way of doing it.

His activities go further than that. On one occasion the water was turned on overnight, flooding the cellar. On another, a valve on a beer pipe was opened, emptying an entire keg of beer. And when the landlord ran a bar in the marquee at the village fair, Roger went along too, switching off each tap in turn as he tried to use them. 'There is nothing logical to explain it,' he told me.

With Roger to support you, then, who needs enemies? But the landlord remains remarkably patient. 'It's very aggravating, but I just go down in the cellar and have a chat with Roger, and give him a telling-off.'

There is a blocked-up archway in the cellar, and he wonders if there is something beyond it which may explain it all. But my own theory is based on the inn's name. The present Royal Oak has been traced back only to the early 1800s, but footings have been found of an earlier building on the same site, which could well date back to Charles I. Was Roger the Roundhead actually a Cavalier – they wore long boots too – who found himself in an area of Norfolk which was very pro-Cromwell and had to hide in the cellar? Does he still support the inn for that reason? And does he play about with the gas taps because he thinks the landlord is still a Cromwell supporter?

Well, you think of a better one.

No longer owned by bishops - but you'll be impressed by the boss

'Behold the Lamb of God' – the great central boss in the ceiling dates back to its days as a guesthouse for the Bishop's Palace up the road.

The Lion
Buckden, Cambridgeshire

Just off the A1

The Lion is not an average village inn, but then Buckden is not an average English village. Both of them have had two previous existences, first when the Bishops of Lincoln lived in Buckden Palace and the inn was their guest-house, then during the coaching era when the Great North Road passed through the middle of the village and the inn was a posting house.

The inn's name has changed along with its function. Because of its ecclesiastical connection it was first named the Lamb or the Lamb and Flag, recalled by the great central boss in the ceiling of the lounge bar, which bears the sacred symbol of the Lamb and the inscription *Ecce Agnus Dei* – 'Behold the Lamb of God'. During its coaching days in the last century the name was changed to the Lion, but it is still known locally by a compromise between the two, the Lion and Lamb, and both names appear over the door.

Now that Buckden has been bypassed it is a peaceful village again, and there are no longer bishops at the palace, just up the road from the Lion. It is now a retreat and conference centre, and the home of the Claret congregation. (Claret has no connection with the wine list at the Lion; it is the name of the group's nineteenth-century founder, St Anthony Claret, and pronounced quite differently.) The Tudor gate-house of the palace remains as a reminder of the days when Catherine of Aragon was imprisoned there after falling out of favour with Henry VIII.

The Lion was built in 1492, some forty-odd years before Catherine's arrival, and even if she was not allowed out of her quarters to take a glass of ale at the inn, her friends and visitors may well have refreshed themselves under that splendid ceiling, with its five moulded oak beams meeting at the central boss. Certainly, it is the oldest part of the building, originally the grand entrance hall where guests were welcomed – and still are – by an open fire in the huge hearth.

There were several alterations and additions during the eighteenth century, and the entrance hall was divided into separate rooms, with the hearth acting as a kitchen fireplace. The hall is now restored to its original size, and although the fireplace is slightly smaller than the original its ten-foot chimney beam remains, carved with rose decorations at each end.

At the turn of this century the proprietors of the Lion extracted full value from the carved ceiling and the history attached to it. All the available space on the front walls was taken up with unashamedly garish advertising slogans. Even in those days it featured the inevitable term, 'Ye Olde...', in this case 'Ye Olde 15th Century Lion Hotel – Formerly a Monastery', which was bending the facts a little. Alongside that, filling the entire space between two more windows, there was the clarion announcement: 'Worldfamous for its Historical Oak Beams and Carving'.

The management did not run to an artist, and the inn sign itself had no picture of a lion, just another 'Ye 15th Century Lion Hotel' and, incongruously, 'Garages'. What they lacked in artistry, though, they made up for in sheer repetition; even the chimney stack was inscribed with the name of the inn.

This all looked distinctly down-market, and perhaps it is the reason why the present proprietors chose the word 'rescued' for their brochure: 'Rescued from corporate ownership in 1982'. The painted slogans on the wall have been reduced to a modest 'One of the oldest posting houses', the chimney stack is restored to its original brickwork, and there is not a 'Ye Olde' in sight. From the outside, in fact, the Lion looks like just another pleasant old inn and, consequently, the impact of the splendid entrance hall-cum-lounge is all the more dramatic for its unexpectedness.

Indeed it can be a little daunting to a newcomer, and if you are looking for a basic public bar with traces of sawdust on the floor, you will not find it here. But the bar itself, in the far corner of the lounge, is welcoming enough, and it is perfectly acceptable to come here just for a drink or a bar lunch, without worrying that you are not dressed a little more smartly. But I would not advise putting your feet on the armchairs.

Will the rebels be deducted, and the twenty changed to ten? Probably not

The Twenty Churchwardens
Cockley Cley, Norfolk

On the Swaffham Road

In the 1930s the village school at Cockley Cley was closed, well ahead of the wave of school closures which has swept through Norfolk in the past decade. That was the bad news. The good news was that in 1968, after serving as a temporary Methodist Chapel and a store-room, it was linked up with the two adjoining cottages and converted into a village inn, replacing one which had been closed. The two classrooms now form the main bar, and the former cottages provide extra seating space and other accommodation.

Before the inn was opened by the local Lady of the Manor, there was much discussion about a suitable name. I think the Cane and Mortarboard might have been rather fun, or even the Teacher's Rest. It could have remained simply the Cockley Cley Inn, but the village's name can be a little confusing for strangers. There is a Cley on the North Norfolk coast, and Cockley has a seaside flavour too – that part of the coast is famous for its cockles – whereas Cockley Cley is actually thirty miles inland. It also used to remind me of Eliza Doolittle's 'Not cockle-likely', until I found it was pronounced rather differently. One way or another, a new name was needed.

It was Bishop Hugh Blackburne, then the rector, who provided the answer. Cockley Cley was just joining his group of parishes, making the total up to ten and bringing the number of his churchwardens up to twenty – something of a record in those days, though Norfolk benefices have grown even larger since. 'Why not call it the Twenty Churchwardens?' he suggested, and the name caught on. There is a photograph in the bar of the original churchwardens – or as many as could be gathered together at one time – and with Bishop Hugh they are armed appropriately for the occasion with churchwarden pipes.

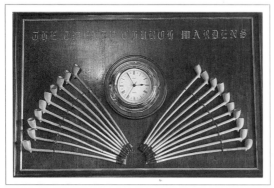

The inn can no longer muster twenty churchwardens, but at least it has twenty of their pipes.

The Twenty Churchwardens does not have an inn sign, though its name appears boldly on the walls. Inside the bar, however, the landlord has erected a plaque over the door displaying twenty pipes. The name took on a particular appropriateness in 1991, after the tower of the church collapsed, just beside the inn. For the next three years the services were held in the bar of the Twenty Churchwardens, until the church was usable again.

The novel name of the inn was much enjoyed by the local press at the time, and I hope the churchwardens enjoyed it too. But at the end of 1994 they, or their successors, were back in the headlines again, and this time the headlines were much larger and nobody enjoyed it at all. Cockley Cley is part of the Hilborough group, whose rector, the Revd Kit Chalcraft, was removed from his living by the bishop because he planned to marry for a third time after two divorces, and was deemed to have broken an undertaking to reside alone at the rectory.

The rector was a popular man, and the bishop found himself with a full-scale rebellion on his hands,

while the churchwardens found themselves equally divided between the rector and the bishop. Five parishes broke away from the diocese and held independent services in their churches; the remainder accepted the appointment of the Archdeacon of Lynn as temporary priest-in-charge. And throughout the controversy, understandably, one of the main debating forums was the Twenty Churchwardens.

One might have expected Cockley Cley to be among the rebels, because it is linked with a much earlier and rather bloodier insurrection. Near the inn is a reconstruction of an Iceni settlement from which Queen Boudicca's followers sallied forth to take part in her revolt against the Romans. The present village grew up around it and, for all we know, some of the locals are descended from that warrior tribe. The reconstruction is a wooden-walled enclave reminiscent of the stockade on Treasure Island, except that it also features a snake-pit, a little extravagance that Robert Louis Stevenson somehow missed. The pit even contains an imitation snake.

Cockley Cley, however, remained loyal to the bishop, perhaps because its links with the diocese go back longer than most, to Saxon times, when the See was based in the little village of North Elmham, before moving to Thetford and then to Norwich. Cockley Cley's first church was built about AD 700, and was converted into a cottage in Tudor times after the present one was built. It has now been restored to its original character, making Cockley Cley the only village in the group, I imagine, with two churches, which may make it doubly conscious of its allegiance to the bishop.

And, of course, it also has the Twenty Churchwardens; should its name now be changed to Ten? I think not. When I visited it a couple of months after the breakaway, I found one of the rebel churchwardens from another parish in the group – an ex-BBC man, as it turned out – enjoying a pint at the bar with the landlord. Some things can transcend an ecclesiastical upheaval – and a pint of beer in a pleasant village inn is high on the list.

The last guide house – and a Poet Laureate who liked his ale

The Leagate Inn
Coningsby, Lincolnshire

Leagate Road

Coningsby has a main road passing through it, which is quite rare for a village in the Fens. The road runs from Sleaford to Horncastle, with a side road to Spilsby and another to Woodhall Spa. But not too many people commute from Sleaford to Horncastle, even fewer go to Spilsby, and there are easier ways to get to Woodhall Spa. So it is not too difficult, as you stand outside the Leagate at the entrance to the village, to visualise the inn in the sixteenth century before the Fens were drained, when the road was just a boggy track across a flat, featureless marsh, and at night the only way that travellers could locate the village was to follow the glow of the blazing torch high up on the gable. It burnt in an iron holder which still projects from the wall, looking rather like a medieval netball goal.

The Leagate is believed to be the last surviving 'guide house' in the Fens. It had other functions too.

The enclosure in which it is set was known as Gibbet Nook Close, and the gibbet used to stand close by what is now a pleasant beer garden. The great yew tree in the garden is thought to be as old as the inn, but instead of the gibbet there is a less macabre attraction, a pond of Japanese koi carp.

The inn was the gateway to Armtree and Wilmore Fens and, until comparatively recently, it had a toll-gate. There is now a reassuring sign on the wall: 'This gate hangs high and hinders none, victual yours'en and pass along.'

Today's travellers can victual themselves in what used to be the stables, now a long, low restaurant at the rear of the inn. Apart from that, the Leagate has retained its original internal layout, three separate rooms off the bar with beamed ceilings, open fireplaces and high oak settles. Its customers have included airmen from the nearby RAF station, and it was one of these, a pilot, who borrowed the inn sign during the war 'to show it to the Germans'. He never came back, and nor did the sign. Its place over the front door remains empty; as the landlady told me, 'Everybody knows the Leagate anyway.'

Having victualled yours'en, it is well worth passing along into the village itself, as the notice on the inn advises. Coningsby is not as well-known as neighbouring Tattershall, because of Tattershall Castle, built about a century before the Leagate, but on a rather grander scale, by Ralph Cromwell, Lord Treasurer of England. But Coningsby church is worth a glance, if only to check the time, because is has the biggest one-handed clock in the country, possibly in the world. The dial is over sixteen feet across, so it can tell the time almost to the minute, with one hand tied behind its back – or wherever. The clock mechanism is on the same scale. The

A blazing torch was placed in the holder high up on the gable to guide travellers across the marshes.

weights on the pendulum are great blocks of stone, and the pendulum itself is so long that it takes two full seconds to complete one swing.

The church has another unusual feature inside, though it is more difficult to spot. High on the wall is a carved head with bands across the mouth and forehead. There are only a dozen such heads in the country, and half of them are in Lincolnshire. One theory is that they are based on a Moorish design and were carved in the thirteenth century by masons who had been to the Crusades. Another is that they are self-portraits, and the bands across the mouths or noses are the protective masks that masons wore to avoid breathing in the dust while carving the stone. A Lincolnshire reference book, however, describes the Coningsby head as 'a scold with bridle, forever silent', which is perhaps more likely. This was a standard punishment for gossips and shrews, and the masons, being men, probably relished portraying it.

Coningsby cannot claim anyone as illustrious as Ralph Cromwell of Tattershall Castle, but it did have a Poet Laureate, who by all accounts was a regular customer at the Leagate. The Revd Laurence Eusdon, an eighteenth-century rector, was not quite in the Dylan Thomas mould, but I suspect from the standard of his poetry he enjoyed his ale. A fellow poet, Thomas Gray, made no bones about it; he called him 'a drunken parson'. Certainly, the couplet the Poet Laureate wrote in honour of George II for his coronation required little more inspiration than a tankard of porter in the taproom of the Leagate:

Thy virtue shine peculiarly nice,
Ungloomed with a confinity to vice.

Sir John Betjeman, eat your heart out.

The eel and the boot can be explained – but what of the Stalingrad connection?

The Eel's Foot
Eastbridge, Suffolk

In lane leading to marshes

The Eel's Foot is an unlikely name for an inn. There are any number of Heads, whether king's or queen's or duke's, and just as many Arms. There is even an inn on the south Devon coast called the Pig's Nose. But a Foot seems a strange extremity to commemorate, and an eel doesn't have one anyway.

There are two explanations for the name of Eastbridge's village inn, one linked to a fourteenth-century Buckinghamshire parson, the other entirely local. Dr John Schorn was a faith-healer as well as a parson, and to demonstrate his power of healing in an understandable way, he used a medieval visual aid, a boot with a figure sticking out of it to represent the Devil. By a little sleight of hand, or simply by pushing it down with his finger, he made the figure disappear, to illustrate how he overcame disease.

The story spread that Dr Schorn used a boot to capture the Devil. Artists depicted him on the rood-screens of some churches, three of them in East Anglia, holding a boot with the Devil trying to emerge from it. Much later, a few inns adopted a figure in a boot as their sign, but the figure was so shapeless after successive painters had dealt with it that it could have been an eel, and thus they became the Eel's Foot. Another still survives in Norfolk, at Ormesby St Margaret.

The local explanation is rather different. The grandson of a former tenant of the Eastbridge Eel's Foot has a letter which appeared fifty-odd years ago in a local magazine, written by a man whose grandfather did some building work on the inn in the last century. 'One day he found all the other fellows in a flummox because there were two or three marks in a heap of mortar and no one could say what made them.

'These boots were made for walking' – but perhaps they now find a refuge for the 'De'il's Foot'.

'My grandfather was a shrewd chap from Scotland, and his guess was that a cow had walked through the mortar, but he thought he would pull his mates' legs a bit, so he told them they were marks of the "De'il's foot". When told who the "De'il" was, they were really scared. Over the years the "D" was dropped and people talked about the E'il's Foot – and that is how that particular pub acquired its name.'

I like both stories. Long may they both survive.

If the second explanation is correct, the inn must have had another earlier name in the eighteenth century, when the Revenue men made it their headquarters – and quite a few smugglers used it too. This lonely coast was ideal for smuggling, and there were plenty of violent encounters between the two, including one at the inn itself. In December 1747 a party of smugglers arrived in the yard, not knowing that a detachment of Welch Fusiliers, reinforcements for the Revenue men, were having lunch inside. In the fighting that followed, most of the miscreants escaped, but two were captured and taken to London by sea – a safer route for the Fusiliers than through the hostile Suffolk countryside. As soon as the soldiers had gone, the smugglers moved back into the inn.

Whatever the Eel's Foot was called then, today the motif of the eel and the boot is firmly established inside the bar – in addition to the array of old boots which line the front garden. It decorates, among other items, the house trophy for darts, a major attraction at the inn. The landlord, a former insurance agent who got to know the Eel's Foot on his travels and took it over in 1990, used to play darts for the county. Folk-singing is another regular feature, achieving national fame in a BBC series a few years ago. The singing, I am told, is enough to charm the De'il from his boot.

There is another intriguing item in the bar among the eels and the boots. It is a framed front page of the *Daily Express* dating back to 1942. The lead story is about the progress being made by the Germans at Stalingrad, which seems to have little to do with this quiet little inn in an obscure village on the Suffolk coast. Many a customer must have puzzled over this, and not liked to ask – so I did. Its significance is entirely sentimental; it was published on the day the landlord was born.

A Saxon welcome, or 'hallo whaler'?

Various whalebones have come and gone at the Whalebone; this is the current offering.

The Whalebone
Fingringhoe, Essex

Opposite village pond

The Whalebone may seem an incongruous name for a quiet country inn several miles from the open sea. It conjures up pictures of Arctic waters, men poised on bowsprits with harpoons at the ready, factory ships sending up smoke and smells – and Greenpeace not far away. You might feel inclined to agree with the learned visitor in the 1980s who suggested to the landlord that the name had nothing to do with whales, but came from the Saxon word 'Walbon' or 'Valbon', meaning 'Welcome'.

The theory is ingenious and rather charming, but,

in fact, there used to be several Whalebone inns in this part of Essex, for the very good reason that a whaling industry existed in the North Sea for centuries. In quite recent times whales have been sighted off the coast or even in the river estuaries.

In 1963 there was a major waste-disposal problem when a forty-foot whale died in the River Colne. The carcase was taken to the rubbish tip at Brightlingsea, but the tip was hardly geared to accommodate such a bulky chunk of decaying flesh, and the smell was quite appalling.

In 1985 two whales spent several days in the Blackwater River, then swam out to sea again – to the enormous relief of residents living near the Brightlingsea rubbish tip.

The earliest reported visitation was in 1677, when 'a monstrous whale two-and-forty feet in length and of bigness proportionate was killed near Colchester, being brought up by the tide', and it may have been this whale which gave the Whalebone at Fingringhoe not only its name but its bone. It is known that the inn existed under that name by 1735, when it is mentioned in the Court Rolls as being the former property of the church, along with its three acres of land. Until about a century ago, on the wall above the front door there was a whalebone, which might have dated back to the 'monstrous whale' of 1677. It was then sent away for restoration, but was too old and brittle to survive, and a wooden 'bone' was erected in its place. That, too, has disappeared but a couple of whale vertebrae still survive by the fireplace in the bar.

Legend has it that this oak tree by the Whalebone grew from an acorn placed in the mouth of a pirate who was executed and buried there three centuries ago. And why not?

The garden of the Whalebone, set on a hillside overlooking a peaceful valley, was the scene of a far-from-peaceful celebration in 1801, when the landlord had the bright idea of celebrating peace with France by roasting an ox. Fifteen hundred people turned up to eat it, and the party got completely out of hand. 'An excited and drunken mob...took the beef even off the plates of those gentlemen that were eating it.'

The party lasted three days, ending with a spectacular finale. 'A vast number of intoxicated men, with flags flying and firing of cannon, paraded about the parish, dragging the cannon with them.' It was probably more peaceful during the war.

Since then the greatest excitement at the Whalebone has been the winning of the Coronation Cup for quoits in 1911. Normally, the inn reflects its peaceful surroundings, the church nearby and the pond across the road where the fishing is good, and a great oak tree which is reputed to be the largest in Essex. According to legend it grew from an acorn placed in the mouth of a pirate who was executed and buried there three centuries ago. Somehow that story smacks less of 'Yo-ho-ho' than just 'Ho-ho'.

After the last war, great changes took place at the Whalebone. Outside, part of the original Church Green was turned into a car park. Two thatched cottages that stood beside it disappeared. The front of the inn was extended, and the sitting room and bar, which were separated by a wood-panelled passage leading from the door to the serving hatch, were knocked into one. One old 'regular' remembers that passage well.

'The panelling was almost black with age, and a form allowed customers to sit in the passage to consume their drink, which they often did if they were unaccompanied village women or if they had come with a jug to take home their supper ale. The large knots protruding from the worn floorboards were enough to stub one's toe on.'

Nobody minded losing the knots, but not all the changes were for the better, and, in 1994, a new owner decided to put back the clock. Roderick Shelton, an architect and historic buildings consultant, who himself lives in a converted inn, set about restoring what he could of the original layout. He also started rebuilding the venerable wooden barn in the garden, which a previous landlord had apparently found useful for kindling. By now, the Whalebone may even have acquired a whalebone again to go over the front door – but it will be the only concession to carnivorous customers. Mr Shelton's bar menu is entirely vegetarian.

A chequered history, from Roman relaxation to a cure for the colic

The Chequers
Gedney Dyke, Lincolnshire

On main street through village

Do not be misled by the name on the sign; this Chequers has nothing to do with draughts. Nor, for that matter, do several other inns with that name, though they do not share the same unusual origin as the one at Gedney Dyke.

A good many of them are based on the arms of the Fitzwarren family, which had the probably lucrative privilege of licensing ale houses in the days of Edward IV. Others date back to the days when innkeepers acted as money-changers, or the inn was used for distributing parish charities, and they displayed an 'exchequer' board outside. It would be rather jolly to see a chequer-board displayed outside the Treasury today, but the nearest we get to it is the

121

name of the Prime Minister's country retreat.

It all started with the Romans, who used a chequer-board sign on buildings which were houses of entertainment as well as refreshment – and certainly you can have a game of chequers at the Gedney Dyke Chequers if you wish. But the real significance of the name can be found in the garden at the rear of the inn, where two berry trees are growing, a tall one which looks a little sorry for itself and a smaller one which is doing rather well.

These are members of the rowan family, and their berries have been described as Britain's most neglected wild fruit. They are called service berries, and the brew which can be made from them is known locally as chequers. They were originally used for fermenting beer before the advent of sugar. Today, a lady in the village with a specialised knowledge of traditional potions makes a powerful liqueur with the berries from an ancient recipe. The landlord gave me a sip, and very potent it was too, but I have to say it tasted uncommonly like cough mixture. It is, in fact, supposed to have medicinal qualities; if you suffer from colic, then chequers is for you – but you may get a hangover instead.

The larger of the berry trees is looking off-colour because it had to be transplanted, but it suffered in a good cause – it was moved to make room for a 'no smoking' extension to the inn. At one time these berries grew wild in woods throughout the south-east of England, but these days they are cultivated by specialist nurserymen. One such nurseryman happens to be a regular at the Chequers, and he was

A toast from the landlord to the berry tree which gives quite a different meaning to the Chequers.

able to supply the small replacement tree.

Gedney Dyke is in the happy position of being on the road to nowhere – unless you count Gedney Drove End, which is the next best thing. Beyond that lies the Wash, and it was off the coast here that King John lost his baggage and treasure after setting out from nearby Sutton Bridge, at the mouth of the River Nene. Since then, not a lot has happened in this remote corner of the Lincolnshire Fens.

There was a bit of excitement, I suppose, when the Fens were drained and Gedney Dyke was dug past the bottom of the Chequers garden, but the dyke no longer plays an important part in the drainage system. There was a mill up the road, once the principal local industry and providing plenty of custom for the Chequers, but the mill is now derelict. The name of Engine Dyke suggests there was a railway here too, but it merely refers to the engine that used to work the mill.

Gedney Dyke is in fact only half a village. It still has a shop, but it is separated from the centre of the village and the church by one of the busiest trunk roads in Lincolnshire. The A17 is the main route into Norfolk from the north – unless you try King John's route and come across the Wash. Thousands of drivers use it every day, most of them bemoaning the shortage of civilised village inns along the sixty-odd miles between Newark and King's Lynn.

A mile off the main road, in Gedney Dyke, beyond one of the earliest Cheshire Homes in its wooded, unfenlike park, they may find what they are looking for – especially if they have a touch of the colic.

A half of bitter and a short back-and-sides please

The Boar
Great Ryburgh, Norfolk

Opposite the church

I doubt that even those who live there would claim that Great Ryburgh is the most picturesque of mid-Norfolk villages. It is basically one long street with a large proportion of modern houses, all of them dwarfed by the maltings that looms over the centre of the village, next to the disused railway line which once connected it with Dereham and thence to Norwich and the main line to London.

On the other hand, nobody in Great Ryburgh complains about the bleak appearance of the maltings, because it is a main source of employment and one of the few substantial industries to survive in an essentially rural area; long may it continue to do so. But casual visitors may not be in too much of a hurry to get out their cameras as they drive through the main street, until they turn the corner at the end of it.

Suddenly, they have stepped back through the centuries. Ahead of them in a tree-lined churchyard is the parish church, its round Saxon tower topped by a fourteenth-century belfry and its short nave and long transepts, unusual in a Norfolk church, forming the almost equal arms of a cross. On the opposite corner is the Boar, another survival from Great Ryburgh's pre-malting days, a traditional low-ceilinged country inn with a huge open fire. The street, now just a lane, continues over the hill to Little Ryburgh, a tiny cluster of cottages with a ruined church, no inn – and no maltings.

The Boar has a curious history. Originally, it was called the Blue Boar but, after the last war, it was

A chance for a quick haircut while enjoying a lunchtime pint. The outside lavatory at the Boar is now a hairdressing salon.

taken over by Americans who named it, rather bizarrely, the Cheval de Trojan. Perhaps they wanted to indicate that, through this Trojan Horse, they had managed to breach Norfolk's alleged antipathy towards foreigners, whether they be from America or anywhere south of Thetford. Actually, Norfolk was inundated with American air bases during, and long after, the war, and after the initial culture shock the airmen were made most welcome.

The American proprietors left in the 1970s and, in due course, the historic inn was taken over by another 'foreigner' – this time a Scot – who in spite of his origins prefers to keep the Boar on its traditional path as an old-fashioned English pub, the role it played for centuries. Nobody is quite sure for how many, but it was the setting for an indenture dated 1777, which occupies most of one wall in what is now the little restaurant. It has over sixty lines of very ornamental writing, each line about two feet

long and full of 'whereases' and 'to have and to holds' and 'in witness whereofs'. The landlord has not managed to decipher it all, and nor could I, but it appears to be a marriage settlement involving an Anne Mack, and it all happened at the Blue Boar, over two hundred years ago.

Although it is being run again on traditional lines, the present-day Boar does have one very untraditional feature, which may be unique. It is accommodated in what used to be the traditional outside lavatory. When the sanitary arrangements were transferred indoors, a new use had to be found for the little building, which occupies a fairly prominent position beside the car park. Generally, such places become store-rooms, or woodsheds, or are just left to fall down, but at the Boar they displayed a little more ingenuity.

It so happened that the landlord's daughter-in-law was a hairdresser, and looking for premises – so what could be handier than the redundant loo? The plumbing and tables were installed – plus some ancient magazines, I hope, to add authenticity – and the outside lavatory was transformed into a unisex hairdressing salon. That was about six years ago, and the scissors are still happily snipping.

This is extremely convenient, of course, for the regular customers in the Boar. They can have a quick haircut while enjoying their pint; the only tricky part is keeping the clippings out of the beer.

One wonders whether this kind of loo-conversion on licensed premises could be taken further. Why not a heel-bar, for instance? Have your shoes repaired while you repair for a drink. Or, given the usual lack of windows in outside lavatories, it should be easy to convert one into a darkroom; have your films developed while you develop a hangover in the bar. There may even be scope for a dentist's mini-surgery, where at least the patients would have something to look forward to when they left.

Meanwhile, the Boar retains its monopoly, as far as I know, on licensed haircuts – the only village inn where you can order a half of bitter and a short back-and-sides.

'A peasant in his daily life, a poet in his joy' - Clare was there

The Bluebell
Helpston, Cambridgeshire

Woodgate

The good folk of Helpston may well have experienced an identity crisis in recent times. Not so long ago the village was in Northamptonshire. Then the boundary was moved and they found themselves in Huntingdonshire. Now Huntingdonshire has disappeared and they have been absorbed into Cambridgeshire. They are just about as far as it is possible to get from the centre and still be in the county, in a remote northern outpost where Cambridge must seem a different world.

At the Bluebell there is no doubt where allegiance still lies. This is where the John Clare Society meets each year, to celebrate the memory of the potboy who became known as 'The Northamptonshire Peasant Poet' – and to them, the Northamptonshire Peasant Poet he will remain. Cambridge after all has plenty of poets of its own.

Clare himself would have deplored these boundary

changes, just as he deplored the Enclosure Acts, which came into force during his time at the inn. He expressed his dismay in his poems. He also wrote sadly about the other major development in the village in his lifetime, the coming of the railway engineers to survey the route of the new main line from London to the north.

Fortunately for the character of the village, if not for the convenience of potential London commuters, there is no station at Helpston and the Inter-Cities ignore its existence. Peterborough, the nearest town, is expanding fast, but still has to absorb several miles of open country before it can gobble up the village. So the lane in which the Bluebell lies, off the Peterborough road, retains its peace and quiet, and

John Clare, the 'Peasant Poet', used to work here as a potboy. Now the pots have given way to Toby jugs, but the Clare Society still meets in the bar to toast his memory.

beside the inn still stands the thatched cottage in which John Clare was born in 1793, though the little row of cottages has now been converted into one.

The Bluebell itself dates back to the 1600s, so it was already about two hundred years old, thatched and somewhat smaller than it is today, when the dreamy young man from next door came to work there as handyman-gardener-potboy. There was a smallholding attached to the inn where the landlord kept a horse and a couple of cows, and Clare looked after them as well as working at the inn. The landlord treated him like his son, and these were probably his

happiest years – 'a peasant in his daily life, a poet in his joy', he wrote. But his life turned sour, and he spent his last twenty-three years in a mental hospital, where he died in 1864.

The present landlord is something of an authority on John Clare, and he will be happy to tell you more but, if you want to see an example of his poems, there is the memorial which was erected to him at the crossroads in the centre of the village. It shares pride of place with the medieval butter cross on the opposite corner. The memorial is engraved with his verses, and one of them expresses his longing to return to his native village:

To turn me back and wander home to die,
'Mong nearest friends my latest breath resign,
And in the churchyard with my kindred lie.

His wish was granted, as a stone in the church porch records, and on the weekend nearest the anniversary of his death in July, the Clare Society meets at the Bluebell to drink to his memory.

John Clare's is a rather sombre story, and Helpston has another sombre tale to tell, the massacre at nearby Woodcroft Castle during the Civil War. It was besieged and captured by Cromwell's men and, perhaps because the defenders were led by King Charles's personal chaplain, a man not greatly loved by the Roundheads, they carried out a particularly ruthless slaughter. The castle has since become a moated manor house, but the cries for mercy, so it is said, can still be heard. Perhaps they added to the depression of John Clare, who worked there for a time as a plough-boy.

Happily, the Bluebell does not reflect all this doom and gloom. The panelled lounge bar is decorated with a very cheerful collection of Toby jugs and teapots, and the simple public bar is as convivial as it was in John Clare's day. Even Clare himself must have had his more relaxed moments. According to the records he once had to ask his publisher for an advance of £8, which he owed for ale – so presumably he enjoyed downing a glass or two between verses.

A stag's head among the cherubs – and the tables hang from the ceiling

It is unwise to jog the table in this amazingly cluttered bar. It is hung on chains,
which increases the legroom but seriously affects its stability.

The King William IV
Heydon, Cambridgeshire

Main street through village

There is no doubt about it, this is a very odd inn. It would not be to everybody's taste, and if you like an open-plan bar with bright lights, lots of space and not too many ornaments, this is not the place for you. I know of no other inn in England which has accumulated such an astonishing collection of improbable paraphernalia with such a total disregard for the convenience of its customers. It has taken eccentricity to the limit, and perhaps it is appropriate that the King William IV should take its name from one of our more unorthodox monarchs, who liked to wear very old hats and was given to spitting from his carriage window. His admirers called him the Sailor King and, indeed, he was a genial, bluff sort of chap, but he was a bit of a blundering oddball too, more popularly known as Silly Billy, and not too many English inns have elected to bear his name.

It was selected for Heydon's village inn, however, long before it took on its present bizarre character. I met a customer there who recalled that twenty years earlier it was basic and unadorned, with only the most essential furniture on its plain earthen floor, and the beer was carried in from the next room. Then it was taken over by two antiques dealers, and they must have brought all their unsaleable stock with them. When they retired about five years ago they left it all behind. The place must be a nightmare to dust, but then it is too dark to see the dust anyway.

The outside appearance of the inn is not too inviting, largely because the kitchen, unusually, is at the front, and it is difficult to make kitchen windows look cosy. In fact, I had the impression it was closed on my first visit and, even when I got inside, it was still difficult to be sure one way or the other, it was so dark. The windows were largely obscured by an assortment of bric-à-brac on the sills; the only lights were over the bar itself, an imposing affair with a carved, wooden front which could have been the panelling from a stately home.

To reach it I had to negotiate a fibreglass statue of Jesus holding a baby in one arm, the other hand holding a candlestick; it would have been helpful if it had actually contained a candle. I ducked past a stag's head flanked by a couple of cherubs, and bumped into a copper font with an elegant Gothic cover, which was in use as a table. There were some ordinary table-tops too, but these were hung on chains from the ceiling, which increased the leg-room underneath them, but seriously affected their stability. Woe betide the careless customer who jolts one if it is fully laden; the cost of replacing all the spilt drinks can be prohibitive.

Once the eyes become accustomed to the gloom, you can identify all manner of unlikely ornaments, filling every alcove, lined up along the walls, hanging from the beams. An enormous bellows, a bed-warmer, an iron cauldron, stuffed birds, dried flowers, farm implements, and old tools the purpose of which has long since been forgotten. Somewhere in the vicinity – I heard it but never saw it – there must be a cockatoo. Only the dining area looks comparatively normal, with horse brasses and harnesses on the walls.

None of the other customers seemed to find anything unusual about these slightly weird surr-oundings. I gather that even the fastidious Egon Ronay was not deterred by the dimly lit jumble of inexplicable impedimenta – though he did comment that they were 'overflowing to an almost oppressive degree'. He was more concerned about the 'chips-with-everything bar food', as he described it, which is one of the pub's few predictable features.

It does have others. While I was trying to take it all in, a couple of youngsters came in the door, threaded their way unhesitatingly through all the clutter, and started playing pool in a far corner, on a table I had not spotted before. In this curious bar it was the pool table that looked out of place.

Heydon is not the sort of village where you would expect to find such an unconventional inn. It has a long and unremarkable history, going back to the time when Iron Age travellers trudged past along the Icknield Way. The Heydon Ditch, just outside the village, is one of the many dykes which were dug across it in Roman and Saxon days to deter invaders. The next visitors of any note were German bombers, who flattened the church in 1940. Then in the 1950s the Wood Green Animal Shelters acquired a derelict pig farm in the village, and converted it into a home for unwanted dogs and cats.

The English are, of course, dotty about animals, and the Shelter has attracted many thousands of visitors, but for another variety of endearing English dottiness they should visit the inn just up the road.

With a story like the never-wins, who needs hanging tables?

The Pear Tree
Hildersham, Cambridgeshire

The High Street

I visited the Pear Tree because it was reputed to have tables suspended on chains, and I could not believe there was another inn in Cambridgeshire, even in the country, quite like the King William IV at Heydon. I was right. Instead of a dimly lit Aladdin's cave of quaint old clutter I found a light and airy bar in an agreeably updated inn. The original Pear Tree was further up the village street, and the present one was a private house which sold only ale until about a century ago.

As for the hanging tables, the chains were installed when the bar was refurbished in the 1970s – perhaps to imitate the King William – but when the current proprietors took over they found that the curiosity value of the tables was outweighed by their inconvenience. As at Heydon, they were highly unstable; one nudge and every glass was spilt. Even when extra chains were attached to the floor, it was still difficult to butter a bread roll, for instance, without making the table swing – and people caught their feet in the chains and made them swing still more. There was a cleaning problem too; the table surfaces had deep gaps in the wood which gathered the dirt, and the chains were tedious to dust.

After twelve months the landlord gave up the struggle. The chains were removed, the table-tops were restored to make a smoother surface and were provided with legs. They may not look so intriguing, but they are a lot more practical.

Once I had learned all this, the original point of my visit had gone. But, happily, the Pear Tree has other features which give it a special attraction. If you are whimsically inclined, you will appreciate the coins which the previous landlord embedded in the bar and the floor-boards to irritate the avaricious; there is no way they will budge. If you enjoy an unusual bar game you can try your hand at 'Shoot the Moon', rolling a little ball along two metal arms and dropping it into a 'moonhole', or there is a gadget which tosses sixpenny pieces at a target. There is even one of those 1960s penny-in-the-slot machines on the wall, in which a lever flips a silver ball round and round until it falls on to a line of holes, but some customers got quite obsessed with this and the noise became tedious, so the ball is now kept behind the counter for special occasions.

What I relished rather more, however, was the newspaper cutting on the wall, alongside a cartoon and a faded photograph of the local football team, known as the Hildersham Never-Wins. Back in 1933 Hildersham F. C. never won a game throughout the entire season. Its record was unenviable, but not unequalled; another team in the Peterborough League, Barholm United, had not won a match either.

The publicity-conscious business manager of the *Peterborough Citizen* had an inspiration. Why not pit these two no-hopers against each other in a gala match at the town's football ground, to give one of them a chance of victory at last?

Tom Webster, doyen cartoonist of the *Daily Mail*,

The Hildersham Never-Wins, the local team based at the inn which never won a match all season – and gained national fame. As the captain said: 'The great thing in life is not to win a game, but to play a bad hand well.'

agreed to referee. The Mayoress of Peterborough kicked off – 'easily the best kick of the match', wrote Nathaniel Gubbins of the *Sunday Express*, who had also been lured from Fleet Street by the novelty of the occasion – and, in front of five thousand cheering spectators, including two coach loads of Hildersham supporters led by the rector (whose son played inside-left), the Hildersham Never-Wins broke their duck at last.

Webster's cartoon portrays this epic encounter, with the caption:

After the most strenuous efforts of missing both man and ball, Hildersham Rangers won 6–4; it should have been 19–17! Flushed with success, Rangers now have no intention of playing anyone else except Barholm United.

At the civic reception which followed, one H. Dawson, captain of the victorious team, made the notable pronouncement: 'The great thing in life is not to win a game but to play a bad hand well.' The *Citizen*'s report then adds '(Applause)' – and rightly so.

None of the team is still alive to tell this tale, alas. The last of them, the goalkeeper who let through a record number of goals that season, died two or three years ago. Their photograph might not have survived either. The previous landlord of the Pear Tree, he of the hanging tables, got tired of seeing it on the wall and tore it up. Happily, his successor salvaged the pieces, had them put together and rephotographed, and restored the team to its place of honour in the bar.

I am delighted that he did. It is one of those delightfully English episodes which deserve preserving, the saga of the Hildersham Never-Wins – who finally did. With a story like that, who needs hanging tables?

The bishops' guest-house with a hymn-board on the roof

Not so much a bar, more a baronial hall. Actually, it was used by bishops rather than barons, to entertain their guests.

The Swan
Hoxne, Suffolk

In the main street, off the B1118

For such a small village Hoxne has an unusually action-packed history and some widely assorted claims to fame, stretching over two thousand years. The recently uncovered Hoxne hoard is the biggest collection of Roman relics ever dug up on one site. It was at Hoxne in AD 869 that Edmund, King of East Anglia, when he refused to renounce Christianity, was tied to a tree by the Danes and pierced with arrows until he died. And the Bishops of Norwich had a palace there from earliest Norman times, where they held courts and instituted clergy. Later bishops, however, had a very different interest in

Hoxne – and that is where the Swan came in.

First, the official episcopal history. Hoxne was recorded in the Domesday Book as the seat of the Bishopric, in the days when the See was at Thetford. Bishops continued to have a palace there after the See moved to Norwich, and in 1256 Bishop Walter de Suffield, founder of the Great Hospital in Norwich, 'sat him down in his palace of Hoxne and indited his will', according to the Hospital's official record.

In the fifteenth century Bishop Lyhart 'often resided at his palace at Hoxne'. He died there in 1472, and his arms are still featured on the font in the parish church. One of his legacies was Hoxne vicarage. Other bishops have also been generous to the village church. Bishop Brown, for instance, who made his will while staying at the palace in 1445, left forty shillings (worth rather more than it sounds today) to spend on the bell tower.

There is no trace of the Bishop's Palace now, but it is thought to have stood on the same site as Hoxne Hall, later known as Oakley Park, which was demolished in the 1920s. However, in the early sixteenth century, another building was erected in Hoxne for the benefit of the Bishop, and it still stands in the main street of the village. From the front it is not recognisable as a work of that period, because the front wall and gable ends were rebuilt in brick in the eighteenth century, but the original Tudor timbers are still exposed at the back. There used to be a carriage entry with a room over the top, where the entrance to the car park is now. The garden must be much the same, except it now has a croquet lawn. It is, of course, the Swan, which has been an inn since at least 1619, but it was its original function that involved the Bishops of Norwich.

Architects have established that, when it was built, it was possible to walk from one end to the other on the ground floor, but the first floor was divided into three separate apartments, each with its own staircase. The experts note, discreetly, that this indicates it was a guests' lodging house – and, according to local legend, all the lodgers were ladies, and they were all guests of the Bishop. In fact, the locals have a word to describe it, but to spare the blushes of the current bishop I will not quote it. Suffice to say that his predecessors are widely believed to have come here in order to enjoy a little relaxation in female company.

Of course, nothing like that goes on at the Swan these days, involving bishops or anyone else. But it is easy to appreciate that it has seen some illustrious company in its day. The main bar still looks more like a baronial hall, with its heavy oak floor, the tables down each side, the central area clear, and an imposing open fireplace at one end with an armchair on each side. One can picture a bishop and his companions dining at these tables with, perhaps, a little light entertainment by musicians and dancers in the central space.

The present dining-room is grander still, with a magnificent beamed ceiling, and there is a pleasant jumble of rooms leading off the main bar, along passages where I have more than once lost my way. The whole place retains its original period flavour; even the boards which record the shove-ha'penny champions of more recent years are tucked away discreetly in an alcove.

It is only outside that modern technology has been allowed to change the appearance of the Swan. The garden is a popular venue for pub lunches around the croquet lawn, and to save shouting out a number when a meal is ready, a discreet buzzer sounds and the number appears miraculously on the roof. It has been likened to a cricket score-board; I think in view of its history 'hymn-board' might be more appropriate.

Beer pumps in the pulpit, tankards in the pews

The bar is inscribed to the memory of Alfred Rooke, 'for many years a treasurer of this church'; originally it was a pulpit.

The Red Lion
Lamarsh, Essex

Lane through village

Sitting on the end of the bar at the Red Lion is a little Basil Brush charity collection box, and if you look closely you will see that Basil has a badly singed nose. It is the only visible reminder of the serious fire that broke out at the inn about four years ago, which did considerable damage to the interior and resulted in quite a major reshuffle of the remaining furniture and equipment. Happily, the most intriguing features of the Red Lion have survived, the little two-seater church pews which provide some of the seating, and the bar itself, another example of ecclesiastical woodwork. It was, in fact, a pulpit; its panels have been re-aligned to form a serpentine-shaped frontage to the counter. Along the top of it is carved the inscription: 'To the Greater Glory of God and In Loving Memory of Alfred Bradley Rooke, For Many Years a Treasurer of This Church, Entered into Rest 19th May 1907.'

It would be reasonable to assume that the pulpit came from Lamarsh church which, unusually for a village church, is nowhere near the inn, but at the far end of this straggling and remote little community,

One of the benches in the bar carries an unlikely warning.

perched on the hillside overlooking the Stour valley. It has preserved its remoteness for two reasons. First, the lane it lies on is narrow and winding, and all the through traffic uses the much more convenient road on the Suffolk side of the River Stour, which marks the county boundary. And second, it is situated midway between Sudbury, which is Gainsborough country, and Bures, which is Constable country.

The two great artists kept to their own areas when they were painting the local landscape, and for some reason preserved a no man's land, a sort of paint-free zone, between the two. Lamarsh lies inside this easel-less and, therefore, tourist-free area. So far as I know it does not feature in either a Gainsborough or a Constable, yet the views across the valley to the Suffolk hills are quite splendid, and the village itself has plenty of picturesque features – not least, the sixteenth-century Red Lion and the twelfth-century,

round-towered church, each with its own pulpit.

Unlike many East Anglian round towers, which are Saxon, this one was built by the Normans; no one is quite sure why. I have always understood that the Saxons went in for them because they mostly used local flint, and this is tricky material for making corners. The Normans knew all about importing stone to build square towers, but they may have thought a round one was easier to defend, and certainly the narrow slits in the Lamarsh tower are obviously ideal for archers. But the guidebook quotes another reason. Round towers were built to protect wells, and this comes closer to my own pet theory, that the towers were once wells themselves, but the land gradually subsided until the well linings were exposed above it. In due course the locals were left with a round tower sticking out of the ground, so they built on a nave and a porch, and the round-tower church was born.

But back to the pulpit-turned-bar. The pulpit in the church looks much the same age as the one in the Red Lion, and there is no hint in the guidebook of any link between the two. Nor does it mention the deceased Alfred Bradley Rooke – though there is a note about one of Essex's earliest road casualties, a Thomas Stephens of Colchester, who came to Lamarsh in 1654 to visit a Mrs Grisagone Smith, for reasons not disclosed, 'and received his death by a waggon thrusting against his thigh'. There was obviously a need for traffic-calming, even in 1654.

On further investigation at the Red Lion I found it was not surprising that the bar-pulpit did not feature in the church guidebook. They told me that it actually came from a church in Worcestershire, along with the pews. They were installed about thirty years ago by a landlord who, presumably, had useful ecclesiastical connections. At the same time he acquired another church fitting which is on one of the pews in the dining area next to the bar. Customers tucking into their pub lunches may be disconcerted to find a notice which reads: 'Please leave this pew vacant during Communion service.'

The curious case of the doctor's surgery, the EEC - and the bull

The Bull
Langley Lower Green, Essex

On the green

Langley is not the easiest village to find, and having found it you still have to find Langley Lower Green. The village is in two parts, and there is quite a gap between Lower Green and Upper Green. They are both attractive, with plenty of thatched cottages with decorative plaster work on the white-painted walls, but Lower Green also has the Bull, a pleasant Georgian village inn by the green.

The village cricket club has its headquarters at the Bull, and although the two greens added together seem hardly large enough to raise a team, they actually have two. The official scorer for Essex County Cricket Club used to play when he was not travelling with the county team, which ensured that, even if Langley did not always win, at least it always got the scores right.

They also play pitchpenny at the inn, tossing pennies into a hole in the settle by the bar. It goes back to the days when the Bull was the Black Bull. Nobody knows when the name changed, but it must have been before the current sign was painted, because the bull it portrays is black and white.

The inn was established in 1780 by the Hawkes Company of Bishops Stortford, a dozen miles away, with money earned from supplying malt to the London breweries. They still owned it in the 1870s, when the licensee was George George, a name guaranteed to confuse unwary customers. The George family still farms in the village and, indeed, George George himself was a farmer as well as running the Bull.

A photograph of that period in the bar shows the outside of the inn looking much the same as it does today, though not quite as smart. It has the same narrow-paned lattice windows, which are not exactly convenient, but are listed and cannot be altered. The favourite tipple in those days was called 'Entire', a bitter stout which travelled so well that Hawkes had it in a hundred inns throughout Essex and Hertfordshire. In 1898 they sold out to Benskins – and the Entire stock has long since disappeared.

The story of the Bull so far is unremarkable. It could be just another congenial country inn with a pitchpenny seat and two hundred years of history. It was only in more recent times that it took on a new role, as a doctor's surgery – and brought down upon itself the wrath of the European Economic Community.

The idea seemed eminently sensible. The nearest surgery was eight miles away at Newport. Langley Lower Green, like most other English villages of its size, was almost entirely lacking in public transport. It was difficult for older people, or anyone without a car, to attend the surgery, and when the doctor suggested bringing the surgery to the village once a week for routine consultations, the offer was eagerly accepted.

Every Wednesday afternoon, therefore, the doctor took over one of the two bars at the Bull, after the lunch-time drinkers had left. A curtain was drawn

Patients could play pitchpenny while waiting to attend the doctor's surgery in the adjoining bar. But the EEC stopped all that.

across the gap between this and the other bar, which was used as a waiting-room. For serious problems, of course, the patients still went to Newport, but for minor ailments and check-ups the Bull was ideal.

Then along came the inspectors, bearing a copy of EEC regulations. The inn, they decided, was not suitable for use as a surgery. This was not because it was licensed premises, and the patients might have a crafty nip out of hours while they were waiting. It was not because it was unhygienic or inadequately equipped. The reason, so the landlady told me, was that there was glass in the door of the temporary surgery, so inquisitive visitors might peer through. And as there was only a curtain between the bars, those waiting for treatment could hear what was being said between the doctor and his patient.

There is, of course, a certain logic in this, and in an ideal world surgeries are spy-proof and sound-proof. But I well remember a surgery in a Norfolk village where the doctor's voice was loud, the wall was thin, and nobody was any the worse for what information filtered through. Certainly, if it were a choice between that and walking or hitch-hiking for eight miles, I know which I would have preferred, and I suspect the good folk of Langley Lower Green would have taken the same view.

But the choice was not in their hands. The doctor had no alternative but to stop his Wednesday surgeries, and his patients have to make their own way to Newport, as best they can. The affair has given a particular appropriateness to the name of the inn. No doubt about it, there is an awful lot of it about.

The locals saved it, and the carriage trade (yes, really) just love it

The King's Head (The Low House)
Laxfield, Suffolk

Road off main street at Royal Oak

The sign at the King's Head has a picture of Henry VIII facing you on one side, and with his back to you on the other. A notice on his back reads, 'The Low House', an acknowledgement that this is the name the inn is known by throughout the district and among all its admirers.

This is not just because the Low House is low – though indeed it is, a long, low, thatched inn dating back to 1480 and possibly built, like so many old village inns, to house masons working on the church.

It got its nickname, however, when there were three inns in Laxfield. The General Wolfe at the top of the village was known as the Top House, the Royal Oak in the village centre was the Middle House, and the King's Head, down by the stream at the other end of the village, was the Low House.

The General Wolfe is now a private house, and at the time of writing the Royal Oak is closed. A few years ago a similar threat hung over the Low House, either to be closed and converted into a private dwelling, or – a fate worse than death to those devoted to it – it could have suffered under a twentieth-century successor to Laxfield's most infamous son, William Dowsing. It was Dowsing who wrecked so many Suffolk churches on behalf of Oliver Cromwell, and the Low House might also have been wrecked by the sort of 'modernisers' who rip out the interiors of old inns and fill them with electronic games, loudspeakers and karaoke.

The Low House faced an earlier crisis in the 1960s when the brewers first put it up for sale. Happily, the purchaser had a soul, and kept everything as it was. Beer was still served from the cask in a back room, the hub of the inn was still the 'settle room' with its splendid high-backed, wooden settles round the walls, and the smaller rooms around it retained their bare floors and plain furniture, and the Victorian pictures on the walls. Everyone was happy.

Then in 1991 the Low House came on the market again. Worse, it actually closed, and there was dark talk of it never being re-opened. At this crucial moment, enter Tony Harvey of Tannington Hall, not on a white charger but driving a horse and carriage.

Mr Harvey is a farmer, but he has two other consuming interests. One is horse-drawn carriages, the other is the Low House. He also does a little broomstick-dancing on a Tuesday lunch-time. These three spare-time pursuits are closely interwoven. He started collecting carriages in his late teens and he now has forty of them at his farm. He takes people on carriage rides during the summer, and whether it is for a pub lunch, or dinner, or just a glass of beer, the carriages always stop at the Low House. Conveniently, there is stabling for six horses at the rear; this must be one of the few inns where the stables are still put to their original use.

When the Low House was sold by the brewers Mr Harvey attempted to buy it, but he was quite happy when the new owner left it unchanged. When it came on the market again he decided to have another go. He got together a consortium of friends and relatives who all knew and loved the Low House. They included three farmers, a timber importer, an electrical engineer, a caterer, and even his sister who lives in Australia. Together they raised enough to buy the Low House in 1992; their names are listed on the wall, rather like a roll of honour.

They appointed a tenant under a strict agreement: no fruit machines, no piped music, no pool table, no cigarette machine, no fried food and no modern bar. The beer is still carried through from the back room – and in the taproom, a term often misused, the regulars still tap their tankards when they want them refilled.

Some of these regulars are as much a part of the Low House as the settles round the walls. Visitors have been known to enquire if they are actors being paid to add to the atmosphere. But, if a visitor happens to occupy their favourite seat, their reaction is genuine enough.

Tuesday lunch-time is step-dancing time at the Low House. It is a slightly cumbersome version of tap-dancing, geared to farm workers in hobnailed boots, though these days it is sufficient to wear shoes with toe and heel plates. It is also when Tony Harvey indulges in a spot of broomstick-dancing, with the odd Suffolk song thrown in. He does it for his own enjoyment, but I am sure his clients, literally the carriage trade, love it too. As he says: 'They can step out of the carriage and into the Low House, and the spell isn't broken. They are still living in the past.'

Petanque in the pigsty, and handles with a horizontal hold

*The bar with the horizontal beer-handles. Customers have to lean over
to see them, and the landlord needs a new set of muscles to use them.*

The Star
Lidgate, Suffolk

The Street

Lidgate lies in the border country between Cambridgeshire and north-west Suffolk where it is almost impossible for a stranger to know which county he is in, even with the help of a map. The county boundary meanders vaguely northwards from Haverhill, through farmland and tiny villages, until it makes a sudden swoop westwards to encompass Newmarket and Exning, in a little Suffolk peninsula which miraculously survived the latest boundary shake-up.

The River Kennett would provide a logical boundary line, but sometimes the border follows it, sometimes it veers away. The only sure way to find out which county you are in is to ask. At Lidgate they will tell you very firmly that this is Suffolk, but only by a few hundred yards.

Lidgate is a modest little village. It often gives the impression it is populated more by ducks than people. Its only moment of glory came in the early fifteenth century, when a local lad called John Lydgate took over where Chaucer had just left off, and burst into verse. Unfortunately, it was not quite in the Chaucer class. As one critic wrote: 'Some good grain is to be found in an unconscionable amount of chaff.'

Lydgate himself would not have been too bothered by that. He became a monk at Bury St Edmunds

when he was sixteen, and probably never read the reviews. There is a brass to his memory in the parish church, but I suspect that few of the present-day parishioners have read his poetry, even if they know who he was.

It was almost another two centuries before Lidgate had its next excitement, the founding of the Star inn. It dates from Elizabethan times – some records put it at 1588 – and in its original form it was two cottages, with a tunnel from the cellar leading to the brew-house next door. It still has two separate bars, where the two cottages used to be, but, these days, there is a slightly Spanish bias which Queen Elizabeth, after her unhappy experience with Philip of Spain, would not have appreciated at all.

In one of the bars there are old posters referring to Catalonian ships, and there are one or two fish dishes on the menu which would be more familiar on the Mediterranean than in an English country inn. The reason is that the landlord's wife comes from Catalonia, and since they took over in 1993 the

traditional spit-roasts in winter, over the open fire in the bar, have been augmented by some of her native dishes.

The continental connection has extended into the garden, where the former pigsty has been converted into a covered petanque court. But the garden itself is English enough, with a splendid weeping willow as its centre-piece. There is a similar blending of cultures inside the bars. Alongside those Catalonian posters there are photographs of very English-looking racing scenes; Newmarket is only six miles away. There is also a photograph of Shergar, but I was assured the missing racehorse is not hidden behind the petanque court.

However, it is not so much the combination of European and equestrian decor which inter-ests me in the bar; it is the beer handles. Anyone glancing casually at the bar counter would say, 'What beer handles?' and indeed they are difficult to spot because they are below the level of the counter. The landlord has found this something of a disadvantage, because casual visitors have looked in the door, failed to see the handles, and gone out again, thinking there was no real ale. The handles are in fact horizontal instead of vertical, and instead of being pulled backwards they have to be pushed downwards. This is very handy for short barmen who could not reach the upright variety, but I gather that the landlord found he was using a whole new set of muscles he had never discovered before.

The handles with the horizontal hold were installed by his predecessor, who brought them from another Suffolk inn, the Bull at Barton Mills. He believes there are only three such sets in existence, and nobody could tell me where to find the other two. Nor was it explained why they were designed that way; they do, after all, jut out behind the bar at a most uncomfortable height if you happen to bump into them. One visitor to the Star says they are not quite as odd as the foot-pedal dispenser he came across in a Scottish bar, where the barman had to dance a jig to get a pint, but they are curious enough to make this inn a Star of Wonder for me.

'A miserable inn in a heathen place' - it gave Pepys the crepys

The Swan
Parson Drove, Cambridgeshire

The main road

Those sceptics who maintain – never having been there – that Norfolk is flat, should pay a visit to this remote corner of the Cambridgeshire Fens, which reaches the ultimate in flatness. The roads are all dead straight, because there are no contours to follow and no obstacles to avoid. The River Nene has been straightened too, the principal channel for the network of straight dykes and ditches which keep the Fens drained. It is an artificial, man-made landscape created by Dutch engineers with lots of rulers but very little imagination. If you have seen

one Fen vista you may think you have seen them all – a flat green sea of sugar-beet and potatoes stretching away to every horizon. But in this sea there is the occasional inhabited island, with a church, a shop, a few cottages and an inn. One such island is Parson Drove.

Arriving in Parson Drove is rather like riding into a Wild West frontier town, except it is surrounded by empty Fen instead of empty prairie. It lies at the junction of two roads – straight ones, of course – which like all Fen roads are mostly empty. Parson

Drove seemed empty too. It was mid-morning, but nobody stirred. And at the deserted road junction, where the Last Chance Saloon would be in a Western, was the Swan Inn.

Until 1914 there was a woad mill at Parson Drove. Yes, woad, but for colouring fabrics, not faces; even the Fens have progressed slightly beyond that. The mill must have been a striking landmark in this low-lying landscape – 'walls of sod, three feet thick' – but the First World War came, demand declined, and Parson Drove came to the end of the woad.

The only obvious re-minder of those busier times is the 'cage' or lock-up next to the Swan, which later housed the fire-engine of the volunteer brigade. The clock face on the roof still bears the letters 'SIXTY YEARS VR' to mark the hours. The mill itself has long since gone, and as I parked outside the Swan it seemed that most of the population had gone too.

It all seemed a little eerie, and it occurred to me how utterly outlandish it must have seemed to the stranger from London who found his way to Parson Drove more than three centuries before me, and whose steps I was following into the inn. At that time the Fens had only recently been drained, crossed by boggy tracks 'where sometimes we were ready to have our horses sink to the belly'. Samuel Pepys was not a happy man as he rode to Parson Drove to visit an aunt and uncle on a particularly bleak day in 1663 – and when he arrived he was no happier at what he found: 'a heathen place, where I find my uncle and aunt Perkins and their daughter, poor wretches! in a sad, poor thatched cottage, like a poor barne or stable...'

He decided to cheer himself up by taking them for a drink and a bite to eat in the Swan next door, but

The bar has mellowed somewhat since Samuel Pepys had a depressing supper in 'this miserable inn'.

the day which had started so badly continued to fall away. 'Took them to our miserable inne, and after long stay, and hearing Frank, their son, the miller, play upon his treble... and singing of a country song, we set down to supper; the whole crew and [Frank's] wife and child, a sad company of which I was ashamed.'

There was worse to come. 'By and by, newes is brought in to us, that one of our horses is stole out of the stable.' That was the bad news. Then the good news: 'it proves my uncle's, at which I am immensely glad – I mean, that it was not mine.'

But he had one final discomfort to endure. 'And so about 12 at night or more, to bed, in a sad, cold, stony chamber; and a little after I was asleep they waked me, to tell me that the horse was found.'

I am happy to report that the Swan has mellowed considerably since then. It was refurbished in 1834, and the landlady tells me she sleeps very comfortably in Mr Pepys's 'sad, cold, stony chamber'. And, in spite of Parson Drove's remote situation and its mid-morning emptiness, the Swan has a strong local following, with very lively (and, judging by all the trophies, very successful) snooker and darts teams. They are twinned with a German counterpart and play regular matches against them, so Pepys's 'miserable inn' in this 'heathen place' is now something of an international sporting centre.

No grudge is borne against him for all that bad publicity in his famous diary. On the contrary, the room at the Swan where the teams forgather in convivial celebration is named after him, the Pepys Lounge. A pity the old misery can't return to join in the fun.

'If you can open an inn when others all about are closing theirs'

A new bar in an old building. Some of the fittings are modern, but the sacking on the tractor-seat 'barstools' is genuine enough.

Darby's
Swanton Morley, Norfolk

Main street

Outside its own immediate area, Swanton Morley has been best known for its Air Force base, operated by the Americans during the war and accommodating the RAF for fifty years after that, until its current closure. As I write, nobody is certain what its future will be, or how badly the economy of the village will be affected. But although many villagers have relied on the RAF station for their employment, they have retained their own identity as a community, dating back to the days of the medieval Barons Morley, who had a castle, long since vanished, on the banks of the Wensum.

It was Sir William de Morley who left ten marks and a gilt cup in 1378 towards building the parish church on the hilltop above the river. It may even have been his idea to decorate it with carvings of a swan and a tun, to illustrate the Swanton in front of the Morley. Since 1990 it has had a rather different adornment, a memorial window donated by the RAF station 'in gratitude for the help and support of the village'.

The village has grown up beneath the church, straggling along the road to Dereham with no obvious central point. The inn known as Darby's is in an older group of cottages near the church, and looks as though it has been a part of the community's life for centuries. Indeed it has, but not as an inn. During the 1980s, when village inns were closing all over the country for lack of custom, as in fact they still are, Swanton Morley acquired a new one. That makes it unique in Norfolk, probably in East Anglia, possibly in a far wider area. And in spite of the rundown of the RAF station and the competition from Swanton Morley's two other pubs, it continues to prosper.

Darby's came into exist-ence in unusual circum-stances. The village already had the Angel, at the far end of the village, and the Papermakers Arms, opposite the church. Each had its own clientele. Then, in 1986, the brewers in their wisdom decided to close the Papermakers, on the assumption that its customers would switch to the Angel, at the other end of the village. But life in rural Norfolk does not quite work like that. In some places, so it is said, people living at opposite ends of the same village are still cool to each other because their forebears were on opposite sides in the Civil War. This does not apply to Swanton Morley, but there can be a strong allegiance to pubs as well as puritanism or princes, and the regulars at the Papermakers displayed a distinct reluctance to change ends.

Enter a local farmer, John Carrick, who was also quite an entrepreneur. 'Diversification' could have been his middle name. Recognising the predicament at the Papermakers, he decided to fill the gap. He owned two terraced cottages quite near it and, without altering the exterior too much, he knocked them into one. He created a long bar, leaving the original fireplace with its bread oven still in place. Next to it he created a family room around a well (safely enclosed), and added a dining area and an upstairs meeting-room. Then he persuaded the magistrates to grant him a licence – they had probably almost forgotten how to do it – and named his inn Darby's after the family who used to live in one of the cottages there.

So far, so good. But the brewers, hearing about this new venture, decided to re-open the Papermakers. Swanton Morley, instead of being reduced to one pub, found itself with three. It would not have been surprising if Darby's had set a new record as the shortest-lived inn in the country but, happily, there proved to be enough thirsts to go round, and all three have survived. If customers cannot face the journey home, there is now bed-and-breakfast or self-catering accommodation at John Carrick's nearby farm.

In spite of its very recent conversion, Darby's still retains a period flavour. It was perhaps a little over-whimsical to make bar stools out of tractor-seats, but the old floors and walls are genuine enough, and unsuspecting visitors might believe it had been ever thus. John Carrick, in fact, has achieved in the twentieth century what was happening all over the English countryside in the eighteenth and nine-teenth, when cottages gradually evolved first into alehouses and then into inns, and their original identity was forgotten. He has just done it more quickly.

Watch out in the bar for the Norfolk twister

The Three Horseshoes
Warham, Norfolk

The Street

Warham is one of those discreet little flint-and-pantile villages tucked away in the north Norfolk countryside, often missed by the holidaymakers speeding along the coast road a few miles to the north. Yet it offers a variety of interests for students of early English history, English church architecture and unusual English inns.

The historian will head for the Iron Age fort just outside the village, with its circular ramparts and ditches enclosing an area of over three acres. In the first century it was one of the strongholds of Queen Boadicea's Iceni tribes against the Romans.

Architects have two churches to choose from. St Mary Magdalen, with its triple-decker pulpit towering over the box pews like the bridge of a battle-cruiser, and a Georgian font which looks like a rather superior bird-bath, and, at the other end of the village, All Saints, with its alabaster reredos depicting the Last Supper, and a tablet in memory of a former rector who captained the England Rugby football team in 1900. It was erected by his seven daughters, says the inscription, and one can imagine the slight frustration of an England Rugby captain with seven daughters – and no son.

The unusual inn is the Three Horseshoes in the centre of Warham, though in the 1930s it would not have seemed unusual at all. It has remained virtually unchanged ever since. The beer is still served from the cask, the public bar is still pretty basic, and the two rooms leading off it could well have the original 1930s furniture, pianola and all. The only slight cheat is the gas lighting. When the current landlord took over nearly ten years ago he found fluorescent lighting in the bar, so he installed the gas mantles instead. He does allow an electric light over the dartboard.

The Norfolk Twister is a bar game which requires either very long arms or a very low ceiling.

The Three Horseshoes goes back much further, of course, than the 1930s. It was originally a smithy with stables at the rear – hence the name. The blacksmith probably started selling ale to his customers while they waited for their horses to be shod, and it developed into a full-time job. The inn was part of the Holkham Estate, the vast tract of agricultural land and property in Norfolk owned by the Earls of Leicester of Holkham Hall. In the 1960s the Estate sold the inn and four adjoining cottages for £2,500. The cottages were demolished to make a car park; not much else has happened since.

I had been to the Three Horseshoes quite a few times to enjoy a pint and a pot of shrimps in the very pleasant garden, before I was told that when I next went into the bar I should watch out for the Norfolk Twister. I thought this must be a local counterpart of the Artful Dodger, and cast a wary eye around the benches to see if anyone looked particularly devious. I should, in fact, have looked upwards; the Norfolk Twister is on the ceiling.

It looks like an inverted roulette wheel, a circle about eighteen inches in diameter divided into twelve red and white segments. In the centre is a pointer which you spin with your hand. It is a simple bar game designed for tall players with long arms though, fortunately, the ceiling at the Three Horseshoes is quite low. The idea is to bet on the number or the colour of the segment in which the pointer stops – or it can be used by twelve players to decide who buys the next round. Not too demanding on the intellect, no skill required, no floor space lost; in short, the ideal pub game.

According to a note written in 1948 there were three other Norfolk Twisters in the county at that time, but I have yet to find them. What I have found is a Norfolk Twister in Sussex, though it is known there as the Spinning Jenny. It is in the George and Dragon at Burpham, a former smugglers' haunt on the bank of the River Arun, just upstream from Arundel. It is said they used the Spinning Jenny to decide how to divide their loot.

Warham is not far from the sea either, and it would not be too difficult to start an entirely new legend about smugglers using the Twister at the Three Horseshoes. But the inn can manage very happily without that. It has been named the best village pub in Norfolk, with or without any smugglers; the Twister needs no new twist from me.

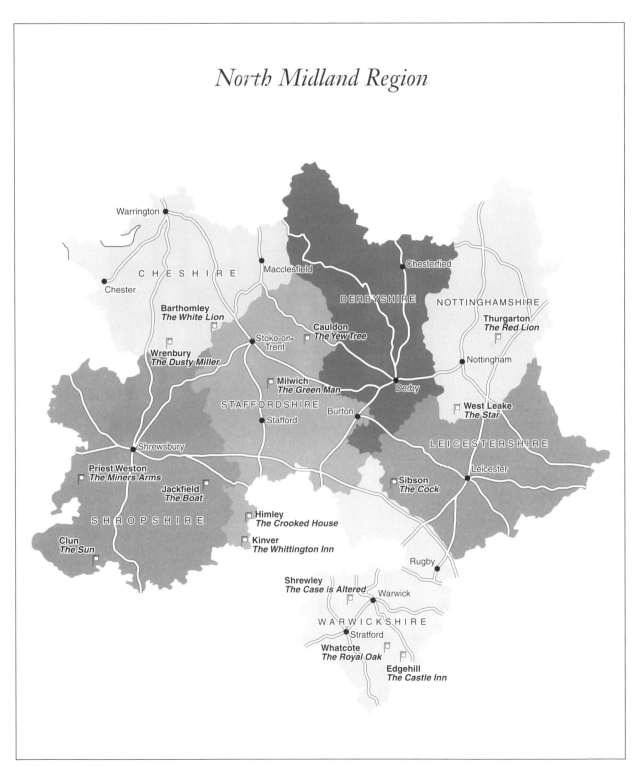

North Midland Region

Warrington

C H E S H I R E

Chester

Macclesfield

Chesterfied

D E R B Y S H I R E

N O T T I N G H A M S H I R E

Barthomley
The White Lion

Cauldon
The Yew Tree

Thurgarton
The Red Lion

Stoke-on-Trent

Wrenbury
The Dusty Miller

Nottingham

Milwich
The Green Man

S T A F F O R D S H I R E

Burton

West Leake
The Star

Stafford

Derby

Shrewsbury

L E I C E S T E R S H I R E

Priest Weston
The Miners Arms

Leicester

Jackfield
The Boat

Sibson
The Cock

S H R O P S H I R E

Himley
The Crooked House

Clun
The Sun

Kinver
The Whittington Inn

Rugby

Shrewley
The Case is Altered

Warwick

W A R W I C K S H I R E

Stratford

Whatcote
The Royal Oak

Edgehill
The Castle Inn

*A landlord who invented a saint, and a
rector's son who provoked a massacre*

The White Lion
Barthomley, Cheshire

Audley Road

There are some confusing names in Barthomley. The village itself sounds like a muddled version of Bartholomew, but it is actually a muddled version of St Bertoline, who in turn sounds more like a cockney Irishman than a saint. The Wulvarn brook, which flows through Barthomley, has nothing to do with wolfram, the element better known as tungsten, which might have been found in it. The brook is actually a reminder that, according to local legend, the last wolf in England was killed near here during the eighteenth century. And the White Lion should more accurately be the Silver Lion, which is how it appeared on the arms of the Crewe family, for centuries Lords of the Manor and at one time owners of the inn.

But these confusions apart, Barthomley is the epitome of a straightforward, unspoilt English village, and the White Lion, with its black-and-white frontage, lattice windows and thatched roof, is the epitome of a straightforward, unspoilt village inn. The same applies inside: oak beams and panelling, open fireplaces, high settles, shove-ha'penny and dominoes on the tables. And for those who enjoy such things, it is encouraging to read in the landlord's brochure that, while they do serve bar meals, 'the pub makes no pretensions of being a catering house'.

This is an unlikely area to find a village like Barthomley and an inn like the White Lion. The M6 motorway is less than two miles away in one direction, the unglamorous railway town of Crewe is only five miles away in the other, and the country lanes between them have become 'rat-runs' for traffic between the two. But the White Lion, in its peaceful setting by St Bertoline's Church, looks much the same as it did in 1614, when it was completed in its present form. Parish clerks lived there much earlier than that, selling ale as a sideline; it was known as 'the clerk's cottage'. Then the ale business built up until it became primarily an alehouse, but the landlords continued as parish clerks and did a little schoolmastering too.

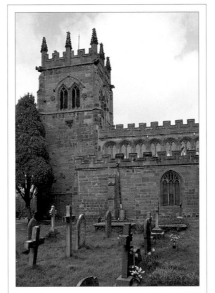

St Bertoline's Church, scene of the Barthomley Massacre in 1643. The customers at the White Lion had a ringside seat.

One of their number, Thomas Smith, who took over in 1726, may have had his own views about St Bertoline, an obscure eighth-century saint who is said to have performed a miracle where the church now stands, but nobody seems quite sure what it was. Perhaps he decided that as Barthomley already had one saint with a vague history, he could get away with inventing another. On the not infrequent mornings when he had a hangover from a heavy night behind the bar, Thomas would tell the schoolchildren to go home and have a holiday, to celebrate St Thomas's Day.

The White Lion had other unorthodox connections with the church. When the Archdeacon made his annual visitation, generally to Nantwich, all the local churchwardens had to attend the service, which was followed by a dinner at the White Lion. It was the tradition after the service for the churchwardens to ride together to the outskirts of Barthomley, then race to the inn. It became known as the Barthomley Races, with considerable prestige for both the winner and his parish. One wonders if the churchwardens of those days were elected as much for their horsemanship as their church-manship.

The most dramatic event in the village's history did not directly involve the inn, though the customers were in a good position to watch it happening, and the details are still recorded in the bar. It took place just before Christmas 1643, during the Civil War, and the vicar of a neighbouring parish left a graphic account of what became known as the Barthomley Massacre, after a Royalist troop attacked the church, where about twenty people had taken sanctuary.

'The men fled into the steeple, but the enemy burning the forms, rushes, mats, etcetera, made such a smoke that, being almost stifled, they called for quarter, which was granted by Connaught [the Royalist officer in command]. But when they had them in their power they stripped them all naked, and most cruelly murdered twelve of them... Connaught cut the throat of Mr John Fowler, a hopeful young man, a minor, and only three of them escaped miraculously, the rest being cruelly wounded.'

There is no doubt where the good vicar's sympathies lay, but the church guide gives the other side of the story too. 'In fairness, it must be said that the villagers were armed, and John Fowler, the rector's son, foolishly fired on the soldiers from the tower, killing one of their number and provoking revenge.' There is nothing new, it seems, about the use of propaganda in wartime.

Her stocking's in the bar among the polyphons – even Queen Victoria might be amused

The Yew Tree
Cauldon, Staffordshire

Lane above cement works

There are two features you cannot avoid noticing as you approach the Yew Tree. The first is the yew tree itself, a venerable giant even older than the inn and so large it almost obscures it from the road. Then you see the second feature – the panoramic view which the inn commands of the biggest cement works in the country. It occupies most of the valley below, and if an invading general were planning an assault on the works, the Yew Tree would make an ideal command post.

But this is hardly what people are looking for when they want to enjoy a pub lunch or a quiet drink; the vista is impressive, but no one could call it picturesque. So the Yew Tree needs something else to make it worth a visit, and once you are inside the door you immediately understand what it is.

Do not expect an amazing array of drinks behind the bar, or a connoisseur's range of real ales; there are just the usual choices. Nor is the bar menu out of the ordinary; indeed it is more basic than most. But the interior of the Yew Tree must be unique. I have seen only one other bar which contains quite so many astonishing items, the King William IV at Heydon in Cambridgeshire, but there the items seem to be deposited at random, and they are more of a jumble than a collection. The Yew Tree is almost as cluttered, but mostly with collector's items, and the man who collected them comes under the same heading. For anyone in search of unusual landlords, Alan East is a must.

Mr East has been at the Yew Tree for over thirty years, but he started his collection long before that, as a schoolboy in 1945. His first acquisition was a polyphon, the elaborate king-size version of a musical box which was developed in the last century. His collection now fills one seating area, and all of them work. You can sit and listen to them on elegantly carved choir pews which he acquired at some stage from St Mary's Church, Stafford. Customers can play the polyphons by inserting a coin, and I tried one that was made in Leipzig, expecting to hear a German drinking song or perhaps a Viennese waltz; instead it gave a rather jolly rendering of 'Way down upon the Swanee River'.

One of the polyphons that provide music for the locals. The choir stalls ensure comfortable listening.

The polyphons are rarely silent, and you might think the constant repetition would become a little irritating, but they do not bother Mr East. 'I've heard them every day for fifty years, and I am still not fed up with them.'

They have to compete for space and playing time with a pianola, which the customers are happy to pedal while the tapes turn, and an assortment of ancient radios which all work too. There is also an antique telephone, but when the bell rang I was a little disappointed to see Mr East pick up a modern one just behind it. Even this collection has its limits.

I suppose it is the polyphons and their close relations, the symphonions, that most people come to see and hear, but his collection does not stop there. Another seating area contains about a dozen circular cast-iron tables, the traditional Victorian design; one fireplace contains so many fire-irons there is no room for a fire. Wartime gas-masks hang from the ceiling, and behind the bar is a serpent, the wind instrument shaped like a snake. But the weirdest exhibit is a Victorian dog-carrier, rather like an over-sized brace and bit, with a muzzle at the front into which to insert the dog's head, and an adjustable wooden spike at the back to secure – rather painfully – the other end of the dog. At least, that was how one of the locals explained it to me but, in fact, he was pushing it a bit. The gadget was actually made only twenty-odd years ago. It is indeed a copy of a dog-carrier, but they were only used on dead dogs.

I suppose the most modern exhibit at the Yew Tree is a shoulder badge from the City of Rye Police Department in New York State. It seems hardly a collector's item until you look at it more closely. After fifty of them had been made, somebody noticed that there were no stars in the Stars and Stripes!

This unusual collection has become quite well known over the years – and not entirely by accident. Alan East is not only an inveterate collector of unlikely objects, but also has a shrewd eye for a newsworthy gimmick. His prize acquisition is a silk stocking once worn by Queen Victoria, together with a lock of hair from Prince Albert's head, supported by a letter from the Royal Household. They are not the sort of items you would expect to find ending their days in the bar of a village inn, and I doubt Queen Victoria would be amused, but their novelty value did not escape Mr East. They cost him £1,200, which is a lot to pay for an old stocking and a few strands of hair, but he told me they had been worth every penny. The press loved the story – not only in this country, but all over the world. One customer brought him a cutting from Tanzania, another read about it in Hong Kong. Overseas visitors keep popping in, the polyphons keep playing – and nobody is too bothered about the cement works down the hill.

'The quietest place under the sun' - but the Sun's hand pumps are much more fun

The Sun
Clun, Shropshire

The High Street

When you have a cluster of villages with such euphonious names as Clunton, Clunbury, Clungunford and Clun, no self-respecting rhymester could resist the temptation to add a second line. Something catty, perhaps:

Clunton, Clunbury, Clungunford and Clun,
Where lots gets said, but nowt gets done.

Or a little more treacly:
Friends to all and foes to none.

Or just:
Whoever named them must have had fun.

But the line which has stuck and is always quoted, perhaps because it came from the pen of the illustrious A. E. Housman, is simply:

'The quietest places under the sun.'

This sweeping claim is contradicted by history and, in the case of Clun, by another local saying about its medieval packhorse bridge, a hazardous route for pedestrians because of the volume of traffic: 'Whoever crosses Clun bridge comes home sharper than he went.' The traffic can be quite heavy too when they are having fun at the Sun at Clun – scope for another couplet there, which Housman never got around to – but, happily, the noisiest and most bloodthirsty period of Clun's history was over before the Sun was built.

This corner of Shropshire was a battleground for centuries. It is dotted with Iron Age forts, and the Ancient British chief Caractacus probably made his final stand against the Romans here in AD 50. Offa's Dyke, the eighth-century earthwork which was the Mercian line of defence against the Welsh, is only a couple of miles west of Clun, and it was constantly attacked. When the Normans moved in, the Welsh attacked them too, and the English earl Edric the Wild joined in. So the Norman Robert de Say built a stronghold at Clun, and in the twelfth century the Fitz Alans added stone defences and a massive keep – but the Welsh kept on coming. Four times between 1200 and 1400 they attacked the castle and sacked the town; if Housman had been around then, he would have amended his couplet to read: '...the bloodiest places under the sun.'

But he wasn't, and nor was the Sun. It was only in the comparative peace of the fifteenth or sixteenth century (opinions differ) that this cruck-truss building was erected, probably as a barn or cowshed for the local farm, which is now the newsagent's shop across the road. Although the exterior is unremarkable, the original crucks – the great beams which curve up the walls to meet in the roof – can still be seen inside, and a section of the wattle and daub wall with its simple floral mural has been exposed and preserved under a glass panel.

Later in the sixteenth century an enterprising merchant acquired the barn, added a first floor and a fireplace, and turned it into an alehouse. The flagstones in the bar are reputed to be gravestones from the old St Thomas's Church.

Not much changed for the next four hundred years. It was only in the 1970s that the local bakery was incorporated to provide a restaurant, bedroom accommodation, and an oak-beamed residents' lounge. The old stables, which had room for ten horses at the turn of the century, have been converted into bedrooms too, but the traditional atmosphere of the bars has not altered; high-backed winged settles, beams in the walls and ceilings, a vast inglenook fireplace. As a bonus, the landlord is firm about no juke-boxes, no pool table and no gaming machines.

This is not an unusual history for a former alehouse turned inn, but one feature of the Sun may be unique. It has an unusual set of hand pumps, which are sometimes called 'cash register' pumps but are,

The knobby little beer-handles started life in a busy Fleet Street pub and have finished up in 'one of the quietest places under the sun'.

unofficially, named after a barmaid called Maggie Marshall. They were manufactured over a century ago by a company called Gaskell and Chambers, and were originally installed in a Fleet Street pub in London, where Maggie Marshall served behind the bar.

In 1939 they were moved to the Three Tuns at Bishops Castle, ten miles north of Clun, then they were acquired by a former landlord of the Sun. Gaskell and Chambers has been taken over by another company, and the new owners could not tell me whether any other Maggie Marshall hand pumps still exist, but it seems unlikely. So, if the shade of A. E. Housman will forgive me, here is a final couplet from Clun:

If you seek a Maggie Marshall there may be only one.
Just look behind the bar at the Sun at (quietish) Clun.

The haunted battlefield where a spectral standard-bearer tries to find his severed hand

The view of the battlefield from the Castle, on the site where King Charles set up his standard, before retiring discreetly to a less-exposed position.

The Castle Inn
Edgehill, Warwickshire

On road between A42 and B4100

Few places look more castle-like than the Castle Inn, and since it stands on a famous battlefield, innocent visitors might assume that it played a role in the battle. Actually, it was built a hundred years later, and it was never a castle, just an ornamental gatehouse. It is, in fact, a folly, the creation of a whimsical eighteenth-century architect called Sanderson Miller, who would probably be amused to know that for the past seventy-odd years it has served as one of England's most unlikely village inns.

Miller was the son of a rich Banbury trader. He owned the Radway estate and lived at Radway

Grange, just down the road from the Castle Inn. It was formerly the home of the Washington family, ancestors of the famous George, and they may well have been living there during the Battle of Edgehill; certainly most of the present house existed at that time. King Charles is reported to have dined after the battle 'at the home of a poor man', which may have been the Grange. The Washingtons were not exactly poor, but by Charles's standards they were probably a little down-market.

The battle was fought on 23 October 1642, the first major encounter of the Civil War, and, when the hundredth anniversary came round, Sanderson Miller decided to commemorate the occasion. Most people would have been satisfied with hoisting a flag, or laying a wreath, or perhaps inscribing a memorial stone. There is, indeed, an inscribed memorial, on the road from Kineton to Banbury, where a Parliamentary horse troop was overwhelmed by Royalist cavalry, but it was not erected until 1949, and it is quite modest in size. Mr Miller had a much more grandiose idea and, according to some reports, an ulterior motive behind it.

He decided to build a near-replica of Guy's Tower, Warwick Castle, on the spot where King Charles is thought to have raised his standard on the Edgehill escarpment, overlooking the battlefield. It would function not only as a memorial and a gatehouse but also, according to local legend, as a convenient rendezvous for secret assignations. The work started during the anniversary year but, builders being what they are – and were in 1742 – it was not completed until 1747, by which time the significance of the anniversary had probably been forgotten.

The octagonal battlemented tower – and everything is battlemented at the Castle Inn, even the toilets – commands the same view across the battlefield that Charles had, before he retired discreetly to a less-exposed position behind the ridge. These days he could just go downstairs into the bar. Thirty thousand men were involved in the battle, and some fifteen hundred were killed – all for nothing, as

it turned out, because it ended virtually in a draw. But some say that was not the end of it. While a good many inns claim to have a ghost or two, the Castle Inn may be beset by thousands, because there have been various reports over the centuries of ghostly armies fighting the battle all over again.

The first sighting was at Christmas time, appropriately by shepherds watching their flocks by night. When they looked up, instead of a star appearing in the east, they saw the Royalist and Parliamentary armies doing battle in the sky. It went on for three hours, before they returned to the village and roused the local magistrate and the minister with the news. These two worthies, with other sceptical villagers, went to Edgehill the following night, and again they saw the armies 'fighting with as much spite and spleen as formerly'. The same thing happened the following Saturday, and the Saturday after that. In fact, these weekly spectaculars only ceased, so it is said, when some bodies were found left behind on the battlefield, and were given a Christian burial.

But the manifestations did not cease entirely. In the 1860s a group of newspaper reporters went to Edgehill to investigate reports of a spectral army lined up on the ridge. 'They all returned shaking and frightened, and went off home as fast as they could' – stopping only, I trust, to file their stories on the way. Then in 1960 a well-known concert pianist, visiting an area of the battlefield where casualties from both sides had been buried together, became very disturbed, 'for I was aware that hundreds of unseen men were watching me'. One of them apparently accompanied him home and stayed with him for a month.

The locals at the Castle Inn have stories of phantom cavalry charges on moonlit nights, of travellers being jostled by ghostly soldiers, and of Sir Edmund Verney, the King's standard-bearer, searching for his severed hand – he was grasping the standard so tightly when he died that Cromwell's men could secure it only by hacking off his hand.

With this going on all around it, perhaps the Castle Inn should be declared a ghost-free zone.

Where even the sober fall over, and bottles roll uphill

The Crooked House
Himley, Staffordshire

Coppice Mill

This greenish corner of the Black Country, where the West Midlands and Staffordshire almost merge, has quite a range of unexpected features. At Wombourne it has the only English church dedicated to St Benedict Biscop and one of the last walled-in cricket grounds in the country. At Pensnett it has the former private railway built by the Earl of Dudley to carry coal from his mines to the iron and steel works at Brierley Hill; since its closure in the 1960s it has become a country walk passing former canal reservoirs which are now wildlife reserves, a former quarry now noted for its wild flowers, and a brickworks which still uses eighteenth-century kilns. Chillington Hall has grounds designed by Capability Brown and Himley Hall was often visited by the Duke of Windsor when he was Prince of Wales. And then there is the Crooked House...

That is not its real name, but it is what everyone calls it, and for the most obvious of reasons. Everything about this former farm cottage is askew. The front door tilts to the left, the one inside tilts to the right. Floors slope, walls lean, the curtains hang away from the windows. The swing of the pendulum in the splendid grandfather clock seems to defy the usual laws of gravity. On one table you can seemingly roll bottles uphill; newcomers stumble and even overbalance as they try to orientate themselves to these bizarre surroundings. No doubt about it, the Crooked House is very crooked indeed.

When it was built a couple of centuries ago it was a perfectly normal cottage. It stood – quite upright at that time – on the estate of Sir Stephen Glynne, owner of the local ironworks and, incidentally, a brother-in-law of Prime Minister Gladstone, which must have been handy when he decided to sink coal-mines under his estate – nobody was likely to argue. It so happened, however, that this cottage was so close to the boundary of his estate that it may even have encroached a little way across it. His mining rights, of course, stopped on the boundary, so his coal-mine stopped under the cottage.

In due course, the mine was abandoned and the workings filled with water. The land immediately above it, under one end of the cottage, began to subside. There came a time when the building started to tilt...

No wonder they call it the Crooked House. The doors tilt, the floors slope, the walls lean, the clock pendulum defies the laws of gravity, and bottles roll uphill.

It is no mean tribute to the solid work of those who built it that the walls did not crack as the process continued. Over a period of time the whole structure tilted gracefully sideways. It finished up with one end several feet lower than the other, but everything still intact.

By this time the cottage had become an alehouse, respectfully named the Glynne Arms in honour of the estate owner. These days the council would probably have condemned it out of hand, but it showed no signs of disintegrating, and the Glaze family who lived there continued to serve their ale,

leaning sideways. Inevitably, it became known as the Crooked House.

When it was bought by the local brewery it was indeed condemned as unsafe, but very shrewdly the brewery did not rebuild it, but reinforced it with steel girders the way it was. With the help of a substantial buttress against its lower wall, the Crooked House has got no crookeder. Instead, it has become quite a tourist attraction, even though it is tucked away at the end of a half-mile cul-de-sac off the main road. After all, it is not often one can drink in an inn which is itself tipsy. One room is preserved as a food-free zone for the benefit of the locals, and this is where you can hear tales of the days when, according to one regular, there were twenty pits within a radius of three hundred yards, until they were closed in the 1920s. The curious location of the Crooked House, right on the boundary of the Earl of Dudley's estate, made it a useful haven for poachers. If they were in danger of being caught in nearby Himley Woods, they reckoned the inn was beyond the jurisdiction of the Earl's gamekeepers. The gamekeepers might have thought that open to argument, but sensibly they did not put it to the test. They would probably have had an uncomfortable reception in the Crooked House, where it is easy enough to lose your balance anyway.

In more recent times an extension has been built behind the inn, which follows the usual specifications of vertical walls and horizontal floors. After spending an hour or two in the Crooked House, this seems distinctly lop-sided. In fact, it is quite a relief to return to the 'normality' of the bar, where doorways tilt in opposite directions, bottles roll upwards, and one of your legs seems distinctly shorter than the other.

The ferry-boat that sank – and even this boat sometimes needs bailing out

The Boat
Jackfield, Shropshire

Ferry Road

It is a very civilised way to reach an inn, walking across a wooden footbridge high above the River Severn, and that is how most of the locals get to the Boat. For visitors it is not an easy place to find. Jackfield does not feature in many road atlases, but you can drive to the inn if you spot the obscure little lane that runs along the west bank of the river from the new bridge at Coalport. It passes a former tile works, now a museum, and an assortment of other sombre buildings which came during the Industrial Revolution and outlived their usefulness. The whole area is, in fact, an outdoor museum, with Iron-

bridge, further upstream, as its focal point. It has a strange 'once-this-was-an-important-place-but-look-at-it-now' atmosphere which can be rather saddening as you pass the derelict kilns and the disused tile and china works in what was once a beautiful and unspoilt river gorge.

For real sadness, though, there is the tragic story behind the name of the Boat. On a foggy winter's night in 1799, eight men, five boys and fifteen women and girls, all employees of the Coalport China Works on the opposite side of the river, lost their lives in a ferry-boat disaster that devastated the local community. The *Salopian Journal* reported:

'As the people from the Coalport Manufacturey, to the number of forty-three, were leaving their work at 9 o'clock at night to go home over the usual passage boat, owing to the inattention of the man who the boatsmen had entrusted to steer over, the boat, unfortunately, went down with all on board. When only fifteen out of the whole could save themselves, the remaining twenty-eight were unfortunately lost. In consequence of the great fog and the darkness of the night, no one was able to give the least assistance. Ten have since been taken out of the water and the Coroner's Inquest is to be held over them this day.'

A fortnight later the *Journal* reported that only nineteen bodies had been recovered. But in a slight amendment to its earlier story it commended a Mr Edward Parker, 'who at great hazard of his life (it had been very foggy and dark) went in and saved two persons from certain death'. Mr Parker, it seems, was not new to this sort of thing. 'This active man has, in the past years, saved four individuals from drowning and has very much contributed in recovering several others.'

One hopes he was bought a few beers at the Boat, but the first record of the inn's existence is thirty-odd years later, in 1831, when George Crumpton 'of the Boat' was buried; another Crumpton, Adam, 'died at the Boat' seven years later. The records also mention a third member of the family, 'William Crumpton of the Boat' who was one of six electors given top coats by the local MP, Mr Forrester, 'to promise their vote'. Mr Forrester was duly re-elected and, indeed, the Forrester family held the seat – one way or another – for nearly two hundred years.

Officially, the Boat was not licensed until 1840, but I doubt the Crumptons worried too much about that. In 1879 it was the only beerhouse in Jackfield, but the competition grew, and by 1901 the nearest pub was only 120 yards away. The Boat, however, was described as 'good and clean' in a County Council report, so it probably still had the edge.

The footbridge leading to it was built in 1922, and when I first read the plaque I assumed it was a belated memorial to the ferry-boat victims. 'This bridge is free, O tread it reverently, In memory of those who died for thee.' It is, in fact, a war memorial, and a very practical one too, but it may have presented a minor problem over where to lay wreaths and plant crosses. The problem was solved in 1977 when a tree was planted in the parking area between the Boat and the bridge; the little wooden crosses from Armistice Day were still around it when I visited in February.

A footbridge outside the Boat now spans the Severn where twenty-eight people died when the ferry-boat capsized.

The tree, however, was not intended as a memorial. Lord Boyne planted it to mark two notable anniversaries, the Queen's Silver Jubilee and – perhaps more importantly – the fiftieth anniversary of the Boat Inn Flower Show. It is, in fact, quite a famous show, and an interesting variation on the usual activities at a village inn.

The other unusual activity at the Boat is bailing it out. It is sometimes flooded when the river rises above its banks, and friends of mine were there in December 1993, when it was being dried out after one of these inundations. It gave them the chance to admire the old stone floors, which are normally carpeted. A roaring fire in the old range was doing a good job, and the bar was still cosy. But the flooding was another reminder of the destructive power of the Severn, which once took twenty-eight lives. And looking down from the footbridge at the speed and force of the water, I could understand why nine of the bodies were swept completely away.

*Famous origins, a ghost, secret rooms, a tunnel,
royalty, a murderer - it's a full house*

The Whittington Inn
Kinver, Staffordshire

On the A449

Forget the story that Dick Whittington was a humble country boy who walked to London to make his fortune, with his bundle over his shoulder and escorted by his cat. He was actually the son of a wealthy landowner who went to London to be apprenticed to a friend of his father. He would have ridden rather than walked, and instead of a cat he was probably escorted by servants carrying his bags. If you want evidence of his affluence, you need only see the splendid old timbered building which was his family's home at Kinver and which, for the last two hundred-odd years, has been the Whittington Inn.

A great many inns look like the Whittington –

from a distance. They mostly date from the 1930s and were built in the style known as Brewers' Tudor. But the Whittington is the real thing, built of wattle and daub on an oak frame in 1310 by Dick's grandfather, Sir William de Whittenton. Mercifully, nothing has been done to destroy the appearance or the atmosphere of the old place, though it could easily have deteriorated into an olde worlde road-house. Indeed, at lunchtime there are more eaters than drinkers in the main bars, but the beams and panelling and great open fires are still a delight, and the little snug known as the Chinstrap Bar remains a safe haven for the serious drinker. The name may baffle anyone under fifty, but wartime radio listeners will remember ITMA's Colonel Chinstrap, played by Jack Train, and this was where Jack entertained his show-business friends.

I am not sure the Whittingtons would have approved of Colonel Chinstrap. Dick's cousin Guy fought at Agincourt, and might not have taken to comical colonels. But the family did have its unconventional moments. Dick's father was outlawed in 1350 for marrying a nobleman's widow without getting the King's consent. He had to sell his manor at Kinver, which was the bad news; the good news was that he just moved to another family estate in Gloucestershire where Dick, in due course, was born.

Queen Anne was a much earlier customer. She was wont to leave her seal on the door instead of just signing the visitors' book.

The new owners of the Manor House, the de la Lowes, married into the Grey family, and Lady Jane Grey, the ill-fated nine-day Queen, spent some of her childhood there. Thus, the old building acquired its inevitable ghost. There have been tales of Lady Jane's footsteps pacing the upstairs corridors, of strange presences being felt, and of the brickwork in one of the hearths being scattered on the floor overnight without a sound being heard.

The most convincing 'sighting' happened at a small dinner-party, appropriately in 'Lady Jane's Room'. All the half-dozen diners maintained that the door handle moved and they felt cold air enter the room, though the door remained closed. They said the temperature went down ten or twenty degrees as the cold air passed them and reached the far end of the room, where the handle of another door was turned. Again the door stayed shut, but the temperature returned to normal. They stressed that this all happened as they were starting their meal, not after they had emptied a few bottles.

Every manifestation has occurred upstairs; Lady Jane may not approve of the lower rooms being converted into bars. Nor would the Jesuit branch of the Greys, who had two secret chapels in the Manor House and installed a secret staircase to a hidden room in the roof, in case of emergencies. As well as a ghost and secret rooms, the old building also had a couple of tunnels, one of which was supposed to lead to Whittington Hall, three hundred yards away. A tunnel entrance in the cellar was explored in recent years, but it had caved in after a short distance.

What else is required of a genuine old English inn? A royal connection, of course, and apart from Lady Jane the Whittington can claim two, though it was still the Manor House at the time. Charles II came this way after his defeat at Worcester, and stayed a night before heading for the precarious concealment of the Boscobel Oak. And Queen Anne was another overnighter, leaving her royal seal on the front door instead of a tip. Perhaps influenced by this up-market clientele the Lord of the Manor, Lord Stamford and Warrington, acquired the licence and the inn sign of the Whittington Inn up the road, transferred them both to the Manor House, and installed a chap called Dunn as licensee. That was in 1783; it has been an inn ever since.

An ancient inn needs one other ingredient, a good villain, and in 1805 the Whittington acquired William Howe. He killed and robbed the local squire in a nearby wood and, believing him to be dead, stopped at the inn for a few pints, hanging his lantern on a beam in the bar. But the squire was found and denounced him before dying, and Howe was arrested at the inn and taken off for trial, leaving his lantern behind. In due course he gained the dubious distinction of being the last man in England to be gibbeted. It would complete the story if the lantern could still be seen hanging in the bar, but it was thrown out by an unromantic landlord in 1926. Not even the Whittington can have everything.

One landlord made pipes from a tea plant,
another pulled out his own teeth

The Green Man
Milwich, Staffordshire

On the B5027

Milwich lies in the virtually unvisited hinterland between Uttoxeter to the west, Stafford to the south, and Newcastle-under-Lyme to the north. Most gazetteers think it hardly worth a mention, and I suspect the good folk of Milwich hope it stays that way. It is a peaceful and attractive little village, and the Green Man is a peaceful and attractive little inn which, in spite of its unremarkable appearance, has seen some remarkable goings-on – a man who sold his wife for two guineas, a licensee who pulled out all his own teeth with a borrowed pair of pliers, a 'regular' who started smoking when he was four and drinking beer when he was five – and lived

until he was ninety-five.

There has been an alehouse on the site of the Green Man for centuries and, although the earliest known reference to it by name is in 1807, it may well have been involved in the sale of Thomas Moss's wife to John Keeling in 1763; the deal may even have been struck in the bar. It was not quite such a cold-blooded transaction as it sounds. Thomas was a Cheadle man who joined the army and was sent abroad, leaving behind his wife Mary and their baby son. Mary came to work in Milwich, and some years later word reached her that her husband had been killed. Either she did not know how to check the story, or she was not too bothered anyway, but she subsequently married a local man, John Keeling, and settled permanently in the village.

Then in 1763 Thomas miraculously re-materialised. He admitted that he had started the story of his own death, presumably because he was enjoying himself so much abroad that he wanted to cut his ties with home. But when his time with the army ended, he decided to rejoin his wife and child. His arrival, understandably, led to 'great Differences and Disputes', according to one report, but these were resolved by the payment of two guineas. Thomas renounced all claim to Mary, and one hopes he then made an excuse and left, so that she and John Keeling could live happily ever after.

Family relationships on the other side of the counter at the Green Man were much more conventional. One family, the Fairbanks, were licensees throughout the nineteenth century. In addition to brewing their own beer they ran a bakery at the inn, groceries were sold, and there was even a carpenter's shop. The premises were actually owned by the Dive family, but they sold them to the tenant, John Fairbanks, in 1871. John had his own speciality, making wooden tobacco pipes from a tea plant which grew at the Green Man. One surviving example of his work has a stem thirty inches long with a silver tip. Mr Pickwick would have looked well with it, but somehow tea-plant tobacco pipes never caught on.

John Fairbanks ran the Green Man until his death in 1905, when the family connection ended, but later another family, the Bennetts, had it for half a century. In between, just before the First World War, there was George Clewlow, a man subject to deep fits of depression. In one such fit he popped across the road to the wheelwright, borrowed his pliers, and pulled out all his own teeth. This may

A roll call of landlords in the bar. One family held the licence throughout the last century.

The Green Man
It was known by this name at least as early as 1815

[1792] – 1825	John Fairbanks	– he died in 1825 aged 65	
[1828] – 1850	Richard Fairbanks	– he died in 1850 aged 55	
1850 – [1871]	Hannah Fairbanks		
[1872] – 1905	John Fairbanks	– he died in 1905 aged 70	

It was purchased by Joules in 1905

[1908] – 1912	Cecil M. Cheatle		
1912 – 1913	A. Wardle		
1913 – 1914	George Clewlow		
1914 – 1915	J. E. Morris		
1915 – 1925	Frederick Wright		
1925 – 1938	Harry Edward Lever		
1938 – 1948	Arthur Bennett		
1948 – 1975	Eliza Bennett	– died 1975	
1975 – 1985	Reg Bennett		
1985 – 1990	Walter Webb		
1990 –	Rod Webb		

have cheered him up for a bit, but the depression returned and, with no more teeth to extract, he tried to drown his wife in the water tank.

His curious activities did not seem to put off the customers, who had their own funny little ways. Ted and Archie Shemilt, who were born in the 1870s and were regulars at the Green Man all their lives, used to recall that Ted started smoking at the age of four and was drinking his father's home-brewed ale when he was five, 'and good stuff it was too'. It certainly did him no great harm; he died in 1971 at the age of ninety-five. Archie, incidentally, was also a smoker – but preferred sugar-beet pulp to tobacco.

Then there was the regular who got drunk every evening, staggered outside and collapsed in his cart, and his horse found its own way home – until one night some jokers unhitched the horse, put the shafts through the bars of a nearby gate, and hitched up the horse again... I have heard the story told at other inns, but they claim it really did happen at Milwich, and for a quiet-seeming village it does seem prone to the unconventional.

Even the ancient church has had its unorthodox moments. At the turn of the century its churchwarden for forty years, William Garle, was also steward of the Wesleyan Methodist circuit, a rare example of early ecumenism which had an appropriate sequel in 1982 when the local Methodist chapel was closed and the congregation invited to share the parish church. They have a Methodist service there every month – using the eagle lectern presented by William Garle in 1904.

But for ecumenism carried to the ultimate, Milwich has seen the baptism in an Anglican parish church by a woman minister of the United Reform Church, of the Venezuelan-born daughter of an English Methodist mother and a Spanish Roman Catholic father. I wonder if they went full circle and wetted the baby's head at the pagan Green Man.

Stone circles, a holy well - and a cow milked into a sieve

The Miners Arms
Priest Weston, Shropshire

North end of village

It is difficult to identify where England ends and Wales begins in this little knob of Shropshire which juts out into Powys. On the route I took to Priest Weston, along the main road to Church Stoke and then up into the hills, I passed a sign welcoming me to Wales, and there was no subsequent sign saying goodbye, but Priest Weston is in Shropshire and so is the Miners Arms – just. The Welsh border is only a couple of hundred yards away.

This was lead-mining country, starting with the Romans, reaching its peak in the eighteenth and nineteenth centuries, now defunct. It was profitable for a time, but it remained on a comparatively small scale. A travel writer observed in 1860 that in one newly opened mine 'the operation seemed to be like playing at mining. There were two boys breaking the ore and one man washing it with a sieve into a tub of water.' It hardly sounds like Rio Tinto Zinc.

The mines left scars on the countryside, but around Priest Weston one sees more stone circles than scars, and the only obvious reminder of the old mining days is the Miners Arms. This was where the miners drank, while the bosses patronised a more up-market establishment up the road. The other inn has closed, and for a time the Miners Arms was closed too, but eight years ago it was bought by Leslie 'Eddie' Edwards who, I discovered, is an ex-BBC technician from Gravesend. Eddie has restored it to cater for both ends of the market, while retaining its original down-to-earth character. He uncovered beams in the ceiling and a blocked inglenook fireplace. There is an anvil beside it as a reminder that this was a blacksmith's shop as well as an inn.

The furniture and the food are basic, and intentionally so. Eddie and his wife do not go in for chintzy furniture or fancy menus. This remains a traditional village inn, where a nineteenth-century miner would feel entirely at home with a pint and a bowl of beef stew – and he would be made as warmly welcome as the walkers who come in from the hills all around, and the archaeology enthusiasts who visit this remote outpost to see the Bronze Age stone circles.

There are four in the vicinity, with a holy well for good measure. The well is supposed to have been poisonous until a Druid priest persuaded a goddess to purify it. He laid on a procession, headed by her effigy, from one of the stone circles, and she duly did her stuff.

The lead miners have long since gone, but they would still feel at home in the bar with a pint of beer and a bowl of beef stew.

The procession was repeated each year in her honour, and when Augustinian monks founded a chapel at the well, they adapted the pagan rite into a Christian festival, with their procession led by a banner of the Virgin Mary instead of the goddess.

The Miners Arms took up this idea and it holds an annual folk festival, which gets a lyrical mention from a local hill walker. 'As I roll down the one-in-five drop to Priest Weston, I hear strains of flutes and bagpipes. Children and dogs are playing in the beer garden and dancing with adults in the lane beside the hollyhocks and hanging baskets.' There might be a

beer or two being drunk as well.

There is another popular folk-tale attached to this area. During a terrible famine a good fairy conjured up a fairy cow, which she said would come night and morning to be milked, and there would always be milk enough for all. But there was one condition. The villagers could use any kind of vessel for the milk, but if anyone tried to fill more than one vessel, the cow would never be seen again.

All went well until a wicked old witch appeared, with a bright idea for cracking the system, without technically disobeying the condition. She brought along just one vessel to fill – a sieve. After being milked into the sieve for a few hours, the cow decided to call it a day, and galloped off in high dudgeon to become the Dun Cow that features on so many inn signs. The witch was, presumably, well satisfied as she splashed about in her milk lake, but the good fairy had the last laugh. She turned the witch into stone, and put more stones around her to keep her in. The witch's name was Mitchell, and the stone circle is still called Mitchell's Fold.

Sceptics will argue that similar tales are told in other parts of the country, and it all goes back to the ancient belief that when the clouds dropped rain upon the earth, heavenly cows were being milked, no doubt through an enormous sieve. But the story was good enough for a former vicar at nearby Middleton, the splendidly named Waldegrave Brewster, to carve scenes illustrating the legend on his font.

The Miners Arms has not devised a festival yet to celebrate the story of Mitchell's Fold, but if a customer turns up asking for his own tankard to be filled, and it turns out to be full of holes, Eddie Edwards will know where he got the idea.

Names can change, but the case for the Case is unaltered

The Case may be Altered, but nothing much has changed in the snug little bar for a century or more.

The Case is Altered
Shrewley, Warwickshire

Case Lane, off Five Ways on the Warwick–Birmingham road

The Case may be Altered, but the inn itself isn't. Nothing seems to have changed for a century, and although the landlady does not go back quite that far, Mrs Mary Gwendoline Jones is an unchanging feature too. This is one of the rare village inns which survive happily without getting involved in bar meals or even a bar snack. There are no fruit machines and no piped music, just an elderly bar billiards table in a back room, which still operates on pre-decimal sixpences.

This anachronistic idyll is not easy to find. It is technically in Shrewley, a hamlet within the parish of Hatton, but it is well outside the village, in a little lane with a scattering of houses which apparently belong to nowhere in particular. If you ask the way locally you will be directed to Five Ways, a confusingly named junction on the main Warwick – Birmingham road where, in fact, only four roads meet. The fifth is a turning a few yards along one of them, but its name offers a helpful clue. It is called Case Lane. It also bears a notice warning that it is unfit for heavy goods vehicles, which looks the real thing but makes me wonder if it was put up by the locals, because Case Lane seems as adequate as most country lanes. But it does cut down the noise past the Case is Altered.

This is not an area where you would expect to find such an unspoilt rural inn. It lies in the triangle formed by Birmingham, Coventry and Warwick, criss-crossed by busy trunk roads linked to an even busier motorway. The main road is only a couple of hundred yards away. Yet the main bar of the Case has survived unaltered from an earlier, quieter age. There are a couple of leather-covered settles, a few plain tables, a poster advertising the products of a defunct brewery, and a clock with letters instead of figures, spelling the name of another brewery long since gone. It is no surprise to find that even the beer pumps are period pieces, miniature versions fitted to the casks themselves.

The approach to the inn has a rather domestic flavour. You enter it through a wrought-iron gate like the gate of a private house, even down to the 'CASE' in wrought-iron letters. Then there is a little paved courtyard, reminiscent of a private front garden. This was, in fact, a cottage back in the 1870s, linked to a baker's and an alehouse. The owner was a William Watts, who was listed as a beer retailer and shopkeeper, with one Mark Harvey as his licensee.

It was Mr Watts, according to one version of the story, who was responsible for the name of the inn.

When he first applied for a licence, the magistrates decided that the premises were too small. He made alterations and enlargements, perhaps by combining the alehouse, cottage and bakery, and returned to the court.

'You've come back about your alehouse,' said the clerk.

'Ah, the case is altered,' said Mr Watts.

He got the licence, and the alehouse got its name.

I have seen another version, however. A later licensee called Mercedes Griffiths had a similar legal battle, not over obtaining a licence but over getting it extended to cover the sale of spirits as well as beer. She had to make similar alterations, and that was when the name was changed.

I can only offer the theory that both versions could be true, and the Case was altered twice. According to old directories and licensing records, it had certainly been altered by 1883, four years after William Watts died, because a Mark Mills is designated 'Baker at the Case is Altered'. Similar entries continued every year until 1897, when the occupant of the Case is Altered was recorded as a Mrs Barnacle. She is recorded again in the following year, but this time the inn is named as the Shrewley Arms.

Could there be some confusion between Mrs Barnacle and Mercedes Griffiths? What a wondrous contradiction in speed-of-movement terms if there was actually a Mercedes Barnacle. But did she go to court again to get the licence altered, and alter the name back again to the Case is Altered? Certainly it was known by that name by the 1930s, and at the beginning of the last war, when it was the headquarters – a highly convivial one, I imagine – of the local Home Guard. But mysteriously, in a letter dated 1968, it is referred to again as the Shrewley Arms.

The deciding factor for me is the venerable sign which hangs outside the inn. It is very faded with age and the weather, but unmistakably it depicts two lawyers arguing over a pile of legal papers. No hint here of any Shrewley Arms; the case for the Case is Altered is unaltered.

'Sorry to disturb you in the chimney, sir,
but is that your horse in the cellar?'

The Cock
Sibson, Leicestershire

On the A444

The Cock claims to be one of the oldest inns in England, 'built about 1250' – and who can say for sure that it wasn't? It is certainly the most attractive old inn in the county, well preserved outside, discreetly modernised inside, and it deserves any history it can get.

There have been plenty of efforts to provide some. The name, for instance, is connected with cock-fighting, and some say a grass mound in the garden

was once a cockpit. One enthusiast has noted that 1250 was about the time that Simon de Montfort, Earl of Leicester, was stirring up trouble among the barons against Henry III – 'and being so close to Watling Street, the Cock could well have been used by the leading noblemen of the day on their travels around England'. Well, possibly.

Then there was the Battle of Bosworth Field, only a few miles from Sibson. Even closer is 'King Dick's

Well' at Shenton, where Richard III is said to have taken his last drink before going into battle, wearing his crown over his visor and crying, 'I live a king; if I die, I die a king.' Which indeed he did, and his crown was retrieved from a thorn bush and placed on Henry Tudor's head at Crown Hill, which is also not far from Sibson. With all that activity going on, it would not be surprising if some of the protagonists paid a visit to the Cock after the battle. Killing people is thirsty work.

It is also possible that Queen Elizabeth stayed there on the way to Tutbury Castle to visit the imprisoned Mary, Queen of Scots. She rarely seemed to miss the chance of trying out a different bed. But, if she did, it would not have been in the same building that de Montfort or Henry Tudor would have known. A former Rector of Sibson, the Revd Frank Best, who was also a local historian, identified the Cock as 'a delightful thatched brick and black timber building of the sixteenth or seventeenth century', though there may be traces of an earlier one. So Elizabeth might have slept in a brand-new bed.

He added: 'There is no documentary evidence of it being used as an inn earlier than 1821, when it was described as a public house and James Peacock as the landlord.' But the lack of evidence does not mean there is any reason to doubt it, and I feel sure it was functioning as an inn by at least the 1730s, because while I am prepared to sacrifice any claim to Simon de Montfort, the Battle of Bosworth, or Queen Elizabeth, I am reluctant to abandon the Turpin connection.

Dick Turpin is principally associated with the Rose and Crown at Hempstead in Essex, where his father was the landlord when it was called the Bell. The bar contains plenty of reminders of the infamous son of the house. But the Cock claims a different kind of link, which is set out in all its literature:

'In 1735 AD the notorious highwayman Dick Turpin would return here after working the Watling Street, taking refuge in the bar chimney and stabling the horse in the cellar when pursuit was close at hand.'

Now, short of finding the marks of Black Bess's hooves on the cellar floor, or Turpin's hat stuffed up the chimney, it would be difficult to provide any proof of this romantic tale, but there is a certain amount of circumstantial evidence. Turpin started his criminal career in Essex, joining a gang of ruthless housebreakers, but when the rest of the gang were caught and hanged, Turpin escaped and moved to Leicestershire, to pursue a new career as a highwayman. He is reputed to have lived with his parents in a cottage just off Watling Street, now the A5 trunk road, which is only about three miles from Sibson. His horse was kept in a clearing at nearby Lindley Wood. It does seem conceivable that, when things got too hot for comfort in the area of his work, he resorted to the chimney at the Cock.

The Revd Frank Best is sceptical. 'The tradition that Dick Turpin used to stable his horse there when not engaged in highway robbery in Watling Street' – a slight variation on the cellar-and-chimney version – 'is hardly the sort of fact that he or anyone else would want recorded.' There is also the thought that the Cock was owned by the church until 1934 – it has opened on Sundays only since the 1950s – and the church authorities would hardly approve of a highwayman being hidden on their premises.

On the other hand, they would probably never have known; Turpin doubtless bought a few rounds to keep people quiet. And once he had moved away to Yorkshire to go in for horse stealing, and been hanged three years later, the story could well have been passed down through successive generations. Even if he only called in for the occasional beer, I will settle for the Turpin connection.

Murder in the Red Lion - not Maria Marten but Auntie Clarke

The Red Lion
Thurgarton, Nottinghamshire

On the A612

Thurgarton is mainly known to tourists because it is on the way to Southwell, three miles away, with its famous Minster. Southwell has aroused mixed feelings among those who know it – particularly punters, depending on whether they win or lose at Southwell Races. Byron lived there as a lad and described it as 'a detestable residence', a view probably shared by Charles I, who spent his last night of freedom there before his surrender, imprisonment and execution, and could hardly have enjoyed it very much.

John Byng, on the other hand, described it in 1789 as 'a well-built clean town, such a one as a quiet distressed family ought to retire to', but it has got a lot busier since then, and families, distressed or not, looking for a quiet retirement, are more likely to consider the surrounding villages like Thurgarton. It is conveniently on the road to Nottingham and the railway line to Newark, but still retains its village atmosphere and its village inn, the Red Lion.

They would not have found it so quiet, though, in the autumn of 1936. The rest of the country was mainly preoccupied with the activities of the Royal Family – it was the period of Edward VIII's abdication – but in Thurgarton the only talking point was the murder of the landlady of the Red Lion, 'Auntie' Clarke.

There have been many murders in village inns over the centuries – there are quite a few in this book – but the Red Lion murder was particularly unpleasant, not least because Sarah Ellen Clarke was murdered by her own niece. Between them they ran the inn after the death of Mrs Clarke's husband, who had also been a butcher in the Shambles at Nottingham. 'Auntie' was eighty-two years old, a frail but domineering old lady, and her niece Rebecca, a middle-aged maiden lady, did most of the work. According to one report, Rebecca could no longer stand her aunt's tyrannical ways and decided to kill her, using a method perhaps learned while watching her late uncle in the Shambles.

'One Sunday night, after seeing her to bed and generally making her comfortable, she stole back to her aunt's room in the dead of night, and carefully and deftly cut the old lady's throat…'

Accounts of what happened next diverge. According to the *Nottingham Observer*, recalling the event twenty-odd years later, 'the niece, in terror and fear of the realisation of her act, hastily collected her cats and flew with them to the water butt, where she attempted to drown herself. Early the next morning the postmistress, on her first round of the week, discovered her wet and bedraggled, but fortunately – or unfortunately as the case may be – still alive.'

There is a more contemporary report, however, in the bar of the Red Lion. A cutting from the *Nottingham Guardian* dated 1 September 1936 is framed on the wall. The headline is not too gripping – 'Notts Village Inn Tragedy' – but the details are much more gruesome. The postwoman did indeed find Rebecca in the water butt, but standing in a stooping position 'with a terrible wound at the throat'. She was shaking her head, with blood pouring from her neck. Beside her under the water was her aunt's cat, with a one-pound weight round its neck.

There is no subsequent newspaper report in the bar to say what happened to her, but I was told that she was tried and found insane, and she died some years later in a home. The 1958 *Nottingham Observer* does add a postscript. 'The old water butt, no longer used and now green with slime, still stands outside the inn, just one of the old relics that help to conjure up the fairy-tale atmosphere of this quaint old pub.'

A permanent reminder in the bar of a 1930s tragedy. The landlady was murdered by her niece, who then tried to kill herself.

Not the sort of fairy-tale to tell the children, perhaps, and later landlords did not, apparently, regard the water butt quite so romantically, because there was no sign of it when I visited the Red Lion.

The inn has been described as sixteenth-century, and there are some old oak beams in the bar, but there have been considerable changes even since Auntie Clarke's day. The photograph in the cutting shows a much smaller, simpler building. A sun lounge has been added, and what used to be an outhouse where customers' horses were stabled is now a lower-level extension to the bar.

Thanks to its proximity to Southwell, the Red Lion has a busy lunch-time trade, but there are enough nooks and crannies, and different levels, to preserve the atmosphere of a village inn – and nobody seems to be put off their food by Auntie Clarke's story on the wall.

No wrestling baronet, no fugitive plotter, no dotty villagers - but it has its own star

The Star
West Leake, Nottinghamshire

Melton Lane

On the face of it, the neighbouring villages in this unpromising area of gypsum mines and plaster works are a lot more interesting than West Leake. The cosily named Bunny, for example, was the home of the 'Wrestling Baronet', Sir Thomas Parkyns. He was so devoted to the sport that he employed two professional wrestlers at Bunny Hall, which he redesigned to accommodate wrestling bouts, and his memorial in the church depicts him in a wrestling stance, beside a pugnacious little figure clad only in a loincloth and a pair of wings, who is looming over a prostrate opponent. 'That Time at length did throw him it is plain...'

Kingston on Soar, a few miles the other side of West Leake, has the Babington chantry where the Catholic knight, Sir Anthony Babington, is said to have hidden after unsuccessfully plotting to have Mary, Queen of Scots crowned Queen. He was later beheaded, aged only twenty-five. On a jollier note, the chantry contains pictorial puns on the family name; the pillars are decorated with babes in tuns.

But the most famous village in the area is Gotham, not because its name was borrowed for the Batman series, but because of the 'Mad Men of Gotham', who shaded a barn from the sun by putting a cart on the roof, disposed of a wasps' nest by burning down the building it was attached to, and built a hedge round a cuckoo in a bush to stop it flying away. In fact, they may not be as daft as they seemed. The story goes that the unpopular King John planned to build a hunting lodge there, and they thought he might be put off by an entire village of village idiots. It seems to have worked.

There is, in fact, an inn at Gotham called the Cuckoo Bush, but one gazetteer described Gotham as 'a very ordinary village', and – not to beat about the cuckoo bush – I thought the same applied to the inn. West Leake, on the other hand, may lack a wrestling baronet, a fugitive plotter or a mob of eccentric villagers, but it does have the pick of the pubs. The Star is a delightful old country inn, set in unexpectedly pleasant countryside just outside the village itself.

It is thought to be eighteenth century, and the public bar certainly gives that impression – low beams, high-backed settles, an uneven tiled floor. The lounge bar is much more recent; it had to be rebuilt in 1969 after the ceiling caved in. The landlord at the time explained: 'In the thirties it wasn't the vogue to have beamed ceilings, so somebody covered this one over with plaster-boards. We tried to strip off the boarding and found there was nothing but willpower holding it together.'

The Star has always been known locally as the Pit House, and there is a popular theory, quoted in some of the guides, that the inn used to be the scene of cock-fighting, or that there was a cockpit nearby; there are even cock-fighting prints on the walls. But that same landlord whose ceiling fell down confessed that this was a story he reserved for American tourists.

The inn is called the 'Pit House' locally, probably because carters taking coal from the nearby wharf used to stop here for a drink, and it became known as the coal-pit house.

A more likely explanation appeared in a letter from a Mr P. Escott North which was printed in the *Guardian Journal* in 1973. Mr Escott North was eighty-four when he wrote it, and he was told the origin of the Pit House by his father, who was born in 1857 and knew the inn by that name when he was a boy. The letter continued:

'When one enters Kegworth (two miles from West Leake) from the Leake road, immediately one has crossed the bridge over the River Soar, there used to be, in days long past, a wharf. It was here that the coal barges used to discharge their loads for distribution by carter over a wide area. Farmers, merchants and coal-dealers brought their horse-drawn sturdy carts to load at the wharf. This accomplished, those carters taking their loads to villagers on the Leake side of Kegworth had their regular stopping places to give their horses and themselves a breather, and a most convenient place for this was the inn at the road junction near West Leake, where a flagon of ale for themselves and water for their horses was obtainable. The inn thus became known as the coal-pit house, later abbreviated to Pit House.'

Which seems pretty conclusive, and although one guide says categorically, 'the name has nothing to do with coal-mines', I vote for Mr Escott North and his father. But he rounds off his letter with another question: 'The mystery to me is, since when has it been named the Star?'

I don't know if he ever got an answer, but I suspect that it was always its official name, and only the locals informally re-christened it the Pit House. But the Star by any other name still gets a star from me.

One of the inns that Cromwell knocked about a (very little) bit

Cromwell's men are said to have stopped here after the Battle of Edgehill, and cut an observation slit by a fireplace to watch out for the Royalists. Why bother, one wonders, when there were already windows?

The Royal Oak
Whatcote, Warwickshire

Village centre

Whatcote is only a few miles from Edgehill, where the first battle of the Civil War was fought, so, with that association, it seems reasonable that the village inn should be called the Royal Oak, commemorating King Charles's famous escape from his pursuers in the Boscobel Oak. It is something of a paradox, however, that it was not the King's supporters who made use of the inn, but Cromwell's, and they would have been very annoyed to see the portrait of Charles in the bar, presented in comparatively recent years by a loyalist customer.

The Royal Oak was probably just an anonymous alehouse at the time of the battle in 1642, and had been for centuries. It is thought to have been built around 1168 to house the masons working on the parish church, which is how so many village inns began. It is built of the local uneven stone, which looks much the same after eight centuries as it does after one, so some of the original building may still exist. Certainly some of the walls are two feet thick, and the roof was thatched until fairly recently. The story goes that the tiles were laid on top of the thatch, 'so adding extra warmth' – a procedure which seems to defy all the usual rules of architectural design, but the tiles look safe enough.

Whatcote has changed greatly around the inn, and the mellow old building looks a little incongruous amongst all the modern houses, but when you are inside the low-beamed bar with its vast inglenook fireplace and King Charles looking at you from the wall, it is the view outside the windows which looks incongruous. The fire-place has a modern coal fire in it now, so it is not possible to look up the chimney and see the iron rungs which used to offer concealment for fugitives, but it is not too difficult to visualise Cromwell's soldiers congregating here after Edgehill. According to Dugdale's much-quoted

Antiquities of Warwick, 'Cromwell and his men sojourned to the Royal Oak, quenched their thirst and filled their bellies after the bloody battle' – but they took the precaution of removing the bread oven by the fireplace and cutting an observation slit in the wall to watch out for the Royalists.

Thus goes the story, but there are one or two historical facts which do not quite tally with it. The Parliamentary forces at Edgehill were commanded not by Cromwell but by the Earl of Essex, at that time captain-general of the army. Cromwell was only captain of a troop of horse at the time, and actually arrived at the battle quite late in the day. The fighting ended virtually in a draw, with both sides still facing each other for a day after it ended, just glaring and probably making the occasional rude gesture, until eventually dispersing. The King headed for Banbury while the Earl of Essex 'fell back to Warwick' – which happens to be in quite the opposite direction from Whatcote.

That's the bad news, so far as the Royal Oak story is concerned. The good news is that not all of the Earl's army went with him. A more recent account of Edgehill written for the Banbury Historical Society says the withdrawal of the Parliamentary forces was quite chaotic.

'Those fit enough to do so either deserted in such numbers that Essex was obliged to write wheedling letters to call back to duty those he diplomatically described as having "gone to visit friends", or scattered haphazardly in all directions... The harrying of Prince Rupert's cavalry seems not to have prevented them looting as they fled, nor quenching their thirst, according to tradition, at the tavern at Whatcote.' So the tradition could well be true, and who can say it was not Cromwell's particular troop of horse who found themselves in Whatcote, did a spot of looting, then finished up at the Royal Oak?

Only a couple of things still worry me. In their situation, would they have bothered to remove a bread oven and hack an observation slit through a two-foot stone wall, when it would have been just as easy to look through one of the existing windows, or just post a man outside? And has the slit been blocked up, or made into another window? I saw no sign of it by the fire.

But let us not carp. Legends have been built on more slender evidence than that. If the Castle Inn on the other side of Edgehill can claim to be on the site where King Charles raised his standard before the battle, why shouldn't the Royal Oak claim Cromwell as a customer after it? It is after all a very pleasant inn.

*You can still sit and dream at the old mill
by the stream - and have a drink too*

The Dusty Miller
Wrenbury, Cheshire

On the canal opposite Wrenbury Mill Basin

It is difficult not to make comparisons between the Dusty Miller and Hoskins Wharf at Shardlow. Both of them are big old commercial buildings which have been converted into licensed premises. Both stand beside a canal and make the most of their waterside situation. Both have moorings for the holiday boats that provide a substantial part of their trade in the summer. Both even have examples of unusual old counterbalanced drawbridges, though on rather different scales.

But there the similarities end. The two inns, as

they now are, have different histories, different settings, different appearances both inside and out, and they probably appeal to different people. Even the canals on which they stand are different in character and were built for different purposes.

Let's take their histories first. Hoskins Wharf is the older building of the two, erected in 1780 as a canal warehouse, but there was a working mill on the site of the Dusty Miller dating back to the sixteenth century, owned by the nearly Cistercian abbey. The original building straddled the River Weaver and had a water-wheel underneath it. When the canal was built early in the last century the mill was replaced by the present building, which also had a wheel worked by the Weaver, but at the side instead of underneath. It ended its days as a working mill at the turn of this century, and became a collection point for local produce to be taken to Manchester in 'fly' boats, the speedy narrow boats designed to carry perishable goods to market as fast as possible, in the days before refrigeration. Even so, it still took them two days to get from Wrenbury to Manchester market.

Most fly boats have long since been broken up, but one has been preserved in another canalside inn only half a dozen miles away, the Shroppie Fly at Audlem; it is actually used as a bar, and must be one of the few Shropshire flies to fall, as it were, on its feet.

Between the wars the old mill building at Wrenbury was used as a warehouse for storing cheese, then it provided storage for the mill on the other side of the canal. It became derelict in 1970 and stayed empty for seven years, until it was converted into the Dusty Miller – just ten years ahead of Hoskins Wharf.

The designers went about it in a different way. At Wrenbury they had a more attractive building to work on, only two storeys instead of four and not quite so looming. With dormer windows in the roof it looks almost homely. And while the Canal Tavern at Hoskins Wharf is a period piece set in the same era as the original building, the large main bar at the Dusty Miller does not attempt to be anything but modern. Much of it is given over to tables and chairs, but happily the area around the bar is a table-free, food-free zone. What both bars have in common are large picture windows looking out on the canal, both have pleasant sitting-out areas on the waterside, and separate restaurants upstairs.

The little river used to work the waterwheel when the Dusty Miller was a mill; now the footbridge provides a route to the garden.

As for the settings, Wrenbury is a very different village from Shardlow, which grew up in the industrial age and has the A6 trunk road running through the middle. Wrenbury is a traditional, and still very rural, village set round a triangular green, and the Hall stands on the site of the abbey which used to own the mill. The Dusty Miller is on the edge of the village with open country around it, on a quiet lane which crosses the canal by a lofty bascule-type bridge.

This was the Llangollen branch of the Shropshire Union Canal, just a rural byway compared with the Trent and Mersey Canal at Shardlow, which was known as the 'Grand Trunk' because of its importance to the canal network. When most of the Shropshire Union system was abandoned in 1944, the Llangollen branch went too, but because of its value as a water-supply channel it earned a reprieve. With no big towns on its route, and two spectacular aqueducts at the Welsh end, it is now one of the most popular holiday canals in the country. Conveniently, the mill opposite the Dusty Miller operates holiday boats from its own canal basin.

While I was there the bridge was lifted for a boat to pass through, and this is quite an impressive entertainment in itself. These bascule bridges are not as picturesque as the humpbacked bridges found on most canals, but they are ingenious pieces of engineering, and fascinating to watch – unless you are waiting to drive across. The little counterweighted footbridge at Hoskins Wharf cannot compete.

But these comparisons will soon be academic. Hoskins Wharf is soon to be closed for refurbishment – I am told it will be 'transformed'. Oh dear…

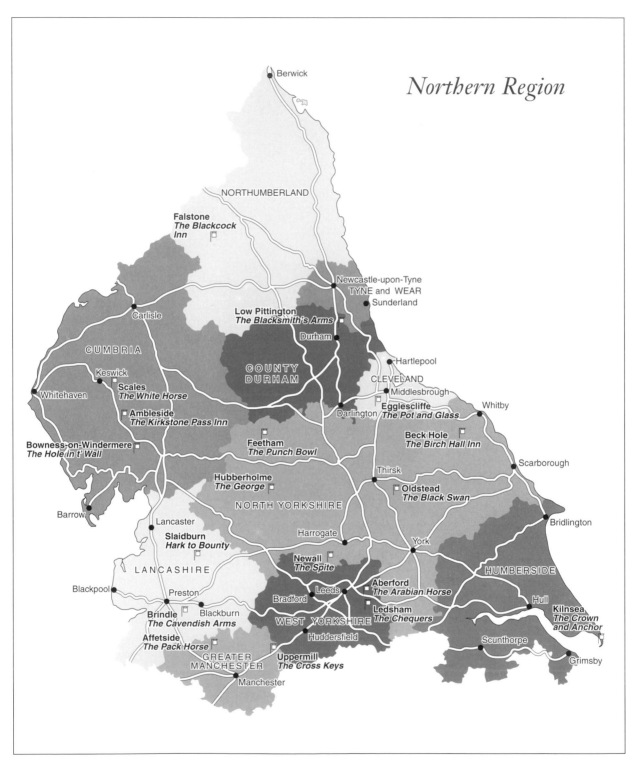

Northern Region

Berwick

NORTHUMBERLAND

Falstone
The Blackcock Inn

Newcastle-upon-Tyne
TYNE and WEAR
Sunderland

Carlisle

Low Pittington
The Blacksmith's Arms

Durham

Hartlepool

CUMBRIA

COUNTY DURHAM

CLEVELAND

Keswick

Middlesbrough

Whitby

Scales
The White Horse

Whitehaven

Ambleside
The Kirkstone Pass Inn

Darlington

Egglescliffe
The Pot and Glass

Beck Hole
The Birch Hall Inn

Scarborough

Bowness-on-Windermere
The Hole in t' Wall

Feetham
The Punch Bowl

Thirsk

Hubberholme
The George

NORTH YORKSHIRE

Oldstead
The Black Swan

Barrow

Bridlington

Lancaster

Harrogate

York

Slaidburn
Hark to Bounty

HUMBERSIDE

LANCASHIRE

Newall
The Spite

Blackpool

Preston

Aberford
The Arabian Horse

Hull

Kilnsea
The Crown and Anchor

Blackburn

Bradford

Leeds

Brindle
The Cavendish Arms

Ledsham
The Chequers

Affetside
The Pack Horse

WEST YORKSHIRE

Scunthorpe

Grimsby

GREATER MANCHESTER

Huddersfield

Uppermill
The Cross Keys

Manchester

Once a bay to shelter in, now an Arabian oasis
for he who dares cross the A1

The Arabian Horse
Aberford, West Yorkshire

Main Street

Getting into Aberford from the A1, if you are approaching it from the north, is not for the fainthearted. Along its entire length there are only a few gaps in the central reservation between the dual carriageways which permit drivers to cut across the oncoming traffic; probably wisely, they are getting fewer all the time. It may mean a detour of several miles to the next junction, but after attempting the Aberford turn I vowed that, in future, I would take the long way round.

This is a particularly busy stretch of the A1, close to the Leeds conurbation and, after sitting in the gap for what seemed like hours, watching the continuous flow of two-lane traffic belting past my bonnet, I would happily have backed on to the southbound carriageway again, had that not been equally suicidal. There came the briefest of lulls and an instant decision; the accelerator went hard down while I prayed that the clutch would not slip and the engine would not stall before I reached the turning on the opposite side.

It was only later, of course, that I read a note in the guidebook which advised gently: 'Best to use A642 junction to leave A1.' The junction is only about three miles further on, and well worth every extra

One of the vast stone fireplaces in the bar, dating back to the days when the Arabian Horse was just a bay.

yard. I still have nightmares about that gap, in which I am sitting there still, marooned for ever between two unbroken and never-ending streams of supersonic traffic.

But having reached the far side, what relief awaits. This turning is the original Great North Road, which used to pass through the middle of Aberford until it was mercifully bypassed, and it is still about twice the width of an ordinary village street. Driving down it after the hurly-burly of the main road is like driving into a ghost town, the broad road empty of traffic, hardly a soul on the pavements, the silence almost eerie. And on the edge of a little green, near an old stone bridge across a quiet stream, stands the Arabian Horse, a sturdy eighteenth-century inn which once catered for stage-coaches, then long-distance motor traffic, now just the locals and the occasional intrepid explorer.

It is an exotic name for a traditional English inn, and it came by it in rather a romantic way. Built in

1770, it was originally called the Bay Horse. Then in 1850, according to one reference book, the landlord of the Bay Horse caught his first glimpse of a thoroughbred Arabian horse. He was a little late in the day, because they were first introduced into Britain during the previous century. Most were crossed with the larger European horses and produced the fast, heavy breed that were ideal for pulling coaches, but three of the Arabian sires which came to Britain were bred only with Arabian mares, and were the ancestors of all the bloodstock in Britain.

The ones which passed through Aberford were on their way north to training stables in Wensleydale, along the old Great North Road. When they reached the village the stream had flooded across the road, and they had to stay there until the water went down. The landlord was so impressed by their beauty that he forthwith changed the name of his inn in their honour.

But little else changed, and this peaceful oasis is Arabian only in name. It still has, for instance, the Bay Horse's great stone fireplaces, one at each end of the lounge bar. The same innovative landlord may also have been responsible for covering one of the fireplaces with an unattractive wooden surround; certainly it was done in Victorian times. Fortunately, the original fireplace was rediscovered during restoration work about twenty years ago; experts say it is almost as old as the inn itself.

Aberford is a pleasant little village which can be enjoyed in peace now that the through traffic is no more than a distant hum in the background. It has another inn, the White Swan, built about the same time as the Arabian Horse but on a larger scale. At one time it was, no doubt, an important coaching inn, and it still has a busy restaurant and overnight accommodation. But the Arabian Horse has managed to retain the homely atmosphere of a village local through the changed circumstances of the village and the change in its own name. As one guidebook says simply: 'It has a comfortable feel.'

Which is more than I can say about that gap on the A1.

First came the Romans, then the packhorses - then the executioner's skull

The Pack Horse
Affetside, Greater Manchester

52 Watling Street

It is called Greater Manchester these days, but Manchester seems in a different world from the little hamlet of Affetside, perched on a hilltop in the open stretch of Lancashire countryside which still survives between Bolton and Bury. It is the highest point on the route the Romans took from Manchester to Ribchester, marching as always in a straight line, regardless of hills or valleys. The old Roman road called Watling Street, now just a quiet lane, passes the front door of the Pack Horse.

Nearby is Affetside Cross which, according to the information in the Pack Horse, is a Roman cross marking the halfway point between London and Edinburgh. Certainly, if you lay a ruler on the map to link the two capitals, the halfway mark is very close to Affetside, but Watling Street was built in AD 79, and the cross has been dated as late seventeenth or early eighteenth century. It is not, in fact, a cross at all, just a round pillar about four feet high, standing on three circular steps, but there is a socket on top where a ball or a crosspiece may have fitted. The official theory is that it marked a halting place for pilgrims, but I prefer the Pack Horse version, except that the present cross is probably a replacement for the original one.

Where the Romans led, the packhorse trains followed, and the Pack Horse was one of the inns which was built to cater for them. Two trails cross at Affetside, and at one time it had two blacksmiths and three inns to cope with all the passing traffic, and plenty of grazing land. The Pack Horse claims to date from 1443, but it is not clear where this date comes from. The earliest indentures for the property are dated 1754, and it is first referred to as the Pack Horse in 1766, when it had a smithy and a cottage.

This must have been the peak period for packhorse trains, and the inn must have done very comfortably until the coming of the turnpike at the end of the eighteenth century. It bypassed the village, and through traffic has taken that route ever since, leaving the old Roman road to become a quiet country lane, and the Pack Horse a quiet country inn.

Well, not completely quiet. It has one regular in the bar who has caused a certain amount of up-heaval over the centuries, according to local legend. His name is George Whewell, and he was the headsman who executed the Duke of Derby in 1651, during the Civil War. But at some stage the executioner must have had a taste of his own medicine, because his body is missing. It is only his skull which looks down on the customers from a shelf behind the bar.

There are some bizarre tales about this skull and what happened when attempts were made to remove it. They were recorded in a pamphlet which was published – entirely in the local dialect – at the turn of this century. One story involves a customer called

One of the 'regulars' at the Pack Horse: George Whewell, the headsman who executed the Duke of Derby at Bolton in 1651, and finished up headless himself. Any attempt to move the skull has dire results, so it stays behind the bar.

Siah Slopp, who got a little drunk and stole the skull as a joke. Later that night the landlord heard a banging on the door, and Siah was there with the skull, pleading with him to take it back.

'When I geet whum,' he said, 'I put th' skull on th' dresser an' went to bed. Aw at once I were wakkened up by summat hittin' me on th' nose. I sit up an' I seed summat bobbin' up an' deawn like a giant moth of a ghostly blue colour, sheinin' like phosphorus an' wi' two greit blazin' red een... I seed that it were a skull, that very skull I'd been sich a foo as to bring away... an' there coom a blood-curdlin' voice saying, "Tak me back to wheer I should be, or I'll tormen thy sowl eaut o' thee!"' So he did.

The landlord told this tale to three customers, who were un-convinced, and one of them decided to test the story for himself. He too stole the skull, and this time he and his two friends were confronted on the road by a ghostly headsman wielding a very solid-looking axe. 'Tak that skull back or I'll chop thy silly yead off,' cried the ghost. 'If I have to ax thee again I'st axe thee wi' this.' Even headless headsmen, it seems, were not above the occasional pun.

The spectral figure followed the trio back to the Pack Horse, and as soon as they handed back the skull to the landlord, it disappeared. 'Yo needn't have any fears that th' ghost ull follow yo any mooar,' they were told. 'Yo're safe neaw it's geet its skull back. Let this be a lesson to yo.'

And it was. How the skull got there in the first place I know not, nor why it is so attached to the Pack Horse, but nobody ever tried to steal it again. On the contrary, I suspect that on very festive evenings, somebody buys it a pint.

Not the easiest place to reach - but the ghostly coachman made it

The Kirkstone Pass Inn
Near Ambleside, Cumbria

On the A592 at Kirkstone Pass

The Kirkstone Pass is the longest and highest of all the Lake District passes, rising to nearly 1,500 feet with gradients of one in four, and the Kirkstone Pass Inn is the highest in the Lakes, one of the most remote and sometimes quite inaccessible. Yet it is still not immune from visitations by ghosts.

In 1993 a lady from Norfolk, a down-to-earth county if ever there was one, wrote to the landlady after a visit, saying that her husband had seen the figure of a ghostly coachman in the bar. Later, when taking a photograph of her in the doorway of the inn, he had seen the figure standing behind her, putting its hands on her shoulders. When the film was developed, the photograph seemed to indicate a whole family of ghosts.

It did not stop there. While having a meal in the bar, she wrote, her husband saw the figure again. The coachman said to him: 'Ask her to take it down,' indicating a hazel branch over the table. Having seen the photograph, she was now writing to the landlady asking for his wish to be granted.

The branch was duly taken down, and the coachman was not seen again at the inn – not that he had been seen before. But in 1995 there was a curious sequel. The family returned to say the coachman had followed them home to Norfolk, and various manifestations had occurred. Lights unaccountably dipped, windows were tapped, the family dog refused to sleep in its customary spot on the porch. The fifteen-year-old daughter said she came to look upon the coachman as an old friend. So they checked the family records, and found there was indeed a coachman ancestor, Benjamin George Webster, who died in the 1890s. Having consulted various psychic experts they returned to the Kirkstone Pass Inn, and by some procedure they did not divulge they managed to shed Mr Webster. Did they leave him behind at the inn, or has his spirit finally departed? Who can tell?

Actually, there was a time when coachmen did frequent the Kirkstone Pass Inn. The front part of

Kirkstone Pass

the inn goes back much further than the coaching days; it was built in 1496 by a priest from Troutbeck, as a refuge for travellers and roadmen, and there are plans for celebrating the inn's 500th anniversary in 1996. Then in 1793, when coaches began to tackle the difficult climb up the pass from Windermere to reach Ullswater and Penrith on the far side, the rear of the inn was extended to provide more accommodation, and it was called The Travellers' Rest. There are still four-posters in the three bedrooms, though not, I suspect, the originals.

Nobody knows any stories to associate deceased coachmen with the inn, but there are other sadly romantic moments in its history. Mark Atkinson and his son Ion kept the inn during the first half of this century, and when they died their ashes were scattered on Caudle Fell, which rises behind it. There is a cairn on the fell in their memory. Ion's wife Renée was involved in a car accident and badly injured while negotiating the difficult minor road

that climbs from Ambleside to the inn. A poem was discovered which gave the accident an added poignancy. It was possibly written by an admirer of one of the Atkinson family, who lived in Ambleside and would have used that road:

If I were a lover and loved a lass
Who lived at the top of Kirkstone Pass
I would swear by all that's true and tried
While I abode in Ambleside,
To love her and love her for ever and ever –
But go up and see her? Never, oh never.

I can understand how he felt about that road, and how Mrs Atkinson fell a victim to it. I drove up it in ideal summer conditions, but even so I held my breath at every corner – and it was worse coming down. In the winter it is often impassable, and even the main road through the pass gets blocked. Normally, in spite of the frequently hazardous conditions, the inn closes only on Christmas Day throughout the year, but in a December blizzard in 1990 it had to shut down because of damage from the snow. Even so, it looked after eleven stranded travellers for three days until the road was reopened. That year the snow was around from October until May, which is exceptional even for the Kirkstone Pass.

Fortunately, the inn is largely self-sufficient. It gets its electricity from two diesel generators, and water is collected from the fells and fed into tanks in the roof, much as it was centuries ago. But technology has lent a hand: the water is now purified by an ultraviolet lamp.

The bar itself is quite small and cosy, ideal in the winter months, but in the summer the customers spill out to the picnic tables and benches across the road, where they can enjoy the stunning views and watch the walkers struggling up the hillsides. The large car park is often full, like most car parks in the Lake District during the summer, and the knowledgeable prefer the Kirkstone Pass Inn in the winter. After all, there are worse places to get snowed up – and you might have a spectral coachman for company.

A pint, some jam, a book of stamps – and a world champion

The Birch Hall Inn
Beck Hole, North Yorkshire

Near the village green

Beck Hole sounds more like a crevasse than a village, but I doubt you could find a better hole to go to, and to the Tommy trapped in the shell-hole in that famous First World War cartoon, this hole would have been heaven. It is tucked away in the heart of the North Yorkshire Moors, and the pleasantest way to approach it is on foot along the disused railway track from Goathland. The countryside around it is wild and rugged, dotted with prehistoric earthworks and standing stones, divided here and there by deep valleys with spectacular waterfalls. One of these falls, Thomason Fosse, is featured in a painting on the front wall of the Birch Hall Inn.

The Birch Hall is not just an inn; it is the village shop and post office as well, a delightful Victorian throwback which I hope will survive the steady elimination of our village sub-post offices. As it is, you can buy a pot of jam and a book of stamps as well as a pint of beer, which is served through a hatch into the small and simply furnished bar. Customers are likely to spill out on to the little lane, to sit on the benches, or stand on the narrow bridge to look at the stream which flows past the inn, or climb the steps to the steep little garden behind.

The homely little inn hardly seems like a centre for international sportsmen, but the photographs on the wall give a clue. They feature members of the Beck Hole Quoit Club, which uses the inn as its headquarters. Each year they take part in the world quoits championships, and the club has produced at least one world champion, Mr Colin Gray, who gained the title in 1990. He actually lives at nearby Grosmont and has a milk round in Whitby, but at that time – and he may be still – he was captain of the Beck Hole club. His prizes inc-luded a handsome trophy, which I hope was put on display at the Birch Hall for a year, and a hundred cans of beer, which I doubt survived quite as long.

The inn is the village shop and post office as well. You can buy stamps and sweets with your pint of beer.

It should be said that for these world championships the 'world' stops at Whitby in one direction, and around Darlington in the other. This type of quoits is a peculiarly North Country affair, played mostly in North Yorkshire, but it is an ancient game dating back to the fifteenth century, and it is still taken very seriously in places like Beck Hole.

Do not confuse it with the gentle game of deck quoits played with rings of plaited rope. These rings are made of solid metal and weigh anything up to nine pounds. This could well be how the American game of horseshoe-throwing began, and indeed the original Yorkshire-style quoits were made from two horseshoes, welded together by the local blacksmith. The modern ones are custom-built and not quite so lethal, but if misdirected they can still inflict a nasty

blow on an unwary spectator's ankle.

The Beck Hole quoit pitch is on the village green, not far from the Birch Hall. It has two iron pins, or hobs, about eighteen yards apart on a clay base. The pins are only an inch or so above the ground, unlike the taller ones in the American version, and although the idea is obviously to throw the quoit over the pin, the trick is not to be the first to do so, because if your opponent lands one on top it is cancelled out – and the pin is not high enough to accommodate a third. The best opening throw, I am told, is a 'gater', with the quoit landing on edge in front of the pin and blocking it from your opponent. Then with luck you can knock it on to the hob with the second and final quoit.

All subtle stuff, a battle of wits as well as skill. Feelings can run high, players can come to blows – and that can be unpleasant if they hap-pen to be holding a quoit at the time. But such occasions, I am ass-ured, are rare; a little gentle barr-acking is as far as it usually goes.

In recent years the sport has become so popular that an indoor league has been formed, so it can be played all the year round. But Beck Hole has yet to acquire an indoor pitch; indeed, when Colin Gray won the championship there was only one such pitch in the country, but it was conveniently close to his milk round in Whitby, and his extra winter practice may have given him the edge.

Most Beck Hole players, however, spend their winters at the Birch Hall, no doubt discussing tactics for the next season. It has not always been their headquarters; they used to meet at an inn on the green, the Lord Nelson. That is now a private house, but its connection with quoits has not been forgotten; guess what it has for a door-knocker.

A thirsty blacksmith, a potty ceiling, and
a fight fan called Charles Dickens

The Hole in t' Wall
Bowness-on-Windermere, Cumbria

Lowside

First, a word of warning. Windermere is one of the most popular lakes in the Lake District, Bowness is one of the most popular tourist centres on Windermere, and the Hole in t' Wall, in spite of its rather obscure position away from the main shopping centre, is rapidly becoming one of the most popular hostelries in Bowness-on-Windermere. It all adds up to a very busy bar during the tourist season, and the best time to visit it is when the holiday-makers have gone, and you can enjoy in peace and comfort the rather special atmosphere and the curious attributes of Bowness's oldest inn.

Its proper name, I gather, is the New Hall Inn, but it has not been called that since the blacksmith next door had a bright idea for speeding up his supply of ale. Hammering horseshoes into shape in the heat of the smithy was thirsty work, and much of his time was spent in nipping round to the inn next door for another pot of ale. He suggested to the landlord that this process could be streamlined if a hole were made in the wall between their establishments. The landlord, no doubt appreciating that this would enable his best customer to become even better, readily agreed, and the Hole in t' Wall was born.

The hole no longer fulfils its original function, of course. The smithy has gone, its site has been absorbed by the inn, and its giant bellows now decorate the bar. But the carefully preserved orifice is still an object of curiosity, and the present landlord will be happy – for the umpteenth time – to point it out to you.

Its story is as familiar to the locals as the one behind that other curiously named inn a few miles away near Coniston Water, the Drunken Duck – beer seeped into the duckpond, the landlady found the ducks lying about looking lifeless, though they were only legless, and started preparing them for the pot. They came round in time, no longer legless but now featherless, and she knitted them woolly jumpers until the feathers grew again.

But while the drunken ducks are the main talking point for visitors at the Drunken Duck, there is more to the Hole in t' Wall than a hole in the wall. In addition to the standard display of farm implements and horse brasses in the bar,

The hole in 't wall in the Hole in 't Wall, where the beer was passed through to the blacksmith next door. He may have needed the odd chamber-pot as well.

for instance, one ceiling is devoted to that other essential feature of rural life until not so long ago, the chamber-pot. There is an amazing assortment of potties – a pot-pourri, one might say – hanging from the beams. Like the blacksmith's hole, they are no longer required to perform their original function; the inn has all modern conveniences.

It also has a third notable feature, a connection with Charles Dickens. Oh no, I hear you cry, not another inn where Dickens ate, or slept, or wrote half a novel, or incorporated it in *Pickwick Papers*! No indeed. This is an inn which he visited after attending a local sporting meeting in 1857, and paid his

respects to a remarkable wrestler-landlord, Thomas Longmire. I do not immediately think of Charles Dickens as a sporting gent, let alone a wrestling fan, so this visit shows him in a rather different light.

The details of Thomas Longmire's wrestling prowess are set out proudly on the front of the inn, together with his portrait. He was the champion wrestler of England, it says, and held no fewer than 174 wrestling belts. That is a spectacular achievement in itself – did he manage to wear them simultaneously, one wonders – but it becomes all the more astonishing when one checks the records.

Professional wrestling did not begin until 1874, so Mr Longmire was presumably an amateur and probably, in view of his location, an exponent of Cumberland wrestling. But according to the *Guinness Book of Records*, the best performances in Cumberland wrestling were by a Mr Baddeley and a Mr Bacon, each of whom won just six titles. In standard Greco-Roman wrestling, the highest number of titles won by anybody is ten. All three of these records seem mere flashes in the pan compared with those 174 belts.

No matter. Perhaps there were other championships in Thomas Longmire's day which Mr Guinness missed, and what was good enough for Charles Dickens is good enough for me. He was cautiously impressed by his host – he warily described him as 'a quiet-looking giant' – and was obviously not going to dispute the number of belts he had won, and nor did any other customer, I imagine, during the eight years that Mr Longmire presided at the inn. They needed an argument with the wrestler-landlord of the Hole in t' Wall about as much as a hole in t' head.

A catholic martyr, Royalist raiders - will they join the Saxons in the bar?

The Cavendish Arms
Brindle, Lancashire

Sandy Lane

For a village which is only three miles from the junction of the M6 and M61 motorways, and lies between the heavily built-up areas of Chorley and Blackburn, Brindle has managed to retain a remarkably rural flavour. This is even hunting country; one of the oldest hunts in England, founded in the reign of James I, comes this way twice a year. In the usual village tradition, the Cavendish Arms is close by St James's Church, and at times over the centuries the landlord has also been a churchwarden. There is another link too; if you are looking for stained glass in considerable quantity, you will find nearly as much in the inn as in the church.

One has to say it is not quite so old; the brewery installed it in the 1930s. But the story it illustrates goes back even earlier than the church, to the victory over the invading Danes by 'the golden-haired Athelstan', grandson of Alfred the Great and the first monarch of all England.

The stained glass is not only in the windows, it is in the wooden partitions which divide the bars of the Cavendish Arms into discreet little nooks and crannies. There are medieval scenes in the glass too, but it is Athelstan's victory which provides the main theme, at the bloody battle of Brunanburg in AD 937.

Nobody is quite sure where Brunanburg was, but the brewery makes a helpful guess. 'Brindle and its immediate neighbourhood is likely to be where the battle was fought, being near the fords and pass of the Ribble, and having a commanding position on the hills in the district.' This seems to be confirmed by the discovery in 1840 at nearby Cuerdale Ford of a chest full of silver coins and ornaments, believed to have been left behind by the Danes as they fled to the Ribble estuary to catch a fast boat to Dublin.

Another likely relic from the battle is across the road from the Cavendish Arms in the church-yard. It is a stone coffin which may have contained one of the more distinguished casualties. The church's unusual treasures, though, are inside. It may have competition from the Cavendish Arms in terms of stained glass, but it must be first in the field with fonts. It has five of them, which could be a record for one village church. They range from the twelfth to the nineteenth centuries, and one is believed to be associated with St Helen's Well (the church was dedicated to St Helen before the Refor-mation), which was thought to have healing powers. The notes from the brewery, incidentally, confirm that there is something special about the local springs: 'A pin thrown into the water appears to defy rust and retains its original lustre.'

The bar has almost as much stained glass as the church next door. The main windows illustrate the Saxon victory over the Danes in a battle nearby, but there are medieval scenes too.

The Reformation brought other changes to Brindle, as well as a new saint for the church. Until then the Roman Catholic Gerard family had been Lords of the Manor and patrons of the benefice, but in 1582, in order to pay for a member of the family to be released from the Tower of London, they sold both titles, along with the village, to the Cavendish family, ancestors of the present Duke of Devonshire. Confusingly, the inn was called the Devonshire Arms before reverting to the family name.

In spite of the Reformation many people in Brindle, as elsewhere, held fast to their old religion, and the village has its own Roman Catholic martyr, Father Edmund Arrowsmith. He was a youthful member of the Gerard family, and returned to Brindle in 1613 after being ordained in France. He found plenty of sympathisers to shelter him, and held clandestine services and heard confessions until he was eventually captured. He was hanged, drawn and quartered at Lancaster Castle, but his severed hand was treasured by his family for many generations, and is now preserved in a church dedicated to his memory near Skelmersdale.

I must record one more violent incident in Brindle's history. During the Civil War Cromwell's troops camped in the fields near the village, which happened to be strongly Royalist. Some of the local youths tried to steal their horses, but they were caught in the act and nearly all of them were either killed or unpleasantly injured.

I mention these unhappy events only because, if the brewers intend to provide another set of stained-glass windows at the Cavendish Arms, there is no shortage of local material.

A peaceful rural oasis - except for the clerics' knees-up in the cellar

The Pot and Glass
Egglescliffe, Cleveland

Church Road

When the promoters of the Stockton and Darlington Railway met at the George and Dragon in Yarm to plan their new project, they could hardly realise the difference that would be made to the area by their railway and the others that followed. Yarm was the most important town on the Tees until the railways helped to industrialise the area. Stockport and Middlesbrough almost merged into each other, Yarm acquired a sprawl of suburbs, and in due course its skyline was dominated by the forty-three arches of the railway viaduct across the river.

Just one rural corner survived, one of the few places where you can look down on that viaduct instead of up at it. Take a little turning off the busy built-up road between Yarm and Stockton, and at the far end of the lane you will emerge on to a peaceful triangular village green, flanked by houses and cottages representing the best of building styles between the sixteenth and twentieth centuries, with the eleventh-century parish church at one end. This is Egglescliffe – not to be confused with Eaglescliffe, which is a nearby industrialised suburb of Stockton – and tucked away beside the church, with a splendid view over that viaduct and the roof-tops of Yarm, is the Pot and Glass.

It is a totally unexpected and most welcome find, a traditional village inn set in a rural oasis. Instead of expanding like the adjoining towns it has actually shrunk. It used to have several cottage industries, from weaving to strawberry-growing, and there was even a paper-mill employing forty people. But the mill closed, then had an ignominious period as a vinegar factory until it was demolished in 1973, and if any cottages still produce cloth or strawberries, they keep them for themselves.

It may have been a matter for regret when all this happened, but the ultimate result is all to the good. Egglescliffe is now a highly desirable haven for those who enjoy relaxing in peace and quiet, away from all the traffic and the noise and bustle at the other end of the lane.

The handsome carved bar front is the work of a previous landlord. He did not actually carve it, just made it from an old sideboard.

Throughout all this, the Pot and Glass has remained almost unchanged, except for its name. Years ago it was called the Pot and Pipe, but perhaps it succumbed to the anti-smoking lobby. The landlord has resisted the temptation to modernise the interior by knocking down the dividing wall between the bar and the next room to make more space. 'The customers don't want changes,' he said, and the customers are right. The only major alteration in the last half-century has been the installation of the handsome carved bar front, made from an old sideboard which a previous tenant acquired in a house sale.

There are, of course, a tunnel story and a ghost story, though nobody is actually sure of either. The tunnel was supposed to run from the cellar to the church, so that either the priest could seek shelter in time of persecution, or he could nip through for a discreet pot of ale without being spotted by his parishioners, depending which version you believe. But it was also used, so it is said, by nuns as well as priests, and strange sounds of nocturnal revelry have been heard, complete with the strains of a ghostly organ. One group of carpet-fitters who were working overnight in the bar to avoid disrupting the customers during opening hours are said to have fled in terror when they heard the unmistakable sounds of an ecclesiastical knees-up down below.

One Egglescliffe rector had more important matters on his mind during the Civil War than sneaking a pint at the Pot and Glass. He was a staunch Royalist, and the story goes that he was asked by the colonel commanding the King's troops in Stockport to demolish the northern arch of the bridge across the river and replace it with a drawbridge, to deter the advancing Roundheads.

The bridge was built by Bishop Skirlaw of Durham in 1400, and perhaps the colonel felt that only another cleric could decently knock it down. The rector duly did so, and each night he went down to the river and pulled up the drawbridge, so nobody could slip across in the dark.

The ploy could not have been entirely successful and, in fact, Cromwell himself is said to have crossed the river and visited the village. That was a good time, I imagine, for the rector to dive into the tunnel and have a few quiet beers in the cellar of the Pot and Glass.

The last inn in England? Robert Bruce would call that debatable

The Blackcock Inn
Falstone, Northumberland

On road through village

In the English countryside it is customary for buildings to change and multiply, while the basic landscape stays much the same. In the area around Falstone it is the basic landscape which has changed, while buildings like the Blackcock Inn have remained. If any of the regulars who drank there before the First World War returned for a nostalgic pint today, they would find the scenery around the village quite unrecognisable. I need only mention the name Kielder, and you will know why.

That war highlighted the fact that Britain needed to produce more of its own timber. The Kielder Forest was the result – 280 square miles of former heath and moorland, now covered by Scots pine, Sitka spruce and Japanese larch. It is not quite the largest man-made forest in Europe, but it comes pretty close. Actually, it is a combination of four forests, and Falstone gives its name to one.

Then came the need for more water as well as more wood, and the Kielder Reservoir was opened by the Queen in 1982. No doubt about claiming the record in this case; it is definitely Europe's largest man-made lake. Between the two of them, the Kielder Forest and Kielder Water have turned this corner of Northumberland into a Switzerland without mountains, which attracts tourists by the thousand, but is, in reality, a vast open-air factory, producing over a hundred thousand tonnes of timber a year and 250 million gallons of water a day.

Throughout this extraordinary transformation,

Falstone and the Blackcock Inn have managed to survive almost unchanged. The village has been luckier than some; the little mining village of Plashett, for example, where millions of tons of rock were extracted to build the reservoir's dam, is now under the surface of the water. Historic buildings like Kielder Castle, which did keep their roofs above water, were affected in other ways; the castle, built in the eighteenth century as a shooting lodge for the

*The resident dog enjoys the warmth
of the fireside at the Blackcock.*

Duke of Northumberland, is now partly a visitors' centre and partly, as one writer rather superciliously describes it, 'a palatial working men's club'.

At Falstone, however, only the views have been altered. It lies below the massive dam wall, which is two-thirds of a mile long and nearly two hundred feet high – not the sort of landmark you can ignore. But in spite of the influx of tourists, and the holiday cabins which have sprung up in the area, Falstone retains its identity as a traditional Northumbrian village, and the Blackcock Inn, although enlarged over the years, still prides itself on being a traditional Northumbrian inn.

This area, after all, has survived dramatic changes before, not in appearance but in allegiance. Falstone was the capital of the Upper North Tyne, in the heart

of what became known as the Debatable Lands. The debate was about whether they belonged to Scotland or England, and Falstone often found itself involved in the argument and the fighting which went with it. The name is actually derived from the Saxon word *fausten*, meaning 'stronghold', and it quite often was.

This was the era when Robert Bruce declared himself king of an independent Scotland, and having driven the last English troops out of his country at the Battle of Bannockburn he spent the next dozen years fighting on the English side of the border, in the Debatable Lands.

It should have all ended in 1328 when the English signed a treaty recognising Scottish independence, but old habits die hard. The Scots regularly came on the rampage long after Bruce's death, and the Debatable Lands continued to change hands. The last time Falstone found itself with a Scottish address was in 1357, but more than thirty years later the Scots were still trying to get it back again, and in that they very nearly succeeded when they scored a notable victory at Otterburn, only ten miles away.

When the Scots were not scrapping with the English, the local clans were scrapping with each other. This was the last district to accept the King's Peace after the Union of Scotland and England in 1603, under the king with the confusing numbers, James VI of Scotland and James I of England.

Nobody is quite sure if the Blackcock Inn existed in those turbulent days. They can only say that 'it is no doubt of a very great age'. Certainly, until the end of the last century it was still thatched, and the oldest part of the building, the bar, which was originally single-storey, is still heated by an old-fashioned black-leaded range. But these days the accommodation runs to en-suite bedrooms, a stair lift and Sky television.

Like many another inn along the borders with Scotland and Wales, the Blackcock has laid claim to being 'The Last Inn in England'. That may well be true, but the older locals will no doubt point out that there was a time when such a claim was, well, debatable.

A toast to the host – in the 'deadhouse' on the hill

The Punch Bowl
Feetham, North Yorkshire

On the B6270 in Swaledale

Feetham and Low Road are two Swaledale villages which adjoin each other so closely that it is difficult for a stranger to appreciate where one starts and the other ends, though the locals maintain that they are two quite individual communities. Similarly, it does not seem too clear whether the Punch Bowl is in Feetham or Low Road; different guidebooks put it in different places. However, there are a great many Low Roads in England, and only

one Feetham; to avoid confusion Feetham it shall be.

Neither village has made much of an impact on history. One or other of them can claim to be the home of Thomas Armstrong, the Yorkshire novelist who based his book *Adam Brunskill* on Swaledale's lead-mining industry in the last century. But he lived on the south side of the River Swale, and both villages are based on the north, so one can argue about that too. The nearest village on his side of the river is called Crackpot, and if I had been Mr Armstrong I would have chosen that as my address without hesitation. The name is not intended to sound eccentric – it actually derives from old Norse and means 'pothole of the crows' – but it would look quite splendid on headed notepaper.

Feetham may not sound such fun, but it does have a strange tale to tell, and at the centre of the tale is the Punch Bowl, perched above the road that winds up the dale beside the river, and with a magnificent view from its terrace across to the hills on what I shall always think of as the Crackpot side. This was where funeral processions used to spend the night on their way to the nearest consecrated ground at Grinton, along what came to be known as the Swaledale Corpse Trail.

They used other hostelries too on the twelve-mile trail from Keld, at the top of the dale, to Grinton church. There was a beer tavern called the Travellers' Rest at the little hamlet of Calvert Houses, and an inn called the Queen's Head at Muker, where special 'funeral mugs' were kept on standby for the mourners. But there is no sign of the Travellers' Rest today, and the Queen's Head became a private house after the First World War. The Punch Bowl is the only surviving inn from those days, and above it on the hillside are the remains of the 'deadhouse', the medieval mortuary where the bodies were left overnight in their wicker coffins while the pallbearers and the mourners spent the night at the inn.

This was not too tedious or expensive for them, because it was the custom that, throughout the journey to the church at Grinton, everyone in the cortège was a guest of the deceased. Special biscuits

Mourners and pallbearers on the Corpse Trail used this door to find refreshment and rest on their way to the churchyard at the end of the dale. It has now been moved inside the inn to preserve it.

and wine were distributed before the procession set out from Keld, and the hospitality continued until the two-day procession was over. The Punchbowl was the main overnight stop, and it was not unknown for two funeral parties to coincide. On one occasion, so it is said, the two processions deposited their burdens in the deadhouse, then repaired to the Punch Bowl together. Next morning, a little bleary-eyed, they climbed the hill and gathered up their wicker baskets. It was only when the bodies were taken out at the churchyard for burial in their linen shrouds that they found they had been carrying the wrong ones.

The Punch Bowl lost most of this passing – or passing-on – trade in 1580, when a church was built at Muker, further up the dale. Funeral parties no longer had to make the long trek to Grinton. The only reminder at the inn of those early days is the elaborately studded front door through which the mourners passed on their way to the bar. It has now been moved inside to help preserve it.

It is just possible to make out the line of the original roof gable of the inn, but the building has been much extended over the years and now incorporates a tea-room, a small shop, and facilities for hiring bicycles and caving equipment. The bar, however, is still a snug and convivial venue, and although it is very much geared to bar lunches during the holiday season, it is still possible to enjoy a quiet beer at the counter, and visualise those funeral parties getting their strength and their spirits up for the last few miles to the graveside.

I hope they always remembered to toast their hosts, lying in their wicker baskets in the deadhouse at the top of the hill.

Parliament sits round a candle on the bar – and a hot poker to keep order

The George
Hubberholme, North Yorkshire

By the bridge over the Wharfe

Hubberholme's admirers have ranged from Hubba the Berserker, King of the Vikings, who gave it his name, to J. B. Priestley, king of the Yorkshire writers, who called it 'one of the smallest and pleasantest places in the world', and asked for his ashes to be buried in the churchyard. At the ceremony his son Tom, with a touch of his father's fluency, said of this remote Wharfedale hamlet: 'Here there is space and beauty. The elements seem to be balanced, the earth seems to touch the sky.'

It is not always as idyllic as that. The Wharfe is only a stream at this point but it is inclined to flood. On one memorable occasion the water rose so high in the church that fish were found swimming in the pews. The weather can be wild and wet too, as any number of sodden walkers can testify. But in the summer one can understand the enthusiasm of the Priestleys and of locals like the Falshaw family, who have lived there for five hundred years.

They may make their mark elsewhere – one built England's second railway, from Leeds to Selby, then became Lord Provost of Edinburgh, another designed the Victoria Falls Bridge over the Zambezi, commemorated in one of the church windows. But they never lose their affection for Hubberholme, and one can imagine the nostalgia felt by a Falshaw serving in the Far East in the last war, who unexpectedly heard the sound of the River Wharfe flowing under the bridge at Hubberholme in a radio broadcast. The presenter was interviewing the vicar, and hung his microphone over the parapet to get an authentic sound effect. The far-flung Falshaw must have recognised it immediately.

Hubberholme is little more than the church, the bridge and the George, forming the smallest conservation area in Yorkshire. Hubba the Berserker was too early for a drink at the George, but it was Priestley's favourite inn, and is still as he knew it – a white-painted stone building with its back turned inhospitably towards the road, but the interior warm and inviting. There are two rooms at different levels with low, blackened ceilings (one of them held up by a couple of tree trunks), copper-topped tables, an open kitchen range – and a candle burning on the bar.

The candle always burns on the bar, a reminder of the annual letting of the Poor Pasture. An auction is held in the bar, and the pasture is let to the last bidder before the candle goes out.

It is the candle which gives the clue to the George's link with the church and the annual ceremony it involves, the letting of the Poor Pasture at the Hubberholme Parliament. The inn belonged to the church until 1965, and the sixteen-acre field behind it, the Poor Pasture, still does; it is held in trust for the poor of the parish. Each year, originally on New Year's Day but now on the first Monday in January, the Hubberholme Parliament meets at the George to let the field by 'candle auction'.

The vicar, his churchwardens and the outgoing tenant, known as the Lords, meet in one room, the rest of the gathering, the Commons, go in the other. Then a fresh candle is lit on the bar, the Lords join the Commons, and the auction begins, with the vicar presiding. Bidding continues until the candle goes out, and the land goes to the final bidder. It can take up to eight hours, depending on the candle, with the ale, of course, flowing throughout. I imagine that by the end of the evening the bidding is not only fast and furious, but frequently incoherent.

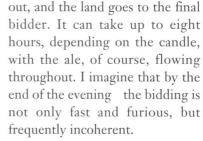

A previous landlady ensured that it never became too furious. The redoubtable Grace Pawson adopted as her badge of office a heated poker, which she brandished under the nose of any potential trouble-maker. It always worked.

Not that Grace was a spoilsport. She was quite content to allow celebrations to continue indefinitely so long as the customers behaved. Two local families once got together for a celebration which lasted six days and nights; Grace was in charge during the night and her maid took over the bar – and possibly the poker – during the day.

The young couple currently running the George have not had to resort to such drastic disciplinary methods. When I met them they had been there for only four months, after the inn had been closed for a spell, and while they were busy getting things going again they also had high hopes and plans for the future. But I am sure the atmosphere will not change – and that candle will be alight on the end of the bar.

Party time on the head that wrecked a thousand ships; never mind 2075

The only modern feature in the bar is the big picture window, which gives customers a better chance to birdwatch in comfort.

The Crown and Anchor
Kilnsea, Humberside

Main Street

It is a bleak, lonely road out to Kilnsea and Spurn Head, and Kilnsea looked bleak and lonely too when I drove out there one rainy Saturday afternoon. The day had started badly. I had visited two Humberside inns which had looked promising on paper, but were disappointing in reality. Both looked run-down and depressing, the stories attached to them failed to stand up, and, unbelievably, neither of them served bar meals on a Saturday – a common practice, I gather, in that untouristy area of

Humberside. So I arrived at Kilnsea in the early afternoon, fully expecting the Crown and Anchor to be already closed and deserted.

Kilnsea itself certainly was, and from a distance the Crown and Anchor at the far end of the village looked much the same – rainswept, windswept and miserable. Having started badly, the day was falling away. But amazingly the lights were on, the car park was full, and through the windows I could see people drinking and chatting and actually looking cheerful. Against all the odds, the Crown and Anchor was jumping!

It was an astonishing and most refreshing discovery in this unlikely setting. The exterior of the inn is not exceptional, and the back of it features quite a lot of corrugated iron, but inside it is a splendidly traditional and unspoilt coastal inn, one bar decorated with ship's lanterns and nautical caps and sea-going mementoes, the other festooned with row upon row of brass spoons and jugs and ladles hanging from the beams, the walls of both covered with decorative plates and old framed notices – 'The Joys of Whiskey', 'The Horse's Prayer' and the like. Only the Lord Nelson knocker on the front door seems a little bogus.

Both bars were packed with people, enjoying themselves without the assistance of blasting music or obtrusive fruit machines. No wonder Kilnsea was deserted; everyone must have been at the Crown and Anchor. And what's more, bar meals were still being served.

While I was enjoying mine, I enquired discreetly if I had arrived in the middle of a party. Not at all, I was told; this was a fairly average Saturday. But there was going to be a party that evening – and indeed in one bar the chairs and tables were already being moved in preparation. In the process, one of the decorative plates was knocked off the wall, and a piece of it came off. One of the helpers wedged the piece back into place, hung up the plate again, and beamed at me cheerfully. 'Happens all the time,' she said. 'Can I get you another beer?'

Spurn Head is not usually associated with such conviviality, more with storms and shipwrecks. The three-mile spit of sand and shingle has had its ups and downs over the centuries – literally. The sea has washed away parts of it, then washed it back again. There used to be a busy medieval port on the Head called Ravenser Odd, but its oddness went beyond its name, because the early map-makers moved it about to different sites at different times until it eventually disappeared. The Spurn Head lighthouses moved too, about half a dozen times, to avoid the encroaching sea. Trinity House finally gave up the struggle and closed the last one in 1985.

The moving shoals and treacherous currents have caused countless wrecks, and not surprisingly Spurn Head has one of the oldest-established lifeboat stations in the country. This may have accounted for some of the crush in the bar. A number of the regulars looked like lifeboatmen, or coastguards, or both. There was a sprinkling of campers from the nearby caravan site, and probably some 'twitchers' too, because most of Spurn Head is now a nature reserve, and the big picture windows at the front of the inn give a magnificent view across the ten square miles of mud flats which are visited by thousands of birds. Those modern picture windows, however, are the only obvious alterations to accommodate the tourist trade. The Crown and Anchor is mainly geared to preserving the traditions of an old-fashioned village 'local'.

So far as I know, there are no strange stories about the inn. I find it strange enough that such a congenial and civilised establishment exists at all in such an isolated and apparently inhospitable location, away from the popular holiday routes, hardly mentioned in any of the guides. It is rather salutary to drive a little further along the road that runs past the Crown and Anchor, out along the Head. The next house you come to bears the notice: 'Built 1847, 534 yards from the sea. Rebuilt 1994, 190 yards from the sea...'

According to my calculations, at that rate it will disappear in 2075. Drink up, chaps!

*Never on Sundays - because madam saw
something nasty near the woodshed*

The Chequers
Ledsham, West Yorkshire

Claypit Lane

If you find the Chequers mentioned in any of the guidebooks you may notice nothing unusual about the entry, until you come to the last line in small type. At the end of 'Hours of opening' are the words 'Closed on Sundays'.

If the Chequers were in some parts of Wales, this would come as no surprise. Sunday opening is still something of a novelty across the border, and around Porthmadog, for instance, where they can sell only

to residents on Sundays, the pubs are still unlikely to open at all. But in England it is rare to find an inn with only a six-day licence, and in West Yorkshire the Chequers is unique.

This is not the decision of the police or the licensee. Ledsham is an estate village, part of the Ledston Estate; the names are similar, but the two villages are a couple of miles apart. Times may have changed in the rest of West Yorkshire, and in the

Ledsham area Garforth and Castleford have grown into substantial towns, and the Great North Road, now the dual carriageway of the A1, skirts the parish boundary. But in Ledsham itself some things have not changed since Pontefract Castle was a Royalist stronghold during the Civil War. The Royalists surrendered, the townsfolk petitioned for the castle to be pulled down, and Oliver Cromwell's men, experts in such matters, reduced it to ruins – but in Ledsham feudalism survived.

One of the network of little rooms off the main bar. They now incorporate the former undertaker's and smithy next door.

It was still surviving in Victorian times, when an unfortunate incident occurred at the Chequers, and the repercussions are still being felt. It was presumably serving beer on Sundays in those days, because the story goes that a party of Sunday revellers were served more than they could hold. Instead of using the available amenities, or even retiring discreetly behind the woodshed, the hapless fellows relieved themselves in the garden in full view of the road – and under the eyes, it transpired, of the Lady of the Manor. Offended and appalled, she ordered the inn to be closed – and it has been closed on Sundays ever since.

The licensee, understandably, is not inclined to be drawn on this subject. I would only say from a customer's point of view that it is sad we cannot enjoy a drink at the Chequers on a Sunday, as at any other village local, because it really is a delightful little inn.

Ledsham is indeed an attractive and remarkably peaceful village, considering the proximity of the A1; perhaps we have the Estate to thank for that as well. It is not easy to identify the Chequers as you drive in, because its walls are covered in dense creeper which is doing its best to obscure the inn sign as well as the inn. Inside there is a network of little rooms around the central serving counter, and leading off one of these is an extra seating area which used to be the smithy next door. The smithy was also an undertaker's, but there is nothing funereal about the furnishings now; it is as cheerful and cosy as the rest of the inn.

The only slightly sobering touch is a fading photograph of children from the local orphanage lined up outside the church in their mob caps – another throwback to feudal times, perhaps, when only church-going was permissible on a Sunday. But one has to say that the children look quite happy about it.

Although the A1 passes so close, it is no easier to get off it to reach Ledsham than it is to reach the Arabian Horse at Aberford, six miles further north. Castleford and Garforth are not far away, but when I was there most of the customers seemed local. Another visiting writer confirms this view: 'There is a local feel about it... and it is just far enough away from Leeds to be spared the great bores of today talking about themselves.' There speaks a southerner, perhaps – or a Sheffield man?

The garden is particularly pleasant, terraced on two levels with plenty of flowers and shrubs. It was here, I presume, that the foolhardy revellers disgraced themselves in front of the Lady of the Manor. If she returned today, and saw the extremely civilised way in which the Chequers is conducted, would she relent?

A Blacksmith's Arms actually run by a blacksmith –
who liked to stay black

The Blacksmith's Arms
Low Pittington, County Durham

Station Road

Let's face it, Low Pittington is not a picture-postcard village, and it is not surrounded by the prettiest of countryside. This was part of the East Durham coalfield, where the opencast mining, which had started in a small way with the Romans, developed in the early nineteenth century into deep mining on a massive scale. Lord Londonderry was the man mainly responsible. His vast Rainton collieries, only a mile or so away, covered the best part – or, more accurately, the worst part – of four thousand acres, and it was he who built the harbour at Seaham to transport his coal around the coast.

These days East and West Rainton straddle the boundary between County Durham and Tyne & Wear, one on each side of it, but in Lord Londonderry's time the boundary did not exist; they were both in Durham and they both breathed, one might say, the Londonderry air.

Low Pittington was there long before he arrived, a Saxon village based on the spring that rises on Pittington Hill and runs down to Keel Well, where the water is still collected in an old iron cauldron. The village was just plain Pittington until Lord Londonderry's miners arrived; then a new village was built to house them, a quarter of a mile away. It was christened, with an eye to the obvious, New Pittington, and that is still its official name, but as it was built on higher ground than the old village the locals called it High Pittington, and Pittington itself took the Low road. Many maps still show it as just Pittington, and ignore its upstart neighbour.

The principal feature of the village, which most visitors come to see, is the church which, confusingly, is not in the village proper but up the road in a little hamlet called Hallgarth. Architects enthuse about its Norman pillars, alternately round and octagonal, all handsomely decorated; the effect, they say, is 'rich and spectacular'.

They are less inclined to enthuse about the other buildings in Low Pittington – 'gaunt' is one description – and they are much ruder about High Pittington. But the Blacksmith's Arms does manage to look more welcoming, and inside it has preserved the traditional atmosphere of a North-country village inn.

The atmosphere is often filled with an equally traditional North-country fragrance. The Blacksmith's Arms is one of those inns which specialise in large Yorkshire puddings, the size of a dinner-plate and smothered in gravy – and that's just the starter. You are likely to get another one, nearly as big, with your main course. In fairness I must add that more sophisticated dishes are also on offer; you could round off all that batter pudding with a Cointreau and orange mousse log.

But there is no doubt they eat heartily at the Blacksmith's Arms, perhaps in the hope of building up their frames to match an earlier landlord, who really was a blacksmith. Jim Barrass was an imposing, moustachioed mountain of a man, who owned and ran the inn as well as the smithy round the corner. According to the present landlord, 'Stories have it that Jim used to come straight from working all day at the blacksmith's shop, and just start serving beer – he was as black as the ace of spades!' Which must have unnerved new customers, but I doubt they complained. He was a very large man.

When Jim died early this century he left a lasting memorial – not a collection of grubby tankards, but the handsome copper fireplace in the front bar. Another legacy from the past is not quite so solid; the landlord says he has seen the ghost of a woman in her fifties, with grey hair drawn back into a bun. 'She was serving a pint of cask beer and turned slowly towards me, smiled, and then just faded away.'

This is the sort of experience, cynics would say, which landlords are inclined to produce when conversation is flagging in the bar, but I gather the cleaning lady has heard a woman laughing behind her, even though the place was empty, and a customer insisted someone kept tapping him on the shoulder when no one was anywhere near.

But at least they have not tried to link this apparently cheerful, even playful, lady with the ill-fated Mary Ann Westhope, who was murdered at nearby Hallgarth Mill in 1830 by a nineteen-year-old employee, Thomas Clarke. His motive was never made clear and he produced a strong defence, but the jury only took twenty-five minutes to find him guilty, and young Thomas was duly executed. The mill was demolished in the 1960s, but Mary Ann is said still to wander the lane between the mill and the inn.

So inside or out at the Blacksmith's Arms you may encounter a spectral lady. Given the choice, I would rather meet the one with the bun, preferably drawing a beer.

In spite of Blubberhouses, no spite at the Spite

The Spite
Newall, near Otley, West Yorkshire

On the road from Otley to Blubberhouses

'Oh yes,' said the elderly gentleman digging his front garden, 'you want the Malice and Spite, just up the hill.'

I had only asked for the Spite, but that was his name for it, and it was a fair reflection of the slight confusion that seems to linger around the name. There is no doubt about the phrase that started it all: 'There's nowt there but malice and spite'; but who said it, and why, seems to vary.

I was asking the way because the first problem is to find the inn at all. It is sometimes listed as Newall-with-Clinton, others just say 'near Otley'. This caution is understandable, because neither of the atlases I normally rely on mentions Newall or Clinton. One guide says 'on the B6451', but another says 'off the B6451', which indeed it is, and quite a long way off at that. It does not help that, although Otley is in West Yorkshire, the Spite, a mile to the north, is across the border in North Yorkshire.

Had I known which road the Spite was actually on, I might well have abandoned the journey altogether, because it is the road from Otley to Blubberhouses, and Blubberhouses holds disturbing memories. I once had to broadcast a traffic warning which said there was dense fog at Blubberhouses, and as I had a few seconds to spare I commented idly what a very odd name it was, and could such a place actually exist.

All thought of fog faded as the heavens metaphorically opened. I was bombarded with phone calls and letters telling me about Blubberhouses, sending me photographs, extolling its beauties, and giving various versions of how it got its name. 'Blubber' was variously interpreted as a sheep, a spring and a berry. There was one reference to whaling, and a romantic suggestion that small children were forced to work in a mill there during Victorian times, and their blubbering could be heard across the moors. But while views on that differed, my correspondents were unanimous in their condemnation of my southern ignorance. It all happened twenty years ago, but I have been wary of visiting Blubberhouses ever since.

Happily, memories must be short at the Spite, and I had a kindly welcome when I eventually found this pleasant stone-built inn, with its splendid views from the back garden across the Wharfedale countryside. It was built in the middle of the last century and christened the Roebuck, and it would have saved a lot of confusion if it had stayed that way, but there was no escaping the 'Nowt but malice and spite' story, and even the brewers had to admit defeat and officially rename the inn.

No malice and spite these days, just a friendly drink under the walking sticks – the modern ornamental equivalent of horse brasses.

The basic facts are that there used to be two inns side by side, the Roebuck and the Travellers' Rest, and a certain animosity existed between the two. One version is that a Travellers' Rest regular ventured next door to sample the beer at the Roebuck, but the landlord recognised him and gave him a chilly reception – whereupon he returned to the Travellers' Rest and commented: 'There's nowt there but malice and spite.' Alternatively, it was the landlady at the Travellers' who rebuked him when he returned from sneaking next door, and he left in high dudgeon, making a similar comment but applying it to both the inns when he got back to Otley: 'There's nowt but malice and spite up there.'

Either way, the Travellers' Rest and the Roebuck became the Malice and Spite. In due course the Malice closed and was converted into cottages, which happily are called the Travellers' Rest Cottages – Malice Cottages might be difficult to market. But the Spite continued to prosper, and these days nobody is too worried about how it all began.

Instead, the Spite concentrates on walking sticks. The walls and ceiling are decorated with a wide variety, perhaps in recognition of the fine walking country which can be seen from the garden. The accent would have been on horses in earlier days, but the stables have been converted into a dining area.

I was discussing the delightful scenery with the lady behind the bar when she casually asked if I knew Blubberhouses. The full memory of that bombardment I had received from irate listeners came flooding back.

'Oh yes,' I said, 'I know Blubberhouses.' And if it had been twenty years earlier, I fear I might have added: 'There's nowt down there but malice and spite.'

*No eccentric vicar, no white horse, no ruined abbey
or public school – just mice*

The Black Swan
Oldstead, North Yorkshire

On road through village

All but one of the villages that cluster in this delightful valley below the Hambleton Hills have their own special claim to fame. Coxwold was the home of Laurence Sterne, the eccentric parson who settled in a very small cottage with a very large chimney, named it Shandy Hall – 'shandy' is the Yorkshire term for wild or unorthodox – and wrote his famous novel *Tristram Shandy*. Kilburn's most obvious tourist attraction is the Kilburn Horse, more than three hundred feet long with a circular eye large enough for twelve people to picnic inside. Ampleforth has its Benedictine public school, Newburgh has its priory, and Wass has the ruins of Byland Abbey.

The odd one out is Oldstead, which is all the more attractive for being virtually unknown. It does have a prehistoric barrow and a disused observatory, but these are rather too specialised for most day trippers. There is really only one reason for visiting Oldstead, and that is the Black Swan. And by doing so, you can see in comfort some samples of the other feature which Kilburn is famous for, in addition to its Horse – the carved mice of the renowned Robert 'Mousey' Thompson.

It is possible that, without those mice, Mr Thompson might have remained just another talented craftsman, but the gimmick became so familiar to the furniture-buying public that it has become the official trade mark of the family business he founded, which is still based in his home village. Mousey's mice can be found in public buildings all over the country, from Westminster Abbey and Peterborough Cathedral to the Black Swan at Oldstead. The Fauconberg Arms at Coxwold has some too, but Coxwold is a busy tourist centre and the Arms is right in the village centre. The Black Swan is better suited to a leisurely mouse-hunt, and you will be rewarded by discovering them on the bar, over a door, by the fireplace, at the back of a shelf – almost anywhere.

The Black Swan has been an alehouse since 1742, and although it has been altered and restored by Mousey Thompson and others, its character has been preserved. Even the mice are nothing new; I am sure they were around in 1742, just more difficult to spot. Even a new fireplace installed in 1994 has merged into the general appearance of the place. It was run for a while by an American, who introduced the unlikely custom of 'Throwing a Bomb on Boxing Day', when the lane outside was closed and a competition was held to see who could throw an American football the furthest. Perhaps he hoped that Boxing Day 'bomb-throwing' would make Oldstead as famous as Olney's pancake race on Shrove Tuesday. Mercifully, he failed.

The Black Swan is on the hillside on the edge of the village, and from the sloping garden which surrounds it there is a splendid view across the valley. The view does not include the Kilburn Horse, but that is not too great a loss, because the horse does not look quite as elegant and immaculate as the model it was based on, in spite of the sterling efforts of the volunteer Kilburn White Horse Association.

One of 'Mousey' Thompson's carved mice, which turn up in unexpected corners of the bar. Robert Thompson lived in nearby Kilburn, so the mice did not travel far – but some have reached Westminster Abbey and Peterborough Cathedral.

It was the bright idea in the 1850s of a Kilburn man, Thomas Taylor, who saw the White Horse of Uffington and persuaded the local schoolmaster to design a larger version and carve it into the side of Rouston Scar, above the village. The work was mostly done by his pupils, who must have been really thrilled.

Unfortunately, while the Uffington Horse is carved into chalk, Rouston Scar is limestone, which means that the Kilburn White Horse is more of a Dirty Grey Horse – and the maintenance problems are enormous. Mr Taylor was not too bothered; he wisely emigrated to Australia. Local volunteers have been left to groom his horse ever since. They have found the gravelly surface easily erodes, it is virtually impossible to paint, and alternative materials get washed away too. There have also been the jokers who pegged rows of black bin liners across the body to turn it into a zebra, and others who caused permanent damage by digging up the turf to alter the shape. This is one gift-horse which should have been looked at more closely, but the Association battles on gamely to preserve what might be renamed the Kilburn White Elephant.

However, the drawbacks of the Taylor horse are more than balanced by the drawing power of the Thompson mice, and the Black Swan is proud of the samples it possesses. I also learned there why Mousey Thompson chose mice in the first place. He was working on the roof of a church when one of his craftsmen observed glumly that, in spite of their skill and hard work, they were still as poor as church mice – so he forthwith carved one on a rafter. Robert Thompson died in 1955, but his business continues to prosper and multiply – and so do the mice.

The family Bible that must always stay in the cupboard: but why?

The White Horse
Scales, Cumbria

On the A66 east of Threlkeld

It is about forty years since a kink in the main road from Penrith to Keswick was straightened, and the kink became a loop. On that loop stands the White Horse Inn, and there must have been some misgivings at the time, in case the traffic flashed past on the new road without noticing the inn was there. The fears were unfounded. Larry Slattery, the present landlord, told me that the slip-road may be difficult to spot and has an awkward camber if you take it too fast, but it has provided useful extra parking protected from the through traffic, and the inn itself is a lot less noisy, thanks to the old

outhouses between it and the new road. Drivers may miss it the first time, but they remember where they saw it, and don't miss it again.

The White Horse, the outhouses, and a guesthouse that shares this little loop are about all there is of Scales, and it is easy to see why. This cluster of buildings is hard up against the foot of Saddleback, which rises for nearly three thousand feet just behind them, leaving no room for anything else. It is so close, in fact, that one imaginative writer has likened the White Horse to Nottingham's Trip to Jerusalem, the famous old inn beneath Castle Rock. 'The steep slated roof seems almost to be a continuation of Saddleback's lowest slope.'

But there the resemblance ends. The White Horse is not built on to sandstone caves, but is a traditional country inn, built in part from ship's timbers which probably came from Maryport on the Cumbrian coast, which is closed to shipping now but once had busy shipyards. It was built around 1660, and has no pretensions to being England's oldest inn, unlike its Nottingham counterpart. And if it tries to open up spaces in the rock behind it for extra cellarage, as the Trip to Jerusalem has, it might run into problems with the Lowther Estate.

This was founded when the first Earl of Lonsdale, a member of the Lowther family, made a fortune from the coal mines at White-haven. It spread across a vast area of what was then Cumberland and Westmorland, and Lowther Cast-le, near Penrith, became their family home. Scales came within the estate, and although Larry Slattery owns the White Horse, the mineral rights are still owned by the Estate. 'If I strike oil or find gold in the garden, it belongs to the Estate.'

The family Bible in the cupboard by the fireplace is part of the fixtures and fittings. It has been there for over a century.

The most important difference between the Trip to Jerusalem and the White Horse is that one is in the heart of a busy city and attracts a lot of sightseers because of its curiosity value, while the other is in the heart of the Cumbrian countryside, with a splendid view across the river to Matterdale, and those who visit it are more likely to come for its excellent pub lunches than to find anything out of the ordinary.

But the White Horse does have an unusual feature, which I found just as intriguing as the Trip to Jerusalem's sandstone bars. It is not the ingenious plaque made of woven and plaited wheat-straw which spells out the name of the inn, though that is unusual

enough, the only survivor of an assortment of corn dollies which used to decorate the inn, made by a Yorkshireman who retired to the Lake District and could not give up his old craft.

Out of sight, however, in a cupboard set in the thickness of the wall beside one of the fireplaces, is an old family Bible, printed in the 1850s, which is said to feature in the deeds of the inn. There is supposed to be a clause that the Bible must never be removed from the premises, on pain of all manner of unpleasant repercussions. I have to say that Mr Slattery, who bought the White Horse from the brewers, can find nothing in the deeds to this effect, but he does confirm that the last tenant told him the Bible had to remain there as part of the fixtures and fittings. There is some fascinating detective work to be done here. The Bible was the property of Henry and Sophie Wood, who married in May 1896 and had three children, Ernest in 1897, Gladys in 1899 and Henry in 1904; the names and dates are recorded on the flyleaf. So is the death of Ernest in 1917, a casualty of the First World War. There the family tree ends.

So who were the Wood family, and what happened to the other children? Presumably they were tenants of the White Horse, but when they left why did they not take their family Bible with them? And how did this tradition grow up that it must never leave the inn?

Larry Slattery has no idea, and different breweries have owned the White Horse since the turn of the century, most of them no longer in existence, so after a hundred years it is not easy to answer these questions. But I rather hope they won't be answered; the mystery of the White Horse Bible is rather more fun if it remains a mystery.

*Never mind Bounty - the Battersbys were noisy
enough to finish up there too*

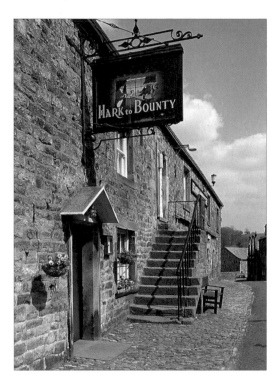

Hark to Bounty
Slaidburn, Lancashire

In the centre of the village

The traditional link between the village inn and the parish church takes a different form in Slaidburn. They do not stand opposite each other, as in so many other villages, and there is no suggestion that one was built to lodge the masons who were building the other – though the Hark to Bounty is said to date back to the thirteenth century, and would certainly have been around when the church was rebuilt in 1450. The link is actually in the origin of its unique name, which involves a Victorian 'squarson', a rector who was also the squire.

The squarson was a great dog-lover, and it seems his parishioners were too, because it was their practice to take their pets to church with them, rather than be parted for an hour or two. The dogs, however, did not always appreciate this privilege, and for over a century a dog-whipper was employed to help keep them under control. It was not just a courtesy title; still on display in the church are two unpleasant-looking whips which were used to quell any dogfights that broke out in the pews, and to silence the noisier members of the canine congregation.

There was, however, an exception. The story goes

that the rector's favourite hound, Bounty, was allowed to make as much noise as it liked – to such an extent that passers-by, hearing the barking inside the church, would nudge each other knowingly and murmur, 'Hark to Bounty.'

The more likely explanation, though, and the one which the inn prefers, is that the squarson, who was also Master of the Hunt, often called at the inn for refreshment after a morning's hunting, leaving the pack outside. On one such morning in 1875 he may have lingered longer than usual over his ale, and the pack became impatient. Above the general baying, one hound could be heard much louder, a distinctive and familiar sound.

'Hark to Bounty,' said its owner benevolently as he ordered another round – and it may well have been that the landlord's business was so governed by the visits of the squarson and his noisy hound that he changed the name of his inn. It was previously called the Dog, and he could have been tempted to rename it That Damned Dog, but Hark to Bounty was more politic.

Incidentally, Slaidburn had a problem at one time with noisy people as well as noisy dogs, and there was an incident in church which caused a far greater disturbance than a mere dogfight. There were two feuding families, the Musgraves and the Battersbys, who fell out over who should sit in the Hamerton Chapel during services. The Hamertons had been Lords of the Manor for centuries, but Sir Stephen Hamerton joined the protest against the dissolution of the monasteries by Henry VIII and was hanged as a result. His estate, which was said to be so large that he could ride from Slaidburn to York on his own land, was split up.

Cuthbert Musgrave got part of it, and insisted on

The jury benches are still in position in the Old Court Room, and the witness box is used as an auxiliary bar.

sitting in the Hamerton Chapel, but the Battersbys, who were tenants of Hamerton Hall, strongly objected. During one service Grace Battersby 'kept bawling, chiding and calling "thief and murderer!"'. Other members of the congregation joined in, with one Battersby supporter shouting, 'Pull him forth out of the quere!'

The case was taken to York, but it might just as easily have been taken to the Hark to Bounty – not to the main bar but to the room on the first floor which is reached by the outside stairs on the front of the building. For centuries this was the only court-room between Lancaster and York, dating back to the days when the packhorse trails along the ancient saltways crossed at Slaidburn, and it was the medieval capital of the Royal Forest of Bowland. Transgressors who were tried here could be put in the stocks for minor offences, or be hanged for something really serious, like poaching. Intermediate crimes were punished by whipping – which at least the local dogs must have enjoyed. But the Musgrave–Battersby case was probably better dealt with at a distance. It went in favour of Musgrave, but the feud continued for many years.

The court-room was used as recently as 1937, and although it acts as a function room these days, it still has the jury benches along one wall, the witness box is used as a bar counter, and there is the heavy wooden door from the corridor which was used by the visiting justices. So, if the main bar downstairs is too full of lunchers for you to enjoy the beams and open fireplace and brass decorations – and I have to say that the accent on food, particularly in the holiday season, does detract from the traditional atmosphere – then ask to see the splendid old court-room upstairs, and have your faith restored.

A community inn - even though the curate poked out the landlady's eye

The Cross Keys
Uppermill, Greater Manchester

Off Runninghill Gate

The re-arrangement of county boundaries played odd tricks in some areas, and none odder than in this corner of what used to be the West Riding of Yorkshire. It already had its peculiarities, in that Uppermill was one of seven villages on the western slopes of the Pennines known collectively as Saddleworth, which, on most maps, does not exist, even though Saddleworth church is very solidly established next to the Cross Keys. Then the boundary changes meant that Saddleworth found itself in Greater Manchester, with the traumatic result that it could no longer provide cricketers to play for Yorkshire, under the old rule that players had to be Yorkshire-born. Of all the severed links with Yorkshire, that was the unkindest cut of all.

Saddleworth fought back. It had, after all, achieved renown in various fields under the Yorkshire banner, quite apart from cricket. It has the longest and highest canal tunnel in England (albeit unused for the last half-century), its band contests are famous nationwide, and it was the Saddleworth rush-cart, drawn through the streets on festival days, which gave rise to the term 'on the waggon', because only those entirely sober could keep their balance on it. Why should all this be credited to Greater Manchester?

It achieved only a partial victory – but it was the important part. Saddleworth is still in Greater Manchester, but it was allowed to retain a white rose as its emblem and local children were still able to play for Yorkshire. Uppermill breathed again.

The Cross Keys is celebrating its 250th anniversary in 1995, having started life under the more sombre name of the Gravemakers, and I imagine it would have liked to do so as part of Yorkshire, but, in fact, it has longstanding links with Lancashire, and the organisations which use it as their base ignore any frontiers. It is, for instance, the headquarters of the

The fire looks welcoming, but in 1794 the local curate made use of it to heat his walking stick, then thrust it in the landlady's eye. He died in an asylum nearly forty years later.

Oldham Mountain Rescue Team, which does not ask which side of the border a climber comes from if he is in trouble and needs help. The quaintly named Manchester Pedestrians Club are not averse to walking into Yorkshire from the Cross Keys, the Saddleworth Runners and Outdoor Pursuits Association do much the same, and the Cross Keys Gun Club, the Saddleworth Historical Society and the Saddleworth Clog and Garland Dancers, all of whom are based at the Cross Keys, do not check the passports of their members.

The wide range of these groups is an indication of the part that the Cross Keys plays in the community; appropriately, they are all taking part in the anniversary celebrations. You might not expect to find this traditional community spirit in an area of such sharp contrasts, because so-called Greater Manchester is a confusing mixture of heavily built-up 'urban villages' and open moorland. Uppermill itself is that kind of village, but if you follow the lane which used to be the packhorse trail up on to the moors, you find yourself in a different world. The Cross Keys is

a mile out of the village, on the edge of open moorland, subject to sudden mists and storms, beautiful in the sunshine but bleak and treacherous in bad weather – and the idea of a mountain rescue team, which can seem a little unreal down in the village, becomes perfectly logical at the Cross Keys.

However, the most dramatic event in the inn's history did not involve a mountain rescue, it occurred in the Cross Keys itself. In 1794 the local curate, the Reverend Charles Zouch, was lodging at the inn when he had a very nasty turn, and suddenly got mad at the landlady – literally. In the public bar, later named Buckley's Kitchen in honour of a subsequent landlord, Parson Zouch heated a walking stick until it was red-hot, then thrust it in the landlady's eye. He was found to be insane, and died in an asylum nearly forty years later.

One might think such an unpleasant event best forgotten, but it has been good for business over the years, and indeed the Saddleworth Historical Society had plans to re-enact it as part of the anniversary celebrations.

The Cross Keys has another criminal association, but happily it is only fictional. A Sherlock Holmes film has been shot here, and there are photographs of Holmes and Watson at the inn to prove it. But, in the main, this civilised inn concentrates on looking after its fell runners and clog dancers, its 'pedestrians' and its rescue teams, and any stray visitors who pass that way. As one verse of the anniversary ode puts it:

Some chaps fancy swell hotels,
But not me if you please!
I prefer the chimney corner
Of the Old Cross Keys.
There I chat with Ned and Charlie,
While we share our 'Hillside Club'.
There's a bit of good old England
In a decent country pub.

Even if you are a Yorkshireman in Greater Manchester...

Other inns mentioned in the book

SOUTH WESTERN REGION
Bigbury-on-Sea, Devon: Pilchard (page 32)
Cerne Abbas, Dorset: Red Lion (page 13)
Cerne Abbas, Dorset: Royal Oak (page 13)
Holberton, Devon: Church House (page 42)
Mary Tavy, Devon: Elephant's Nest (page 30)
Montacute, Dorset: King's Arms (page 25)
Rattery, Devon: Church House (page 42)
St Stephen, Cornwall: King's Arms (page 37)

SOUTHERN REGION
Bucks Green, West Sussex: Fox (page 41)
Burpham, West Sussex: George and Dragon (page 146)
Hartfield, East Sussex: Anchor (page 75)
Holyport, Berkshire: George (page 62)
Lewes, East Sussex: Dorset Arms (page 75)
Pluckley, Kent: Black Horse (page 67)
Yattendon, Berkshire: Royal Oak (page 58)

SOUTH MIDLAND REGION
Birchanger, Essex: Three Willows (page 96)
Dinton, Buckinghamshire: Seven Stars (page 89)
Murcott, Oxfordshire: Nut Tree (page 83)

EASTERN REGION
Hempstead, Essex: Rose and Crown (page 169)
Ormesby St Margaret, Norfolk: Eel's Foot (page 118)

NORTH MIDLAND REGION
Audlem, Cheshire: Shroppie Fly (page 177)
Bishops Castle, Shropshire: Three Tuns (page 153)
Gotham, Nottinghamshire: Cuckoo Bush (page 173)
Shardlow, Derbyshire: Hoskins Wharf (page 176)

NORTHERN REGION
Coxwold, North Yorkshire: Fauconberg Arms (page 208)
Hawkshead, Cumbria: Drunken Duck (page 188)

Index